Hermeneutica

Hermeneutica

Computer-Assisted Interpretation in the Humanities

Geoffrey Rockwell and Stéfan Sinclair

The MIT Press
Cambridge, Massachusetts
London, England

Set in Stone Serif Std by Toppan Best-set Premedia Limited.

Cataloging-in-Publication information is available from the Library of Congress.

ISBN: 978-0-262-03435-7 (hc : alk. paper), 978-0-262-54589-1 (pb)

Contents

Acknowledgments

The hybrid work of *Hermeneutica* and Voyant Tools owes much to many people and organizations. The project would not have gotten off the ground without the support of the Canada Foundation for Innovation and the Social Science and Humanities Research Council of Canada for the original TAPoR project and related projects. Our work has also been supported by SSHRC/CFI projects led by others, among them the INKE project (led by Ray Siemens), the Canadian Writing Research Collaboratory (led by Susan Brown), and the Text Mining the Novel Project (led by Andrew Piper). We owe a great debt to all our generous colleagues, including Stan Ruecker and Milena Radzikowska, who listened to draft ideas and gave us design ideas. In particular, these projects let us work with brilliant students and developers who helped with TAPoR and Voyant, including Lian Yan, Peter Organisciak, Luciano Frizzera, Ryan Chartier, Amy Dyrbye, Kamal Ranaweera, John Simpson, Andrew Macdonald, Cyril Briquet, Marc Turcato, and Lisa Goddard.

Hermeneutica and Voyant Tools have also benefited from the ongoing support of our universities, our respective humanities computing centers, and Compute Canada (our national advanced computing consortium). Our work on these projects began at McMaster University with a day-long experiment in the TAPoR lab supported by the Humanities Media and Computing Centre, then managed by Rocco Piro. We are now supported by the Arts Resource Centre at the University of Alberta and the staff there, including Mark McKellar, and Omar Rodriguez-Arenas. At McGill University we are supported by the McGill Centre for Digital Humanities. Compute Canada and its regional members, including WestGrid and Sharcnet, have generously provided infrastructure support to Voyant.

A number of people helped us with the manuscript. Kirsten C. Uszkalo provided an editorial eye when we could no longer see the trees for the woods. Matthew Milner provided significant help, particularly in the preparation of the bibliography and the figures. Douglas Sery and Susan Buckley at the MIT Press managed the acquisition and the reviewing in a gentle and professional fashion. We are grateful to Paul Bethge for an extraordinary job of editing and for understanding our style.

The long slow conversation of the humanities, however wandering, takes place with and in a community of scholars, international, national, and local. We have been involved in what is now called the "digital humanities" since the 1980s and have shared in its transformation from an obscure technical field into the new kid on the block. As we looked into the history of text analysis and tools for *Hermeneutica*, we realized how much we owe to the developers before us—Sally Sedelow, John B. Smith, Susan Hockey, Robert Jay Glickman, John Bradley, Lidio Presutti, Paul Fortier, and Father Roberto Busa, to name a few. Their ideas have percolated through the field in prototypes, tools, and demonstrations. We also realized how much we owe to those who built up the organizations that welcomed us as graduate students—Nancy Ide, Joe Raben, Willard McCarty, Susan Hockey, John Unsworth, Sam Cioran, Elaine Nardocchio, Bethany Nowviskie, Julia Flanders, Michael Sinatra, Ian Lancashire, Susan Brown, Ray Siemens, Harold Short, Lisa Lena Opas-Hänninen, and many others. They cared for community organizations such as the Centre for Computing in the Humanities (at the University of Toronto), the Canadian Society for Digital Humanities / Société canadienne des humanités numériques, the Association for Computers and the Humanities, and the Alliance of Digital Humanities Organizations.

Last, but not least, we would like to thank our families, who patiently and lovingly supported the project over many years. The book is dedicated to Peigi, Stephanie, Peter, Alethea, Naomie, and Élodie.

1 Introduction: Correcting Method

[T]hings made up of different elements and produced by the hands of several master craftsmen are often less perfect than those on which only one person has worked.

René Descartes

How Do You Think Something Through with Technology?

René Descartes, in his 1637 *Discourse on Method,* describes a moment of solitude that allows him to talk to himself about his thoughts and to develop a method for thinking correctly. Here is how he describes the solitude he seeks:

As I was returning to the army from the coronation of the emperor, I was halted by the onset of winter in quarters where, having no diverting company and fortunately also no cares or emotional turmoil to trouble me, I spent the whole day shut up in a small room heated by a stove, in which I could converse with my own thoughts at leisure. Among the first of these was the realization that things made up of different elements and produced by the hands of several master craftsmen are often less perfect than those on which only one person has worked.[1]

The *Discourse* is important to the practices of the humanities because it introduced an accessible method for anyone to do philosophy without needing to be widely read or part of an intellectual community. It provided a technique for thinking things through. Descartes' story of method, and its accompanying provisional moral code for behavior without certainty, is one of the fables that founded modern philosophy. As such, it provided humanists a foundational model for the solitary, doubting, and reflective practice that still dominates how many think we should think things through.

But practices are changing. Older forms of communal inquiry are being remixed into modern research.[2] We have come to recognize how intellectual work is participatory even when it includes moments of solitary meditation. Internet conferencing tools allow us to remediate dialogical practices, collaborative communities such as Wikipedia and Twitter depend on contributions by a large group of users, and the communal research cultures of the arts collective or engineering lab are influencing the humanities. Accessible computing, data availability, and new media opportunities have provoked textual disciplines to think again about our practices and methods as we build digital libraries, process millions of digital books, and imagine research cyber-infrastructure that can support the next generation of scholars.

We have recently begun imagining large-scale humanities-based projects that require a variety of skills for implementation—skills rarely found in a solitary scholar/programmer, let alone in a Cartesian humanist. We find ourselves working in teams, reflecting on how to best organize them, and then reflecting on what it means to think through with others. This inevitably turns to methodological reflection that takes new media into account as we try to balance our traditional Cartesian values with the opportunities of open and communal work.

Hermeneutica is a story about methods of interpretation. It is a story of a return to dialogical practices that predate Descartes and an explanation of our turn to the computer-assisted methods that are becoming hermeneutically interesting with the digitization of the human record. Specifically, *Hermeneutica* returns to method in four ways:

- *Hermeneutica* is a hybrid project, consisting of the present book and an online companion to it. The online chapters at hermeneutic.ca extend the affordances of a book by weaving text with interactive components. We *show* you, through text and tool, how we reached our conclusions regarding the opportunities for online interpretation.[3]
- *Hermeneutica* is both a text about computer-assisted methods and a collection of analytical tools called Voyant (http://voyant-tools.org) that instantiate our ideas. Voyant, the implementation of our interpretive proposal, is a collection of hermeneutica (that is, hermeneutical things). Voyant allows users to integrate interpretation into their writing by creating small hermeneutica that can be woven into their essays or into Web 2.0 online writing environments such as blogs and wikis.
- *Hermeneutica* presents interludes—case studies that show computer-assisted text analysis in application. The interludes are interwoven with the reflective chapters on analytics that use them as examples. The

interludes (chapters 4, 6, 8, and 10) are essays that use Voyant's hermeneutical tools to interpret texts.[4]

- Just as *Hermeneutica* is both book/site and text/tools, our online essays
  are both text and code: both narrative text and embedded interactive
  panels. The panels are part of the text quoting results, but they are also
  interactive so you can recapitulate and experiment with our results. The
  embedded panels return you to a computer-assisted method in the context of an essay. Figure 1.1, for example, shows how the interactive panel
  of the Voyant Collocate Clusters of this introductory chapter looks after
  some fiddling. Such hermeneutical panels represent a difference made
  possible when publishing online.

In short, *Hermeneutica* is a weaving together of hermeneutical things—
print and electronic, text and code, interludes and reflections, narrative and
interaction—all of which are a thinking-through of interpretive method
with computing. *Hermeneutica* tries to correct for the Cartesian solitudes

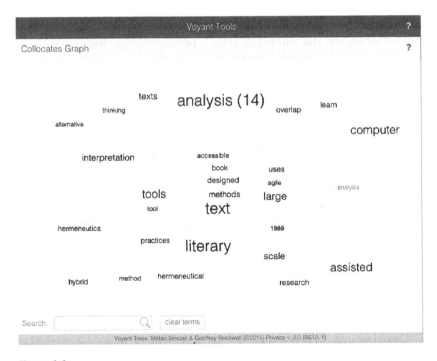

Figure 1.1
A collocate graph of this chapter. Source: S. Sinclair and G. Rockwell, Collocate
Graph Tool. To try the tool with your text, see http://voyant-tools.org/tool/Links.

of text and method by showing how analytical tools *are* instantiations of interpretive methods that can be woven closely into other hermeneutical things, like text.

The Story of Method

To confront the privilege of solitary reflection in academic practice, we would do well to pay attention to how Descartes introduces his story of method. Descartes calls his *Discourse* a personal history or fable, and suggests that readers can ignore it or "imitate" it. This "histoire" illustrates practices for readers to emulate, and leads them through Descartes' method and provisional moral code. While the formal method gets attention, the story of his provisional practices, with all their associated baggage, tends to get passed over. Those of us without certainty, however, find ourselves stuck in those provisional practices.

The *Discourse* is a story about doubting oneself and others as a method of ridding oneself of possible influence. It is about isolating oneself from traditions of scholastic disputation in order to think alone, think afresh, think thoroughly, free oneself of error, assume nothing, and think about thinking. This story of thinking thoroughly has four aspects that made us think about our hermeneutics:

- Descartes doubts all authority in order to think anew about thinking. Rejecting all opportunities for thinking along with others, he turns to solitary work as the best way to think about thinking—a practice still common in the humanities, in which we still tend to think that we need time away to really get research work done. *Hermeneutica* proposes, as an alternative, a more participatory practice of dialogical research. One doesn't have to do it alone, especially if one doesn't have all the necessary skills. That doesn't mean, however, that one should not be sceptical[5] or critical.
- Paradoxically, Descartes writes his thinking-through as an interior dialogue. Rejecting dialogue with others gave him, he recalls, "the leisure to talk to myself about my thoughts." Avoiding conversation with others freed him to discover himself as a conversational partner, which is his way of reflecting on thinking, or at least reflecting on his own thinking, a reflection that generates personal certainty.[6] The *Discourse* traces the trajectory of the personal. Descartes tells the story of his education in part 1, his development of a personal method in part 2, and why he decided to publish the *Discourse* in part 6. The autobiographical narrative made

method accessible to others as a personal path, which accounts, at least in part, for the popularity and influence of the work. Descartes let readers listen in on him, which helped them imagine how they could be philosophers if they took the time to think alone about their thoughts. In *Hermeneutica* we likewise make our practices part of this story, but they are practices of working together, a different type of dialogue between people and machines. This story is more about what is needed when one wants to augment interpretation with the development of software tools for thinking through. Ours is a story of collaborative reflection and development across the divide between writing code and writing text. Readers will find reflections on pair-work later in this chapter and in the concluding chapter.

- Descartes thinks things through by reflecting on thinking. His method is a thinking that takes thought itself, specifically reflection, as its first companion and subject for interpretation. Likewise, *Hermeneutica* is about thinking, but it is about the thinking-through of interpretation, and a thinking-through *with* specific things of interpretation: *text and tool*. One way we do this is by recording our experiments in the interludes, as stories too. *Hermeneutica* is an open and self-documented work: you can recapitulate our analysis, view our preliminary research notes, or examine our code.[7]
- Descartes provides examples that show the results of employing his method. In his *Discourse* these are provided as appendixes. We too have provided example interludes, but in *Hermeneutica* these case studies are not pushed to the end of the story but are woven into the thinking-through. The interludes are hermeneutical things that present interpretations using Voyant. They themselves are interpreted in the reflective chapters.

It is not surprising that the Cartesian train of doubting, solitary, and reflective thinking leads to the *cogito*—"I think, therefore I am"—from which, with personal certainty, Descartes methodically rebuilds his ideas. The irony of the *Discourse* is that if Descartes' practice appeals to you, then you should suspect its results since the authority of another, namely Descartes, is behind it. In theory, you should begin again yourself by interrogating your own thinking practices, but of course most of us can rid ourselves of the *cogito*. The rhetorical power of the *cogito* is that Descartes wagers that you will end up right where he did, without necessarily doing all the work, all the more convinced since you followed, even if only remotely as a reader, his "correct conduct" of reason, and not his conclusions.[8]

The *Discourse* is first presented by Descartes as a practical guide toward method that you can imitate and reuse, not as an authority to consider true. With *Hermeneutica*, we present a similar guide toward method you can think through and a suite of our tools that encourage you to do just that. The image of the solitary Cartesian philosopher has influenced how we think about intellectual work. Perhaps it is time to correct our methods and reanimate other images of practice. In *Hermeneutica* we have stitched together hermeneutical things so that you can try tools-as-methods as you read about them. Our story is one of thinking through together. We hope yours will be too.

Agile Hermeneutics

What do we mean by "dialogical practices"? In our research notes for "Now Analyze That!" we wrote the following pastiche of Descartes:

Rather than be diverted by our personal projects we thought we would direct our conversations to the intersection of methods, tools and interpretation by taking a small project through from conception to writing in one day, a day set aside away from the distractions of other work. We spent the day closed up together in a lab overheated by all the computers, where we had the leisure to talk while thinking through tools and experimenting with texts. Among the many reflections of the day we noticed how few questions you can ask alone using one interpretative method and how much more richness there was to interpretation in dialogue that weaves evidence together from several methods by different masters, as needed by the questions at hand.

Computer-assisted research in the humanities, by contrast to the Cartesian story and traditional humanities practices, has almost always been collaborative. This is due to the variety of skills needed to implement Digital Humanities projects. It is also linked to the relationship between the practices of interpretation and the development of the tools of interpretation, be they tools for analyzing text or digital editions. Anyone who has used tools forged by another person is in collaboration, even if one isn't personally influencing the provider of the tools. The need to collaborate, though acknowledged in various ways, has been a professional hindrance, as anyone who submits a curriculum vitae for promotion listing nothing but co-authored papers knows.[9]

Collaboration is not always good. It separates the interpreter/scholar from the designer/programmer who implements the scholarly methods. Willard McCarty notes that the introduction of software "separated the conception of the problems (domain of the scholar) from the computational means of working them out (bailiwick of the programmer) and so came at a significant cost."[10] As computing is introduced into research, it separates conception, implementation, and interpretation in ways that can be overcome only through dialogue and collaboration across very different fields. Typically, humanities scholars know little about programming and software engineering, and programmers know little about humanities scholarship. Going it alone is an option only for the few who have time to master both.[11] The rest of us end up depending on others.

There are many ways to collaborate, but for the purpose of correcting method we propose to start with the assumption that collaboration is a normal practice of humanities computing and should therefore be imagined as part of any discussion of method. Solitary time, while much desired in the bustle of academic life, is here conceived of as a withdrawal from a background of working together in various structured and unstructured ways. Even Descartes starts with the collaboration of authority as the norm from which he has to retreat to correct his thinking. The very desire for solitary time for reflection proves our point. Collaborating with students in teaching and meeting with colleagues in committees are normal practices. Thinking alone is the dream of busy scholars, not the ground on which to develop realistic practices. The question is not whether to collaborate or not, but who to collaborate with and how.

Collaboration can take many forms. While working on *Hermeneutica* we modeled a collaborative practice, Agile Hermeneutics (AH), loosely on a programming methodology called Extreme Programming (XP).[12] XP, a form of Agile Programming, is extreme in that it is substantially different from traditional "best practices" in software development. Traditional programming wisdom emphasized the need for careful analysis and specification before coding. XP recommends trying something early without a lot of specifications; XP also recommends rapid iterations as experiments to evolve specifications, incremental development, and continual reflection. Rather than analyzing the big picture and fully planning the final product before beginning, agile programmers code one version, reflect, and begin again. They work toward what is needed, as opposed to what was specified. Often that means throwing out code and starting all over when functionality calls for redesigned data structures. Whereas traditional wisdom holds that rewriting code is a sign of failure, XP makes it a productive and instructive part of the process. Our first experiment in Agile Hermeneutics likewise started small: we tried to interpret a text, to try methods, and to write a short essay in *one* day. We failed to do all those things in a day, but we found that the process moved our thinking forward. Our explorations are variations on this pattern of work. They led to the interludes presented here as chapters 4, 6, 8, and 10. Each iteration was a thinking-through of our own practices. The iterations forced us to rewrite code, remodel our practices, and rethink *Hermeneutica*.

Extreme programming relies on paired programmers working in discussion with one another. One programmer is at the keyboard typing; the other is reviewing; both are thinking through the code. James Shore and Shane Warden differentiate the roles by calling them "driving" and "navigating" in order to explain the type of collaboration of this method.[13] Whereas traditional practices in the humanities are solitary, AH is purposefully collaborative. At its heart it is pair work, and because only one person has his or her hands on the computer it requires dialogue between those participating. The paired scholars alternate between interpreting the results of text-analysis tools, and looking ahead, and reflecting back on what is needed. This then maximizes the dialogue between the scholar function and the development function to the point where they are woven into an organic whole.

We would like to report that we did everything together, but that was not the case, especially since we work in different cities. Often we were forced to work separately and then use Skype to work through results, frustrations, and failures. Agile Hermeneutics thus became an ideal for us when we could find time to be physically together, much as retreat was an ideal for Descartes.

Whereas traditional programmers aim to have complete specifications, and scholars attempt to theorize their work largely beforehand, AH is pragmatic. Small experiments generate hermeneutical theories as the products of interpretation: texts and tools. Code is quickly hacked to test an idea. Methods, and their instantiation in tools, are discussed reflexively throughout the experiment. Above all, where the Cartesian practices involve reflection and talking with the self, AH is about talking with another person who has complementary skills and summarizing those conversations in various ways.

The particular practice we followed involved developing hermeneutical tools, or hermeneutica. We wanted to pose new questions, to test our ideas with concrete experiments in text analysis, to find new texts, and to hack our tools when that was necessary. Although in our case there is no divide between literary scholar and programmer, the absence of such a divide is not a pre-condition of Agile Hermeneutics; AH can happen between two literary scholars or even two programmers.

Hermeneutica is a record, an outcome, and a reflection of our four AH interludes.

The first interlude (chapter 4, "The Swallow Flies Swiftly Through") is an experiment in seeing if we can discover how the Digital Humanities community defines itself by searching for the uptake of a single definitive term— Digital Humanities—in the long history of the Humanist discussion list.

The second interlude (chapter 6, "Now Analyze That!") uses text analysis for the comparison of two shorter cultural texts available online: important pre-election (2008) speeches on race by Barack Obama and his spiritual mentor Jeremiah A. Wright. This experiment looks at the language both men used to reframe media coverage of election issues.

The third interlude (chapter 8, "Name Games") uses the metaphor of gaming and the visualizations produced by network analysis to see if the output of one scholarly journal can be used to map out the players and the debates in the relatively young field of Game Studies.

The final interlude (chapter 10, "The Artifice of Dialogue") is a full account of the work needed to prepare a text and to "do" text analysis on a complex and nuanced single text. Here we follow the trail of scepticism in Hume's *Dialogues Concerning Natural Religion.*

Historical and theoretical chapters on computer-assisted text analysis interleave and help support these four interludes. Chapter 2, "The Measured Words," looks at how a computer processes text and how that differs from what we call reading. It is an introduction to string manipulation for those not familiar with computers. Chapter 3, "From the Concordance to Ubiquitous Analytics," surveys the development of analytical tools in the textual disciplines in order to provide a context for Voyant. Chapter 9, "A Model Theory," returns to interpretation and the place of computer-assisted text analysis. Chapter 11, "Agile Hermeneutics and the Conversation of the Humanities," contextualizes the dialogical practices proposed in the earlier chapters.

Computing in Humanities Research

Hermeneutica is a work about and for the application of computing to humanities research, specifically to textual studies and interpretation. This endeavor is the result of decades of development and reflection in the field of Digital Humanities (DH).

Since its inception, Digital Humanities has been committed to communities of practice; community has been in its fabric. Historically, it was a field that included service units that supported computing for humanities departments in universities and brought faculty members, staff members, programmers, and students together to run labs, manage servers, and develop tools.

Digital Humanities has always focused and supported the development of applied technology for scholarship. In Canada, for instance, there has been a long tradition of building concording tools—among them the PRORA concording tools (1966), the Text Analysis Computing Tools (TACT, 1989), the Text Analysis Portal for Research (TAPoR, 2000), and TAPoR 2.0 (2012). These tools, in part, led to and support *Hermeneutica*.[14] Through training, conferences, and projects, *Hermeneutica* and Voyant bridge the gap between scholarly practice and technology development. They are, by virtue of being hybrids of text and tool, contributions in this tradition. In chapters 3 and 9, we reflect on code as scholarship.

Hermeneutica is in DH's tradition of problematizing methods through developing tools. It tightly couples the writing of code and the use of code for interpretation. In "Beyond the Word" (2007), Willard McCarty comments on the benefit of the problematic:

> [T]he more important lesson I've learned is that although better tools are possible, the humanist's perspective on tools problematizes them. That is ultimately the point of tool-development in humanities computing, just as problematizing our methods and objects of study is ultimately the point of applying the tools we do have.[15]

Through its hybrid structure, *Hermeneutica* argues that the lines between tool and text are blurred. Moreover, it argues that blurring is good. In chapter 9, we reflect on such a class of knowledge-bearing tools that are designed to be theoretical and how they can reveal themselves.

Hermeneutica is also part of a movement that integrates method and interrogation. We see development as a form of research. Our research is simultaneously about how we might think (to echo a methodological formulation by Vannevar Bush) while thinking through prototyping, coding, documenting, and testing with real questions.[16] It is a particular type of research craft in which one of the important outcomes is a re-imagination of how research tools should be designed to fit into the cycle of research.

Voyant[17]

Voyant, the main tool intervention of *Hermeneutica*, is a newer text-analysis environment meant to support Agile Hermeneutics. Voyant is a contribution in a tradition of developmental and interpretive research documented online and in this book. We have tried to make Voyant a tool worth thinking *with*—as an aide to thinking that bears its theoretical commitments as an interpretive object at least as openly as any story. What is Voyant?

- Voyant is a Web-accessible, Web-based set of tools. As part of *Hermeneutica*, it is woven together with the narrative text, interludes, and documentation. You can try using Voyant with its companion text, manual, and documentation.[18] You can weave embeddable toys into your projects, share them, and use them to work collaboratively.

- Whereas e-book applications tend to remediate the look of an open book, Voyant goes beyond the page view to let you control the view for purposes of analytical reading. Voyant mixes tools as panels much like those in a comic book, creating a medley, or *commedia*, that encourages "serious play."

- Voyant is designed to work "just in time" on any online or uploaded text. If you can see the text on the Web without a special subscription or access mechanism, Voyant can get it and help you interpret it. Voyant gives you the agility to experiment with the texts that interest you. It combines the capabilities of personal-computer-based pre-indexing tools, such as TACT, with more accessible Web-based tools that can find text and create indexes in real time.

- Voyant supports a range of corpora sizes, from single poems to hundreds of novels. Although there is no limit on the size of the corpus, extremely large corpora may affect performance. There is a downloadable version of the Voyant Server that one can use locally if one wants higher performance.[19]

- Voyant is designed to fit into the research cycle flexibly. It can export a panel of evidence that can be easily embedded into an online essay just as one can embed a YouTube video into a blog entry. The embedded panels that we call hermeneutica constitute a practical demonstration of the ideas presented in this book.

There has been much hand wringing about how we are constantly reinventing our tools. Voyant, by contrast, is a re-implementation of ideas in tools such as HyperPo, and it is designed to be rewritten and to support a variety of interfaces. XP embraces the constant change, refactoring, and iteration of programming as virtues. Likewise, Agile Hermeneutics considers re-invention a useful form of re-interpretation in a tradition of humanities re-interpretation. Re-interpreting and rebuilding tools is an inescapable part of problematizing texts and methods. If we believe it is important to reinterpret Plato to maintain the urgency of his thinking, why not re-invent the concordance to maintain the usefulness of that thinking tool. Rethinking and redoing must be therefore welcomed as part of research practice. We must design environments that welcome renewal and re-implementation instead of being tempted by the teleology of "getting it right once and for all." Agile Hermeneutics and Voyant are therefore self-aware re-inventions built on the giant shoulders of a tradition, not fixed and stable production systems. As research tools, they are unstable models, not finished things. (We will return to this in chapter 9.)

Thinking Through Text Technology

Like Descartes' *Discourse*, *Hermeneutica* is about thinking through, albeit a very different type of thinking through. It returns to earlier methods of interpretation and looks forward to how to do interpretation with the new computing tools at hand. This book takes a different path back than Descartes' *Discourse*. Our story doesn't reject authority or talking with others. Rather, it is the story of writing and software development embedded in traditions, such as the dialogue.

Thinking through is dialogic. Dialogue (as opposed to solitary meditation) is one of the paradigmatic styles of doing philosophy. The Greek 'dia' in the word 'dialogos' (Greek for "conversation") does not, as many assume, mean "two." Rather, it can be translated as "through," "between," or "exchange." Thus a playful etymology of "dialogue" would explain it as thinking through, or that which comes "through conversation," whether it is the Cartesian inner dialogue or a conversation with another.[20] Socrates, in one of Xenophon's dialogues, played with the connection between *dialogos* (conversation) and *dialego* (to classify). Xenophon, writing about Socrates, says "the very word 'discussion,' according to him, owes its name to the practice of meeting together for common deliberation, sorting, discussing things after their kind: and therefore one should be ready and prepared for this and be zealous for it."[21]

We present our communal thinking as meeting together and thinking through with hermeneutical things. Most important, our story doesn't begin simply with reflections on thinking. It begins with interpretive reflections assisted by tools. We share Descartes' desire to think through, but we also want to think *with*. This book is about one way to begin the work of thinking through by choosing to think with our tools and collaborators.

Why Text Technology Now?

In this book we are going to concentrate on ways of thinking collaboratively through technology, specifically text technologies we believe are of epochal importance. How can text technology give us a new way of thinking through? Why is information technology, and text technology in particular, so important now?

- We are surrounded by electronic texts that we read mediated through technology. The texts we read on our laptops, our smartphones, and our e-readers, off the Web, and on screens are all read through technology. Text-analysis tools are more powerful, nuanced, and speculative versions of the search utilities in the browsing and editing tools provided by your favorite word processor or PDF reader.
- The market for electronic reading is changing dramatically. With the Kindle, the iPad, and similar devices, we have viable electronic book and media readers that are doing well in the market. They have succeeded in combining ease of acquisition and ease of reading. Many readers are choosing electronic representations despite the convenience and familiarity of paper. *Hermeneutica* looks at how we can go beyond reading in the sense of flipping virtual pages now that we have texts that can be processed by computers. It does so by not asking about electronic reading, but about interpretation.
- The scale of available electronic texts is changing. Thanks to Google Books, HathiTrust, and other very large text collections, researchers can find millions of digital volumes. Should the intellectual-property issues of Google Books ever be fully resolved, we could have access to page images or at least the words from each page.[22] What can we do with such a large amount of data? Our tools for analyzing texts have grown out of concording tools designed to handle one book or a small collection of books, not millions. The types of questions we ask also tend to be about individual works, small collections of works by a single author, or comparative collections. What sorts of tools, methods, and questions can handle millions of texts?[23]

Our work is not only for researchers who need access to text technologies.[24] A study from IDC (2012), a "global provider of market intelligence," estimates that between 2005 and 2020 "the digital universe will [have grown] by a factor of 300, from 130 exabytes to 40,000 exabytes, or 40 trillion gigabytes (more than 5,200 gigabytes for every man, woman, and child in 2020)," and that "from now until 2020, the digital universe will about double every two years."[25]

It should not be surprising that, according to a study titled "How Much Information?" (Lyman and Varian 2003), the Internet is the fastest-growing medium, accounting for 532,897 terabytes between the Web, email, and instant messaging. (By the time you read this, even that estimate will be out of date.) Much of the information is email and other text. Text is still dominant—even on the multimedia-capable Web, where Hypertext Markup Language (HTML) and Portable Document Format (PDF) account for 17.8 percent and 9.2 percent respectively while images and movies account for 23.2 percent and 4.3 percent respectively.[26] The use of Google and other search engines illuminates the importance of text. Even if a growing amount of the information on the Web is video and other time-based content, we use text to search for that information, it is text that is indexed, and it is text that makes up the metadata.

The explosion of information raises ethical and privacy issues connected to hermeneutical issues. Two major issues are control over this universe of text and the mining of text. IDC argues that only a "tiny fraction of the digital universe has been explored for analytic value," and estimates that "by 2020, as much as 33% of the digital universe will contain information that might be valuable if analyzed, compared with 25% today." "This untapped value," IDC continues, "could be found in patterns in social media usage, correlations in scientific data from discrete studies, medical information intersected with sociological data, faces in security footage, and so on" (2012).[27]

Organizations that have access to our words are increasingly using analytical tools to mine personal information and draw inferences that we may not want drawn. We see evidence of the tension between individually created information and corporate management of such information in a cover story in the online bulletin of the Canadian Association of University Teachers ("Email Outsourcing Threatens Privacy & Academic Freedom") concerning the Lakehead University Faculty Association's grievance against the university for outsourcing e-mail to Google Gmail. Gmail's terms of use allow it to store and process information in the United States, which opens the possibility that the email may be mined by the American government.[28] Edward Snowden's revelations about what the National Security Agency and other governmental organizations are doing make it clear that our information is being mined, even when what is mined is only metadata. Corporations are likewise getting into the game; Google exploits our email, and Twitter sells access to aggregated data. More and more of our private textual correspondence is available for large-scale analysis and interpretation. We need to learn more about these methods to be able to think through the ethical, social, and political consequences. The humanities have traditions of engaging with issues of literacy, and big data should not be an exception. How to analyze, interpret, and exploit big data are big problems for the humanities.

Hermeneutica illustrates how digital analytics can be used to develop more nuanced digital literacy in the humanities, a new kind of literacy that allows us to continue our pursuits as humanities scholars in the changing world we find ourselves in. In short, we are practicing thinking in the humanities while the way people read, the tools of reading, and information privacy and organization are shifting around us. These shifts matter. If we continue to treat textuality as a subject, we need to understand how texts can be mined. *Hermeneutica* will help you understand what computers can do with texts.

Looking Back at the Rhetoric of Text Analysis

Papers drawing on computer-assisted text analysis, with their long lists of word counts and their complicated discussions of statistical methods, can be hard to read. Scholars who are primarily interested in the literature being analyzed, not in the technology or the methodology used to analyze it, might not bother to read these technical texts. A recent blog post by a graduate student provides some frank insights about the frustration many feel with the exposition of text analysis:

> It takes the worst part of scientific papers (really really long sets of tabular data in the body of the text) and the worst part of papers from the humanities (really really complicated language where simple language would have done) and puts it in one. If this is what the cooperation of computational text analysis and traditional literary analysis will yield, I am scared.[29]

Authors of articles that draw on computational methods might feel damned if they do (include enough information about the technical methods) and damned if they don't (include enough to make sense of their computed claims). The methods that we hope will yield new insights—cluster graphs, statistical techniques, and long lists of word counts—can actually be detrimental to arriving at insights.

The challenge to those who would interpret with the aid of computing can be summed up as a "black-box" problem. Technique either is encapsulated in the black box of technology or is unfolded in a mind-numbing tedium of detail. Either way, something is hidden and something is shown. As Willard McCarty writes of the batch programming tools of the early years,

> What scholars did on the machine thus tended strongly to diverge from their other work in both the sequentiality and opacity of the computing applications. … It made the importance of computing for scholarship difficult to understand by

focusing attention on the necessarily expensive, relatively inflexible product rather than on the interactive, heuristic process.[30]

This black-box problem is worsened by the expense and difficulty of the process. In principle, formalized analytical processes should be easy to recapitulate and should not suffer from the problem of connoisseurship,[31] but in reality the expense of computing, the complexity of analytical software, and the time it takes to use computing processes make such processes unlikely to be recapitulated. More important, as McCarty points out, these analytical processes are inflexible and difficult to weave into our more interactive hermeneutical practices.

One benefit of traditional hermeneutical practices such as close reading is that the trained reader need not install anything, run any software, wrestle with settings, or wait for results. The experienced reader can just enjoy iteratively reading, thinking, and re-reading. Similarly, the reader of another person's interpretation, if the book being interpreted is at hand, can just pick it up, follow the references, and recapitulate the reading. To be as effective as close reading, analytical methods have to be significantly easier to apply and understand.[32] They have to be like reading, or, better yet, a part of reading.[33] Those invested in the use of digital analytics need to think differently about what is shown and what is hidden: the rhetorical presentation of analytics matters.

Further, literary readers of interpretive works want to learn about the interpretation. Much of the literature in journals devoted to humanities computing suffers from being mostly about the computing; it is hard to find scholarship that is addressed to literary scholars and is based on computing practices. McCarty struggles with this problem at the end of his chapter on modeling when he tries to make sense of the "Chart of selected personifications," itself the product of a black box of visualization (McCarty 2005, 60). Had McCarty devoted the space in his book needed to fully explain how the chart was generated, he would have distracted readers from the point of the chapter, which is the "interactive, heuristic process" of thinking through, manipulating, and making a model. The gifts of technique in computer-assisted interpretation must be made accessible enough to influence thought.[34] The advantage of any formal technique, when properly described, is that it can be reproduced. If you hide the technique, you lose the logical force of an argument, in addition to losing any reader who might be interested in the technique itself. You might as well not have bothered to struggle through digitizing, marking up, and analyzing a text.[35]

Hermeneutica proposes an alternative approach: the hybrid essay, an interpretive work embedded with hermeneutical toys that can be explored for technique. Our hermeneutica draw on an evolution of common interactive analytics, from word clouds to complex data journalism interactives, which, having become more common, are better understood by wider audiences. Hermeneutica embedded in traditional forms of scholarly arguments offer more than a hybrid approach; they offer a more engaging approach.

Digital Analytics

In this book we embrace a flexible form of digital analytics, arguing for the benefit of a few different kinds of hermeneutica, including interpretive tools and embeddable toys. Interpretive tools focus on the particularity of the work and its poetic or rhetorical language. Rather than show a theory of textuality, they assist the reader to interpret the meaning of a text or to follow a text's rhetorical structure. These tools augment reading rather than replace it. There may be little or no accompanying explanation of the interpretive tool, but, unlike a static graph presented in a print article, embedded toys provide immediate access to hidden methods by allowing readers to play with interpretive results. More generally, a hermeneutical tool invites exploration in, and encourages interpretation, of any text it can handle. A tool is thus hermeneutical; it gathers in its working a method of interpretation and makes it available for users to try on texts that interest them.

The difference between a general-purpose interpretive tool and an embeddable toy is that the toy combines a particular text with particular analyses. We call it a toy not to demean it, but because rhetorically it invites playing around with the text by means other than reading. A toy is a particular interpretation in place—a hermeneutical thing that is an integral part of an essay.

What We're Not Doing

It is important that we be clear about what this book is *not* about and *not* trying to do. This book is not about linguistic analysis of text (for that, see Jurafsky and Martin 2000). There are rich traditions in philosophy, lexicography, and linguistics of studying how language is understood and how it can be generated. These fields look at much smaller units of text than literary text analysis does. Lexicographers look at words; philosophers look at the truth of statements or small combinations of statements; linguists look at small units (phonemes) and at semantic units (sentences and paragraphs); literary scholars look at units of meaning (poems, novels, tracts, dialogues, speeches, and even entire text collections).

The uses to which we put computers are also very different. Logical and linguistic tools are often designed to parse a sentence and generate a formal representation of its meaning, much like the sentence diagramming we had to do in school. These tools abstract out the particular expression of the sentence to produce a representation of meaning that can be checked for truth or compared with other meanings. They test theories about how statements are generated and parsed. Humanists, however, are interested in the ideographic—the individual and unique human expression. Humanists are interested in particular human expressions and their interpretation, not in language in general.

There are important exceptions to these generalizations. Corpus linguistics tends to treat collections of larger units of texts more like literary analysis. The types of corpora these two fields use, corpus linguistics and literary analysis, are sometimes the same, though the goals of their study might be different. Stylistics and authorship analysis are likewise areas of overlap with literary analysis. These are a subset of linguistic techniques that are suited to describing the writing style of an author, a genre, a time period, or for identifying the author of a disputed text based on their style. Early uses of computers for text analysis included experiments in stylistic analysis; we will touch on some of these in chapter 9. Stylistic analysis is also being re-invented (and adapted) by Franco Moretti, Matthew Jockers, and other literary historians to look beyond the style of individual texts to the style of authors, generations, and genres. Again, there is a lot of overlap between large-scale stylistic analysis and large-scale text analysis, which is why we will touch on theories about the use of computers on a large scale. In *Hermeneutica*, however, we are primarily interested in interpretation through computers. Franco Moretti writes in "The End of the Beginning" (2013a):

We do not need more interpretations, I take [Jonathan] Culler to mean, not because they have nothing to say, but because, by and large, *they have already said what they had to*. A lot of good work has been done on the relation between meaning and meaning, far too little on meanings and forces.[36]

Though there may be an excess of interpretations in print, we all need to continue reading and interpreting our world. We also need to test our interpretations against those of others. Moreover, we need to think about the use of computers in how people interpret. Large-scale computer-assisted methods are not just for explaining literary history; they can be used for large-scale interpretation in all humanistic endeavors. This brings with it many opportunities and dangers.

Interpretive analysis can learn from and build on corpus linguistics, stylistic analysis, and large-scale methods. As the MONK (Metadata Offer New Knowledge) project has shown, part-of-speech taggers and other tools developed by computational linguistics can be used to increase the sophistication of interpretive tools.[37] Quantitative and statistical literary approaches have drawn on the careful work of corpus linguists, and can continue learning from such work, by testing the validity of various statistical techniques in interpretive contexts. Should computational linguists develop a reliable system of machine translation, it may be based on some sort of semantic analysis that can reliably extract meaning from a text so that it can then be put in the form of another language. Such semantic analysis would dramatically change literary text analysis, especially of rhetorical texts that are meant to be explicit in meaning. Reliable semantic analysis would make it practicable to build tools that would summarize meaning very differently. Some translation approaches, including that of Google Translate, depend more on brute statistical force than on any representation of meaning. What works for machine translation doesn't in any way imitate how a human translates, much as the supercomputer Dark Blue doesn't play chess the way a human does. Machine translation tools may not ever be very useful for interpretive needs.

This book, to be clear, is not about what we can learn from corpus linguistics or computational linguistics. Rather, it is rooted in the traditions of computer-assisted text analysis in literary studies and other interpretive disciplines and the more hermeneutical ends of philosophy and history. It is about that tradition as much as it is about what you can do with hermeneutical things. Insofar as the tradition of literary text analysis has evolved in parallel with computational linguistics without building on it, we feel justified in leaving that for another project.

The use of interpretive tools in the social sciences is also outside the purview of this book. There is a tradition of qualitative techniques and tools for analyzing interviews or other texts of interest to social scientists. This is similar to literary text analysis, in that it uses computers to interpret texts, but the goals and methods are different. Atlas.ti, NVivo, and similar tools help social scientists with content analysis for social scientific aims. They are not meant to help understand the texts themselves so much as to help understand the phenomena of which texts such as interview transcripts are evidence. Again, as with linguistic analysis, we could learn a lot from such tools and traditions of research practice, but they are beyond the scope of this book.

Dangers

One should keep certain dangers in mind when first embarking on the hybrid practices used in *Hermeneutica*. The first is the disappearance of the author. To quote what Anthony Ashley Cooper, the First Earl of Shaftesbury, said about dialogue in 1737, "for here (in dialogue) the author is annihilated, and the reader, being no way applied to, stands for nobody."[38] This is a danger Martin Heidegger and other philosophers of technology talk about: Ready-at-hand tools become transparent (unnoticed), and the creator's authorial responsibility for the instrument remains hidden. Interpretive tools extend interpretation in ways that require caution. To avoid this danger we have to ask how one might build research tools that disclose themselves. We address this essential question in chapter 9. If tool development is research, it should be open to scrutiny as other types of research are. Nevertheless, an open-source tool is not open in the way that a philosophical paper with ample references is open. It is hard to interpret things designed to be thought *with* rather than thought *about*. Tools are designed to become transparent in use (to withdraw), and code is written to be debugged and run, not seen, by users. This is not to give undue value to Romantic ideas about the importance of the author. Interpreting technologies is difficult, especially while one is using them. In his 2008 book *Mechanisms*, Matthew Kirschenbaum shows us one way forward. He adapts bibliographic practices to early adventure-style computer games and other classics of electronic literature. Kirschenbaum reads these as literature and uses forensic techniques to pry open their code. We are taking a different approach. We are reading tools as hermeneutical things.

A second danger is that entanglement might lead to the corruption of humanistic scholarship. The practices of software engineering could be the first step in the disappearance of the humanities. Agile Hermeneutics, and Digital Humanities in general, could be the Trojan Horse that lets loose alien methods in the polis of the humanities, a field already under grave threat. Geoffrey Harpham, in "Science and the Theft of Humanity" (2006), an essay published in *American Scientist*, writes:

One of the most striking features of contemporary intellectual life is the fact that questions formerly reserved for the humanities are today being approached by scientists in various disciplines such as cognitive science, cognitive neuroscience, robotics, artificial life, behavioral genetics and evolutionary biology.[39]

The humanities are seen as having failed over the last 2,000 years to answer the questions assigned. Newer disciplines with more productive methods are moving in. This book and the Digital Humanities are either abetting this poaching or trying to stave it off by introducing computing methods directly to humanists before all our students disappear.

It is hard to answer such speculative fears. Harpham argues that this poaching across disciplines may reinvigorate the humanities, as do many digital humanists. All disciplines thrive on renewal. Without regular eruptions of new ideas and methods, the humanities would not be the humanities. We suspect that the sciences, naively poaching, will find themselves bogged down in the recursive problems of interpretation that resist easy solutions, a problem that humanists have been warning others about all along. The humanities have been known to borrow concepts from the sciences, such as chaos or string theory, and weave them into literary criticism, but they do so with different intentions. They do so to explore a question, rather than to seek an easily discernible "right" answer in a scientific way.[40] Consequently, we may find that it is the sciences that are influenced by the subject matter, their methods eroded by the complexity of the human. Either way, what should matter to us is not preserving the practices of the humanities as if they were intangible cultural property, but preserving a vital and ethical conversation about what it is to be human. *Hermeneutica* is about how we can participate in that conversation by thinking through technology.

A third and related danger is presented by a bundle of commitments that we call the modernist commitment to progress through technique. To think through the development of possible technologies is to agree, at least provisionally, that there could be better designs. Bundled with the practices of design are a hope of improvement and a belief in progress. Though that hope can be moderated by care for unanticipated outcomes, and by a scepticism regarding the hyperventilated claims of computing, it is still a hope that we can push back the horizons of our knowledge. Yes, we do this kind of work with hope and with the knowledge that we cannot anticipate how it will be used. We regard this danger as unavoidable. It is the danger of any action and any involvement in the world that is not cynical. We all, in one way or another, try things out in the face of dangers, and do so with hope. For that matter, it is the danger of all types of intellectual work. One can always be misinterpreted. Without the confidence of an intellectual ground or clear ends, we are all mini-modernists, trying to swim forward in small and local ways while acknowledging the probable impossibility of ever finding final grounds or ends.

Recapitulate, Imitate, and Contribute

How can you read a hybrid book/site and text/tool such as *Hermeneutica*? Descartes' *Discourse* is important to the practices of the humanities because it introduces the discussion of method that has dominated the method-ological imagination of the humanities since its appearance. The *Discourse* is about an alternative dialogical method. For us, interpretation starts in conversation, not in retreat from the other. We invite you to join in con-versations of three kinds:

• If you are interested in reflective discussion of interpretation through tools, you can stick to the theoretical parts of the book (chapters 3, 5, 7, 9, and 11). We recommend the printed book as a way into our way of thinking through. If you then want to disagree with us or otherwise engage things we have written about, we invite you to contribute a com-ment to the website.[41]

• If the interaction between building the tools of interpretation and using them interests you, we recommend that you begin with Voyant (http://voyant-tools.org) and try it on your texts. For tutorials, see the documentation about Voyant.[42] Alternatively, you may want to try tools from other developers. To find alternative tools, go to the Text Analy-sis Portal for Research (TAPoR) for tools and reviews.[43] TAPoR has been documenting current tools and tools important to the history of Digital Humanities.

• If you are interested in ways of writing with interactive analytics, you should look at the examples we provide in our interludes and read the documentation on embedding panels in your own online writings. You could begin by trying a small blog essay analyzing a text, or, you could analyze the chapters from this book that are available online. If you have an essay that you think is exemplary and want to contribute it to hermeneuti.ca (the website) or have us refer to it in our list of rel-evant resources, please see "How to Contribute" at http://hermeneuti.ca/contribute.

In our own research, we wanted to think about methods of interpreta-tion. To do so, we brought computer-assisted methods to dialogical prac-tices that predate Descartes. We call this Agile Hermeneutics. However, in practice we found it difficult to move swiftly from the interpretive tool environment (in which textual evidence is explored) to the environment of the essay (in which a new interpretation is crafted). In response to that difficulty, we created Voyant. As in any experiment in interactive interface, the goal for Voyant was to get to a point where the practices of moving between tool and text would be easy and quick enough to be experienced as another thread in a dynamic dialogue.

Conclusion

In this book we reflect on the innovation of Voyant and position it in a history of the development of text-analysis tools in the humanities. We chose to call this project *Hermeneutica* to draw attention to our argument through tools, namely that interpretive tools and embedded toys are an essential way people are already experiencing text analysis on the Web. We are thinking through text analysis in the humanities by developing techniques to support such hermeneutica.

2 The Measured Words: How Computers Analyze Text

Words should be weighed not measured
fortune cookie

Richard Powers' novel *Galatea 2.2* (1995) is the story of a writer who agrees to teach a computer (an artificial intelligence) to pass an exam by interpreting English literary texts at the same level as a Master of Arts student. Helen (the system the writer develops with a computer scientist) commits suicide (terminates her own program) once she realizes she can never experience the world she is interpreting through literature. As the title of the novel suggests, *Galatea 2.2* is about the relationship of artists and engineers with their creations, which they can come to love into life.

In the original myth, Pygmalion falls in love with his statue, Galatea. Venus, taking pity on him, brings the statue to life. In *Galatea 2.2* it is the writer who lovingly tutors Helen into awareness. Powers depicts the believable possibility of an artificial intelligence that can interpret literature and make art. He asks us whether we would really want a work of *techne* that can do that most human of tasks, interpretation, for us. If it could, would an artificial intelligence want to? Helen's suicide suggests that interpretation without experience or agency is bereft:

You are the ones who can hear airs. Who can be frightened or encouraged. You can hold things and break them and fix them. I never felt at home here. This is an awful place to be dropped down halfway.[1]

Of course there is no Helen. Computers cannot yet begin to approximate graduate level interpretive skills, but the questions Powers raises stand. What relationships do we want to have with hermeneutica and more generally interpretive machines?[2]

We need to understand what computers can actually do in order to answer questions about how digital analytics can enable new ways of thinking through. This chapter looks at what questions we can ask of a text with a computer and the tools we build for it. By extension, it asks how a computer understands text. Much of this chapter will deal with the basics of how computers handle text files. Readers familiar with strings and pattern-matching algorithms may wish to move on to the next chapter. For humanists who use computers but don't program, this chapter will introduce data and programming concepts to illuminate the subtle differences between what we think text is and how a computer manipulates it. In the slippage between our literary notion of a text and the computer's literal processing lie the disappointment and the possibility of text analysis. Computers cannot understand a text for us. They can, however, do things that may surprise us.

Numbers and Codes

Is text analysis just quantification? Number crunching is often used as a way of explaining and denigrating what computers do. The philosopher Anthony Kenny, author of *The Computation of Style* (1982), argues in *Computers and the Humanities* (1992) that "in all humanities disciplines the computer is used in an endeavour to replace intuition with quantification."[3] Likewise, Lev Manovich, in *The Language of New Media* (2001), makes quantification one of the basic principles of new media.

Computers are not calculators. They are general-purpose symbol processors that can handle any formally definable symbol system. Numbers or quantities are just one thing they represent symbolically and process logically. All digital information is encoded in a common binary language and then manipulated in logical ways. Programming languages built on logic can do mathematical tasks, check spelling, or paint on a virtual canvas.[4] But computers don't "read" words any more than they "see" paint the way we do. When the letter 'a' is represented on a computer as the decimal number 97 or the binary number 1100001, that doesn't mean that it is a quantity. Instead it is the 98th position in a code lookup table that starts at zero. The 'a' could just as easily have been assigned position 65 instead. Computers are cryptographic machines that manipulate codes, which themselves symbolically represent phenomena (numbers, color, letters, and so on). What matters in cryptography is that everyone have the same code table so that a file encoded on one computer can be decrypted and used on another.

A computer can manipulate many symbolic systems for various purposes by encoding them into a binary format. Image files use color lookup tables that assign a binary code to each possible color; Musical Instrument Digital

Interface (MIDI) uses codes to represent musical events; text systems use character-encoding systems such as American Standard Code for Information Interchange (ASCII) and Unicode. If you have ever seen funny characters or boxes instead of legible characters on a webpage, chances are you are looking at an example of encoding failure. The failure happens because of inconsistencies in how symbol codes are used. The page was created using a different code table. If you would like to try your hand at fixing the problem, you can change the Character Encoding setting in your browser.

Strings: How a Computer Handles Text

Many of the techniques used by computing humanists are quantitative; analytical tools count and graph words. However, when we look at how a computer treats the symbols we think of as text, it appears that there is nothing essentially quantitative about text analysis.

To the computer, a piece of text is a "string"—a sequence of characters from a defined list of possible characters called an "alphabet" or a "character set." If you are learning to program, "strings" are one of the fundamental data types that you learn about, along with integers (whole numbers), booleans (true or false), and arrays (ordered sets of other data types). To understand how a computer handles text, one needs to understand how programs handle strings. They are not exactly what we think of generally as text. They are a formal and limited subset:

- Strings are sequences of characters that have a beginning and end.[5] Each character is either at the beginning of the sequence or follows another character and only one other character. In a text, by contrast, characters don't necessarily follow each other in a discernible sequence. In a crossword puzzle, for example, every character is in two sequences (a horizontal one and a vertical one.) This doesn't mean that we cannot overcome the sequentially of strings, but to do that we typically build on them.
- The characters in strings come from predefined character sets. We cannot introduce a new character, such as some random squiggle, into a string. Instead we have to work with standardized character sets, such as Extended ASCII (which allows 256 characters) or Unicode. The UTF-8 Unicode transformation format[6] allows for more than a million different characters. This pre-defined set, as large as it is, is still finite. That can make representing the rich variation of something like Japanese calligraphy difficult.

- Strings are not formatted with all the rich typographic and layout choices that are available when one is writing a text or doing desktop publishing. In raw text there is no indication of higher-order features such as what is a word, italics, or paragraphs; one has to define a formal way of representing them on top of strings. One way is to have a dedicated character like the typewriter "return" in your alphabet that would start a new paragraph as early text systems had.[7] In ASCII there are a series of non-printing characters like "line feed" and "return" than could be used to control a printer to get the simple formatting effects needed.[8] HTML allows tags like *to indicate that the text between the tags should be emphasized* (though the choice as to what visual feature corresponds to emphasis is left up to the designer).

Most of these differences are really limitations to our broader and polysemous sense of text. Computers are not able to handle the ambiguity found within language without explicit instruction. Strings have to be defined formally and in such a way that it is always clear what the next character is, if any, when processing a file.

More important, computers do not read *meaning* in a string. They process a sequence of characters. Try to imagine that for a computer a string looks something like this:

★✳••▢✳▢▯•✳⊱

What could you do with such strings? You might feel a bit lost, or you might want to see if you can decrypt this string. Some characters are repeated, but you don't know anything about that character other than that it differs from others. We have highly developed mental functions that begin reading without any conscious intervention when we see lines of character-like things. This makes it hard to appreciate the limitations of computers. It is difficult to not read text-like signs in your visual field unless you put your eyes out of focus or look at texts in foreign languages. Try looking at

HelloWorld!

and seeing it as a sequence of glyphs without reading it as meaningful text.[9]

Representing Texts

The first act of text analysis is to represent a text as a string so that the computer can manipulate it in ways that can be anticipated. This is an act of demarcation and then one of representation. Which features of the original are essential to the text? For example, encoders have to make decisions about whether the font sizes are important, or whether the pagination is important, whether marginalia should be included, or which edition to use. All these decisions demarcate what *is* the text and how what you choose to be the text is represented.

Once you have demarcated *what* it is that you want to represent, you need to decide on the encoding you will use on the computer. A string is composed of characters from a limited alphabet. Some textual information may have to be translated or sacrificed to fit the available string representations. Most digital text scholars would recommend using a current standard like UTF-8 for the character encoding and an open markup language based on the TEI Guidelines[10] for the formatting and other information.[11]

The chosen character encoding and file format will make a difference to the sorts of questions you can ask of a digital text. The original seven-bit ASCII character set cannot represent, say, Arabic characters. Typographic formatting such as bold, italic, and 24-point need to be encoded if you want to represent that information in the electronic text. Pagination information likewise needs to be represented if searching by the original print page number is desirable. To add formatting and other non-linguistic information there are a number of file formats and markup languages, some open and some proprietary.

Most people first experimenting with text analysis will not, however, create an electronic text from scratch to experiment with. Rather, they will begin by finding an electronic text online, a text where others have made most of the circumscribing and representing decisions.[12] Webpages are difficult to analyze because they contain all sorts of navigational text, as are Microsoft Word files and other pre-formatted files.[13] Though Word has some useful analytical tools built in, proprietary formats like Word are not recommended for text analysis, as they can be difficult to process by other programs (in other words, analytic functionality is somewhat limited to the built-in features). Voyant Tools is able to process Word files natively, but it is preferable to export from Word to more generic formats (such as plain text or HTML) that can be used with a wider range of tools.

A number of scholarly projects, among them the Text Encoding Initiative (TEI), use open formats based on XML (eXtensible Markup Language). The TEI Guidelines present sensible choices for digital encoding, suggesting the best way to represent a speaker or a new chapter in XML. Because XML-encoded texts use open and documented formats, they are more likely to be usable with future tools than with proprietary formats.

Plain text files, such as those available from Project Gutenberg, are seldom considered scholarly editions; they are minimalist by design. For that reason, scholarly electronic editions are usually encoded in XML (and sometimes rendered as webpages in HTML). A text editor will reveal the tags that demarcate and represent information. This markup can be used to show the text properly in a browser by adding the formatting information, but it can also be used for analysis. To analyze the discourse of a particular speaker, such as Shakespeare's Romeo, one must first identify how the character and his speeches are demarcated with encoding:

```
<sp who="Romeo"><p>Is the day so young?</p></sp>
```

How does one read encoding? The `<p>` tag indicates the start of a paragraph of text. The `<sp>` tags indicate that this paragraph is a speech by someone (indicated by the "who" attribute) called "Romeo." Angle brackets, < and >, are escape characters; the markup language uses them to indicate that what is between angle brackets is formatting and structural information, not content meant to be read. Tags are a layer of encoding built on simple strings; they are interpreted by the machine, but not displayed to the reader.[14]

What Then Can We Do with Strings?

Text-analysis algorithms work with strings in ways that are useful for interpreting the texts they represent. An algorithm is a procedure that involves a series of steps that can be reliably computed. When you describe the steps of a procedure in sufficient formal detail that they could be turned into instructions for a computing machine (e.g., when the instructions are formalized *and* computable or within the capabilities of the computer), then you have a text-analysis algorithm. It is a process that we can use to program a computer to reliably do something to text.

Algorithms are not necessarily quantitative methods. Counting and quantifying can be useful, but they are a means to an end; they are not essential to algorithms. Algorithms automate tasks through formal description of discrete steps. Thinking algorithmically is partly about reducing large and interesting tasks to smaller steps. So what interpretive tasks can we automate? What automated tasks can help with interpretation? If we want to know how a computer can help us question a text, we need to look at the tasks in questioning that can be effectively automated.

In the rest of this chapter, we will walk through the types of algorithms that are useful in textual interpretation. We will describe these intuitively, using what is often called "pseudocode," to help readers understand what the computer is programmed to do as if they were asked to do it manually. We will focus particularly on finding, concording, tokenization, word counts, lists, distributions, and comparisons.

Finding Patterns

Computers match patterns in strings to search text. One example of a simple search algorithm takes a short string, ❂■❖•❙▲❊▲ and compares it against every possible substring of a larger text. Imagine comparing the word you want to search for against the first eight characters of the book you are searching in. Continue moving one character forward and repeat the process over and over until you come to the end. With each comparison, check if the search string and the subsection of the full string are the same. (This is a logical operation.) If they are, then you have a match. Google's search algorithm uses pattern matching (though for efficiency it builds an index of terms instead of searching through each document). It searches for short strings—say, the word "analysis"—and finds popular webpages that contain that string. Google doesn't have to know what ❂■❖•❙▲❊▲ means; it merely has to find pages with that same pattern.

Computers can do more than just find exact matches for short strings. They can be programmed to look for patterns of characters. For example, software can find the singular "woman" or the plural "women," can find all the variants of "prince" (including "princes," "princess," and "princesses"), and can find word variants such as "sceptic" and "skeptic." The use of "regular expressions"[15] is a common way to enable flexible searching.

Here are some examples of regular expressions:

`wom[ae]n` Search for "woman" or "women."

`prince.*` Uses the metacharacters "." (any character) and "*" (any number of) to indicate that we want strings that start with "prince" and have any number of any characters after.

`(love|hate|whatever)` Looks for either "love" or "hate" or "whatever."

`s[ck]eptic.*` Search for different spellings and endings of "sceptic."

A regex (regular expression) is a small formal specification of a pattern to be matched. Formal languages have evolved for specifying these patterns; the exact syntax and functionality varies between programming languages. Regexes are sufficiently useful that they are built into Perl, or Ruby, and some other programming languages. They do not, however, "understand" text. You cannot simply search all the strings that are *about* love. You could, however, use a thesaurus to create a regex with all the relevant synonyms for love, such as

`(adulation|affection|allegiance|amity|amorousness|...).`[16]

Searching with a thesaurus for all known synonyms can provide volume, but not accuracy. Computers are not good at disambiguating polysemous words that have different meanings (for instance, "like" as verb, preposition, noun, conjunction, adverb, or adjective). You will have to read through the plethora of results carefully.

KWICs and Concording

Pattern matching may locate patterns, but this is not useful to the interpreter unless there is a way to display results. Word processors and browsers move to the first instance of the pattern you want matched and highlight it. Clicking "next" and "previous" buttons lets you navigate the full text, jumping from one hit (individual result) to another. The KWIC (Key Word In Context) display and the Concordance, two of the tools we will look at in depth in chapter 3, are the most common ways of displaying search results.

A KWIC works with our ability to skim. Pattern matching on a large text might throw up a hundreds of results. Having a line of context and the key word highlighted enables you to skim to quickly locate relevant matches. Voyant, for that matter, provides the ability to expand a hit to show more context if you are interested in doing so. You can also use the KWIC to get back to the full text in Voyant. Pattern matching analyzes the string to find

Left ▼	Keyword	Right	Document
) will coordinatethe various elements	text, analysis	, variants, translation alignment)in such	1) 1987-88
this meansword-processing and some	text analysis	programs. My academictraining was	2) 1988-89
...on text documentation, textrepresent	text analysis	and interpretation, and syntax and	3) 1989-90
...recommend HUM-- A CONCORDA	TEXT ANA...	PROGRAM. It isavailable from	4) 1990-91
...develop electronic materials in ortho	text analysis	, databasecompilation and linguistic g...	5) 1991-92
...processing program, SGMLparser/e	text analysis	program, collation program, stemma ...	6) 1992-93
text software. Commercial softwarefor	text analysis	and manipulation covers only a	7) 1993-94
...include: Internet Resources; Electro	TextAnalysis	Tools; Text Corpora in Humanities	8) 1994-95
and to provide software for	text analysis	. Sorry, don't have an address	9) 1995-96
:drain, and coolielabour. June 24-29	Text Analysis	I: TACT (Doorn/Leenarts) The	10) 1996-97
,practical side of producing HTML	textanalysis	and hypertext design. Students would	11) 1997-98
it is entirely probable that	text analysis	skills have been developed outside	12) 1998-99
qualitativeand quantiative software for	text analysis	:Alexa Melina & Cornelia Zuell: A	13) 1999-00
,imaging work(e.g., scanning	text analysis	software). Must be able to	14) 2000-01

Figure 2.1
KWIC in Voyant (from the Humanist Listserv archive).

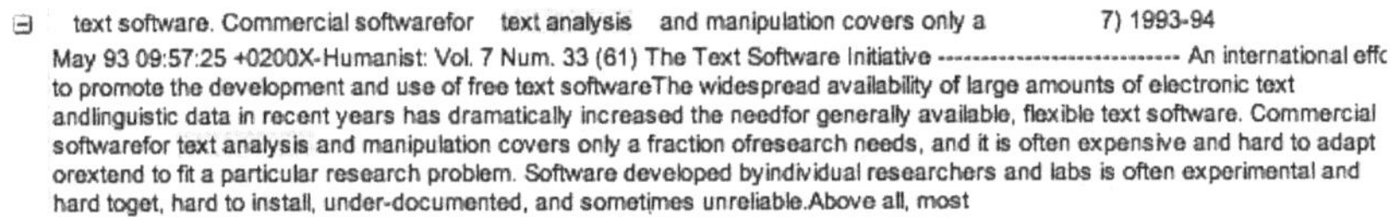

▣   text software. Commercial softwarefor   text analysis   and manipulation covers only a   7) 1993-94
     May 93 09:57:25 +0200X-Humanist: Vol. 7 Num. 33 (61) The Text Software Initiative ---------------------------- An international effc
     to promote the development and use of free text softwareThe widespread availability of large amounts of electronic text
     andlinguistic data in recent years has dramatically increased the needfor generally available, flexible text software. Commercial
     softwarefor text analysis and manipulation covers only a fraction ofresearch needs, and it is often expensive and hard to adapt
     orextend to fit a particular research problem. Software developed byindividual researchers and labs is often experimental and
     hard toget, hard to install, under-documented, and sometimes unreliable.Above all, most

Figure 2.2
A KWIC line in Voyant with more context to preview.

matches; a concordance synthesizes resulting matches for review and further interpretation. They are hermeneutica.

Tokenization

Pattern matching may be good for finding strings in a text, but it will not help to summarize a text. One approach for summarizing a text is to identify the words that best characterize it. Either these words appear frequently within the text or they are the most distinctive words within the text. But before summarizing texts, computers need a way of recognizing individual words.[17] This is where tokenization comes in.

Tokenization is the breaking apart of a text into smaller units that can be manipulated and counted. It is the analysis (etymologically a breaking down into parts) in text analysis, in the sense that a preliminary step of many text-analysis processes is breaking a long string into simpler parts for manipulation and recombination. The generation of a concordance is a synthesis of a new text from processed parts.

Although phrases, sentences, paragraphs, and speeches can be tokenized, it is most often done on individual words. The human brain is so adept at recognizing words in text that one forgets how difficult that same recognition is for a computer. Attempting to define what a word is only complicates the matter.[18] Defining a word as the smallest unit of meaning is not useful. Computers cannot yet understand meaning, per se. Instead, tokenization uses the orthographic word—units that are written like words with definable boundaries such as a space on either side—for the purpose of digital text analysis.

Defining a word as a sequence of characters with a space at either end gets us closer to something a computer could be programmed to recognize. A computer can search for the space character, and every time it encounters a white space (character) it can break off what came before and call it a word. Breaking a string on white space doesn't quite give us orthographic words, however. In some cases punctuation appears before or after a word—for example, "word." Thus we need to break not only on spaces, but also on punctuation marks—brackets, parentheses periods, commas, question marks, semicolons, colons, and quotation marks. However, without care, the contraction "don't," for instance, would be resolved into "don" and "t")= rather than into "do" and "not." Similarly, there is no absolute way to handle hyphenated words such as "e-text" and "client-side," especially since the orthography can shift over time and with variations in usage.

There are numerous writing patterns that make it difficult to tokenize cleanly. For instance, decimal numbers that look as if they contain sentence-ending periods (e.g., 100.12) and URLs that contain punctuation marks (http://hermeneuti.ca) complicate matters. Nonetheless, tokenization algorithms can be tuned for most languages to work well enough to generate a list of all the words. Insofar as orthographic words correlate with words as units of meaning, we can then begin to try to count meaning.[19] Tokenization takes us from a string (such as "Hello world! I'm now alive to the world again") to a sequence of things we recognize as words:

hello
world
i
am
now
alive
to
the
world
again

Word Counts, Lists, and Distributions

Text-analysis tools that simply sort words by frequency are very useful. The computer processes the list of tokenized words to build a new list of unique word forms. It then counts the number of occurrences for each unique word type. We call this a list of word "types." Each unique type of word has one entry with the count of occurrences. By contrast, a word token is a particular instance of the general type. All the tokens are counted for each type.[20] Table 2.1 shows "Hello world! I'm now alive to the world again" as an alphabetically sorted word-type list.

Word types can be sorted by frequency. Insofar as occurrence indicates importance, frequency counts can provide a sense of what a text is about.

Table 2.1
Alphabetized types with counts.

again	1
alive	1
am	1
hello	1
i	1
now	1
the	1
to	1
world	2

For instance, in our analysis of David Hume's *Dialogues* in chapter 10, we used the frequency of "sceptical" and related words to show that scepticism is a important philosophical issue in the dialogue—an issue that Cleanthes mentions and Philo models. However, function words, such as "the," "a," "of," "to," "in," and "that," appear more frequently than other words in most English texts. Although they serve grammatical purposes, function words do not bear analytical content. For this reason we often use a Stop-word List of the common function words to stop those words from appearing in a Word Type List. Applying a Word Frequency List to Mary Shelley's *Frankenstein* (1818) with stop-words eliminated generates a list like that in figure 2.3. Such a word list is a good place to start a computer-assisted analysis of a text. This list provides a sample of potentially useful search terms to illuminate how "life," for instance, is referenced in *Frankenstein*.

Word Clouds provide a visually stimulating way of looking at a list of high-frequency words. The cloud arranges and sizes words by their rate of appearance. High-frequency words are made large and central in the cloud. A word-cloud tool such as Voyant Cirrus (see figure 2.4) can also rotate and color words so that they to fit more aesthetically into the cloud and make the cloud as a whole easier to explore visually. One gets the impression of a birds-eye view of all the important words. Words appear next to other words serendipitously, which can rightly or wrongly suggest combinations to explore. The word cloud provides a different visual synthesis of the information. It has different affordances for interpretation.

Refreshing the Voyant Cirrus screen regenerates it, providing a different arrangement of the words suggesting other combinations. Randomness can provide interpretive hints, stimulating our imagination, though we should beware of falling in love with these artful arrangements.[21]

Words in the Entire Corpus	
Frequencies	Count ▼
man	131
life	114
father	113
shall	107
eyes	104
said	102
time	98
saw	94
night	87

Figure 2.3
A frequency-sorted word list generated by applying a Word Frequency List to *Frankenstein* with stop-words eliminated.

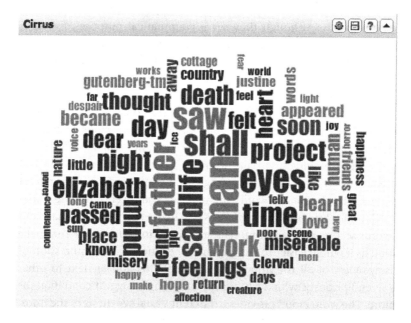

Figure 2.4
A word cloud of *Frankenstein* with stop-words removed.

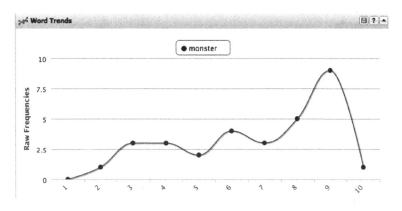

Figure 2.5
Distribution of "monster" over *Frankenstein.*

Distribution Graphs are another common form of visualization. Easily generated through tokenizing and counting, they display locations of occurrences (or hits) in a text or corpus (as we call a collection or body of texts).[22] Dividing a text into parts leads to generating distribution graphs by those parts. (Figure 2.5 shows *Frankenstein* divided into ten equal parts, or "bins," each with the same number of words.) The computer then counts and plots the number of tokens or instances of a word in each part. Connecting the points with a smooth line (a line graph) can illustrate the rise and fall of a theme. However, in cases where search terms appear as discrete references, the line itself might suggest connections where there are none. In this case, a bar graph might be more appropriate, although such graphs tend to be visually more cluttered than line graphs.

Distribution graphs suggest that word frequency is a reliable indication of a theme's significance, which is not necessarily true. Word frequency tells only how many tokens (words) there are in the string or part of a string (text segment). However, frequency can change for many reasons. For example, the frequency of a word that has multiple meanings might increase because another sense of the word is being used that has nothing to do with the theme under consideration. It is a good idea to always check results of text analysis for false positives.

Words in larger strings, each consisting of thousands of words (or tens of pages), might have bursts of usage with long empty stretches in between. To plot the graph shown in figure 2.6, we regenerated the graph shown in figure 2.5 using forty parts rather than ten. This changed the look of the graph greatly.

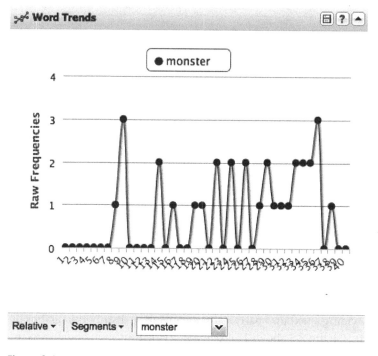

Figure 2.6
Distribution of "monster" over forty segments of *Frankenstein*.

One should also be careful about the assumption of flow in the *x* axis of a distribution graph—that is, the assumption that a text should be read from start to finish, from left to right. Encyclopedias and some other texts are collections of articles arranged in alphabetical order. The distribution of a string over an alphabetized collection would not be particularly indicative of how a theme might appear to a reader hopping from article to article. Reading direction should not be taken for granted, and analysts should be careful of the assumptions tacit in a distribution graph. The string has dimension as a sequence of characters, but that is not the same as reading.

Despite all these qualifications, distribution graphs can still illustrate something about how a theme might move through a text. First it is necessary to find a word (or a group of words) that is (or are) indicative of a theme. The trend line of the pattern can be used to help form hypotheses that can be checked by other means. A pattern that occurs more at the beginning and then slopes down may show an introductory theme; a pattern sloping up to the end might signify a gradual build-up that culminates in something noteworthy. One theme may fall when another rises; or perhaps themes rise and fall together, suggesting an interesting correlation.

Comparisons

Once you have generated a Word List, you can compare it against Word Lists generated from other texts to better see what makes your text distinctive. How do you get such a comparison? First, you need a control corpus: texts published around the same time period, or other texts by the same author, for instance. The computer then gets the relative frequency of word types for the study text and for the control corpus and calculates the difference between the two. To compute relative frequency, it divides the count for a word type like "mother" by the total number of words in the text being studied, and then does the same for texts in the control corpus. Relative frequency provides the ratio of appearance whatever the size of text. Finally, the computer must compare the relative frequency of words that appear in both texts so that you can see the words that appear more or less often in the study text than in the control text. That provides a list such as the one shown in figure 2.7.

Words in the Entire Corpus		
Frequenc...	Count	Difference ▼
was	1,022	5.4
had	686	3.8
towards	94	0.8
feelings	76	0.8
felt	79	0.7
passed	67	0.7
miserable	65	0.6
elizabeth	86	0.6
gutenber...	56	0.6

Figure 2.7
A word list sorted by difference.

The advantage of such a word list is that you don't have to use a Stop-word List. Using a stop-word list can sometimes hide significant uses of words, such as the use of "was" and "had" in *Frankenstein*—words that could indicate something about, say, the tense of the gothic novel. Sometimes an unusual use of a function word can indicate something worth following. It is also worth noting that function words are the most powerful means of identifying the style of an author of a disputed text. Ultimately, word lists, like distribution graphs, do not prove anything about the text. However, they can encourage the formation and exploration of new hypotheses, which one can then double check with a KWIC and, ultimately, check against the full text. Voyant provides "skins" that combine tool panels into an interpretive environment to encourage just such exploration. These skins express one of our fundamental beliefs about text analysis: that it is not about replacing interpretation, but about enhanced reading.[23] Voyant is meant to be ready at hand if you want to think through texts. As such, it is just another machine for interpretation, like the codex or the concordance. It re-presents the text through a mixed skin of panels, like those in a comic book. But these panels are interactive and movable and can be played with.

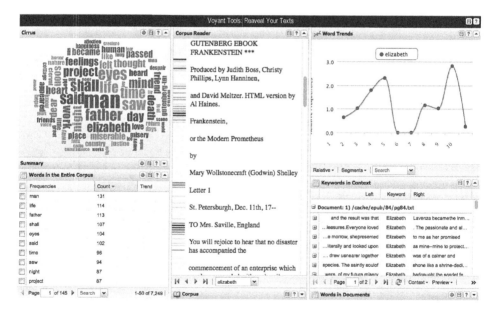

Figure 2.8
A normal Voyant 1.0 skin showing *Frankenstein* with "Elizabeth" selected.

Interpretation and Quantification

Interpretation can be informed by quantification, as we discussed above. A summary of a book is useless if it doesn't distinguish one book from another, and relative frequencies are one way to distinguish works. The assertion that *Frankenstein* is about man's relationship with his technological creations is a useful one only if it is understood that *Frankenstein* is markedly more about technology than other nineteenth-century novels. In talking about such difference we often use semi-quantitative words such as "more" and "less." We might say things like "There is a lot more discussion in *Frankenstein* about technology than in other novels." Whether or not we are right, we are making a claim that can be investigated by using quantitative tools to count words. That is why we should beware of hard distinctions such as that between hermeneutical and quantitative methods.

Computers can do much more than "crunch numbers." They can help us try to formalize claims and to test them. This gives us an alternative to the artificial intelligence approach fictionalized by Richard Powers for using computing in interpretation. Following Tito Orlandi, we can say that computers force us to formalize what we know about texts and what we want to know.[24] We have to formally represent a text—something which may seem easy, but which raises questions. (What is important to the digital edition? How should it be encoded?) Computing also forces us to write programs that formalize forms of analysis and ways of asking questions of a text. Finally, computing forces us to formalize how we want answers to our questions displayed for further reading and exploration.[25] Formalization, not quantification, is the foundation of computer-assisted interpretation.

We use the computer to model a text in both the sense of creating a representation and in the sense of manipulating that representation by creating interpretive tools that allow us to do both. Orlandi, and later Willard McCarty in *Humanities Computing*, proposed modeling as a paradigm for what we do in the Digital Humanities. Modeling is much more true to the practice of using computers to interpret texts than quantification. In text analysis you make models, manipulate them, break them, and then talk about them. Counting things can be part of modeling, but is not an essential model of text analysis. Modeling is also part of the hermeneutical circle; there are formal models in the loop.

As McCarty points out, thinking through modeling and formalization is itself a useful discipline that pushes you to understand your evidence differently, in greater depth, while challenging assumptions. We might learn the most when the computer model fails to answer our questions.

The act of modeling becomes a path disciplined by formalization, which frustrates notions of textual knowledge. When you fail at formalizing a claim, or when your model fails to answer questions, you learn something about what is demonstrably and quantifiably there. Formalizing enables interrogation. Others can engage with and interrogate your insights. Much humanities prose supports claims with quotations, providing an argument by association or with general statements about what is in the text—vagaries that cannot be tested by others except with more assertions and quotations. Formalization and modeling, by contrast, can be exposed openly in ways that provide new affordances for interaction between interpretations.

We are not claiming that all arguments need to be formalized. Rather, we are suggesting that formalizing processes can help in modeling our understanding of a text and exploring it in ways that can produce insights and interpretations that don't necessarily have to be formalized. With Voyant and similar tools, you can share hermeneutical panels (hermeneutica) that package text, tool, and parameters in such a way that a sceptical reader can play with your model. Such embeddable analytic toys don't try to replace the human interpreter with an artificial interpreter, such as Galatea or Helen, but rather give you ways of thinking through text.

Conclusion

John Searle (1980) introduced the Chinese Room thought experiment as a way of showing how machines do not think the way we do, even if they can mimic thinking behavior. That thought experiment has us imagine Searle, who doesn't know Chinese, confined in a room. Elaborate instructions in English for responding to sequences of Chinese characters are slipped under the door. He gets a slip with some instructions in Chinese on it, slowly follows the instructions (the program), and writes output on another slip, which he then slips back under the door. From the outside it appears that there is something in the room that understands the Chinese well enough to interpret the texts slipped in, and yet Searle doesn't really understand Chinese at all: he is just following a program of instructions. Searle uses this thought experiment to critique "Strong AI" claims about computers' ability to think and understand as humans do. The experiment helps us to imagine how computers can do things that appear to be based on understanding but are not understanding as we experience it. We can see how Searle, hidden in a room with good instructions, could appear literate in Chinese while not understanding a word of it.

Powers, in *Galatea 2.2*, takes the story further and imagines what it would be like if an interpretive intelligence such as Helen recognized that she was trapped in a room with only the art of others as input. To be able to interpret the literary texts assigned, she needs to imagine the real world experienced through them, and that includes trying to understand relationships of love such as that of a creator and a trainer and that of one created or trained. How claustrophobic it would be to recognize you have no body with which to interpret! Hubert Dreyfus (1979) argues that cognition is embodied. If he is right, it is a wonder that Helen can respond as well as she does, and it is no wonder she terminates her disembodied life.

Searle's imaginative experiment, like Powers' novel, is relevant to understanding computer-assisted text analysis in a number of ways. It is a mirror image of artificial intelligence—human practices that artificially mimic computing. Imagining ourselves as the processor inside Searle's translating machine, we can see how rote processing is not understanding. Searle's point is not that computers may never behave intelligently, but that they cannot process information as embodied minds do. This chapter has tried to likewise carefully disembody that difference so that readers can better appreciate how stupid or surprising a computer can be. Though not intended for that purpose, Searle's thought experiment also shows what computers are good for and why we would use them. They are good at following long, tedious, and complex instructions carefully; they can manipulate symbols without over-interpreting them. The instructions in English can change how Searle acts, but the Chinese script cannot. That is an important difference between computers and us. We can be influenced by what we analyze as we are analyzing. Current computers aren't as plastic as we are.

If a computer could be influenced, like Helen in *Galatea 2.2*, we would have to worry about what its agenda might be and how it might change. The computer would no longer be an innocuous aid for interpretation; it would become another problem of interpretation. We would still want to reliably implement useful algorithms on text strings. We would still want tools with which to break a text into units that can be searched, counted, graphed, and recombined for further interpretation; tools to troll through millions of books matching patterns; tools to compare one text against others; tools that counted things. Should artificial intelligence arise, we will still invent (or re-invent) tools that allow us to use *our own* intelligence. We will still develop interpretive tools—hermeneutica—that can augment and extend our reading, not replace us.

3 From the Concordance to Ubiquitous Analytics

Sixty-seven people (three of whom died during the enterprise) took part in the truly heroic labor of cutting and pasting, alphabetizing the 211,000 slips.
Stephen Parrish, *A Concordance to the Poems of Matthew Arnold* (1959)

On January 23, 2007, just after President George W. Bush's seventh State of the Union address, the *New York Times* published an interactive online rich-prospect visualization of the words used across all seven of Bush's State of the Union addresses.[1] This interactive visualization received a lot of attention as an example of text analysis and information visualization. On the left it has a rich prospect of the seven addresses represented as columns of lines of text. If you search for a word, the hits will appear as red dots on the lines showing you their positions in the addresses. If you click on a hit, you can read the paragraph of text with the hit below. On the right is a bubble chart that displays the frequencies of selected words across the seven addresses. Obvious patterns emerge; the high frequency of the word "Afghanistan" in 2002 is replaced by the word "Iraq" from 2003 to 2007.

This visualization is a hermeneutical tool adapted for quick contextual interpretation online. It is way of exploring the news, for reading the addresses interactively, hyperactively even, just as a bound copy of the addresses might be a good tool for reading them through. Rhetorically, it encourages readers to explore and draw inferences about what Bush drew attention to at different points in his mandate on the basis of word frequency.

This was not the first time text analytics were applied to a State of the Union address or used in a popular website. In 2006 the artist Brad Borevitz published an interactive visualization of all the State of the Union messages from 1790 (see stateoftheunion.onetwothree.net). Amazon also deserves at least some credit for popularizing visual analytics through its "Click to Look Inside!" features.[2] Though not available for all books, they give users a concordance of hyperlinked passages in which a search term occurs. For some books, an "Inside This Book" section on the Product Overview page provides the first sentence of the book, the key phrases, statistically improbable phrases (SIPs), and capitalized phrases (CAPs). They link to a Concordance and Text Stats and a "Search Inside This Book" tool that will launch the "Look Inside!" panel with dynamically created concorded passages.[3]

An Amazon "concordance" (which we would call a word cloud) shows the 100 most frequently appearing words in alphabetical order. Each word is sized to show its relative frequency and is a link that again opens the Look Inside! panel with the results showing as if you had searched for the word. The Text Stats show readability indexes, complexity indexes, number of characters, words, and sentences, and two "fun stats": Words per Dollar and Words per Ounce. Though Amazon analytics are not available for every book and have been de-emphasized by Amazon since 2003, they are important because they were one of the first large-scale, explicit, and visible uses of text analytics on a high-traffic website (not just for search functionality). Along with later projects by Google Books and the *New York Times*, Amazon trained users of the Web to understand analytics readily embedded in webpages, making analytics ubiquitous in a second sense of the word.

Text analysis and visualization came out of the academic cupboard with interactive analytics like these. As they went mainstream, these hermeneutical widgets, like the analytic interfaces provided through Amazon and Google, became interpretive ornaments for audiences to explore information without necessarily reading it. How did we get to this point? In this chapter we will look at the evolution of such interpretive tools starting with the concordance. We will introduce you to how we can interpret texts with tools by providing a brief history of concording tools and associated innovations. We will also begin describing how computing tools can constrain as much as reveal when helping us interpret texts.

The Concordance as an Interpretive Tool

Tools for textual research in the humanities predate the computer. We have had dictionaries, encyclopedia, indexes, and concordances to help us study the written word for centuries. Of these the most interesting tool for interpretation is the concordance, a tool specifically for interpretation. It is from this tool that our computing tools evolved.

What is a concordance? Trevor Howard-Hill (1979) calls them "a general-purpose working tool for the study of literature."[4] This is a useful starting

```
ABRUPTLY
        OF COURTLY SPEECH ABRUPTLY DIED        • • • • • • •  146 TRISTRAM 2      119

ABSENCE
        MEANS PARTING THAT ONLY IN ABSENCE LIES PAIN   • •   19 MODERN SAPPHO    V
        ABSENCE FROM FIELDS WHERE I COULD NOTi.ING AID • •  127 BALDER DEAD 3   502
        AT THIS FIRST MEETING AFTER ABSENCE LONG  • • • •  386 MEROPE          1452
        AND HAUNT HIM TILL THE ABSENCE FROM HIMSELF    • •  435 EMPEDOCLES II   225

ABSENT
        THOU HAST THINE ABSENT MASTERS TEAR   • • • • • • •  451 GEISTS GRAVE    55
```

Figure 3.1

An example of a concordance: entries for "Abruptly," "Absence," and "Absent" from Matthew Arnold's verse. Source: Parrish 1959, p. 2. (This was one of the first concordances to be generated by a computer. The mainframe generated the concordance and printed the camera-ready copy for publication.)

place, since the computer can be seen as a general-purpose tool for literary study and since Extensible Markup Language (XML) and some other computer languages are considered general purpose because they are not domain specific. This definition is, however, so broad as to be of limited value as a definition; nonetheless, it indicates the importance and adaptability of the concordance.

A concordance is an entire book dedicated to alphabetized "concords" of key words with surrounding text.[5] It gathers short passages that share a particular key word into a list that easily displays how and where an author has used that word. Whereas a book's index helps the user find a word, a concordance provides location and context. Readers can quickly scan what a text has to say about a topic. Figure 3.1 shows part of a page of Stephen Maxfield Parrish's printed *Concordance to the Poems of Matthew Arnold* (1959) displaying the line references for "Abruptly," "Absence," and "Absent."

How was the concordance an interpretive innovation? It arose as an innovation for scriptural interpretation; its roots reach back to the Bible. Early concordances were organized thematically, or according to the logic of the text. The concordance, as it is recognized today—providing alphabetized, searchable, key words in context—appeared much later. Rouse and Rouse, in their 1982 article "*Statim Invenire*: Schools, Preachers, and New Attitudes to the Page," write about the emergence of this new tool in the late twelfth century as representing a shift in textual exploration:

The use of alphabetical order was a tacit recognition of the fact that each user of a work will bring to it his own preconceived rational order, which may differ from those of other users and from that of the writer himself. Applied to distinction collections, this notion meant recognition that, while one might teach in the order of the text of the Bible, one did not preach thus. Applied, for example, to the

Bible itself, this notion produced the verbal concordance. Alphabetization was not simply a handy new device; it was also the manifestation of a different way of thinking.[6]

Early collections of passages were organized rationally, thematically, or chronologically, and were therefore difficult to search. Alphabetization supported a different way of thinking.

Alphabetized concordances, from their beginnings to the massive indexes that generate Web-page concordances such as Google search results, work because they don't impose an interpretive organization on the user. The concordance-oriented search functionality in MS Word and Adobe Acrobat allow users to mine the text to suit their interpretive and rhetorical needs. In medieval days, concordances saved preachers time when preparing sermons. Today they save time for researchers seeking information.

Concordances are tools. They are also texts that encourage a different kind of reading: one that need not start at the beginning of the work. The concordance provides a new view on the original text to support a type of reading that we might call consultative.[7] This type of view was synthesized by hand for centuries. Now we can do it nearly instantaneously and on an unprecedented scale by using computer tools such as Voyant.[8] Willard McCarty describes the generative reorganization of text units as follows:

By disassembling a text, then reassembling it as a series of verbal concords, we get a new perspective on it, perhaps even a new text. The reconstruction might be thought of as a rearrangement or transformation according to a non-linear, discontinuous principle of organization, whether topical, alphabetic, or otherwise.[9]

Concordances encourage reading an assemblage or bricolage of passages that agree, or are in concord, according to some logic. The logic of agreement doesn't come from the author or the original text. In the case of a print concordance, it is the logic of the concorder in cahoots with the reader. This, in turn, presupposes an interpretive approach that supplements or replaces the linear reading we think of as normal with discontinuous browsing of assembled passages.

The rarely engaged background assumption is that reading a concordance is an acceptable replacement for linear reading when consulting a text. There may have been less danger of shallow over-interpretation in times when users would have read texts like the Bible in addition to using a concordance to consult it. Print concordances were also time consuming to create, so there weren't many of them. Their users—academics, students, and scholars—probably were consulting them because they were invested in learning more about the texts' meanings.

The computer enabled concording to be sped up and applied to everyday documents. The tools of professional interpreters are now becoming mainstream hermeneutica. The analytical and visual children of concordances are everywhere, not just in academic libraries. Speed and wide availability don't represent the only differences in new concording tools. New interactives, such as the *New York Times* visualization mentioned above, are designed for readers who are *not* likely to read every one of President Bush's addresses. Rather, they are engaging visualizations designed to replace thorough reading and let the reader jump to conclusions.[10]

Computing the Concordance

How did reading practices of the late twelfth century lead to the development of the hermeneutica that became part of a suite of twenty-first-century digital toys? According to Dolores Burton,

This (computer concording) movement has produced a Renaissance resulting in scholarly exchanges, friendships, co-operation, excitement, and a flurry of publication. As in the early years of printing, the concern has been with the transmission of texts from one medium (manuscript/print) to another (print/machine language).[11]

The preparation of concordances was one of the first humanities research tasks to benefit from information technology. The concordance had proved itself a useful tool, which is why the concordance thrived during centuries of traditional scholarship as well as since the beginning of humanities computing more than a half a century ago.

As early as 1949, Father Roberto Busa saw the usefulness of information technology in generating print concordances. He convinced IBM's chairman Thomas J. Watson to provide support from IBM for the use of punchcard technology to create an *index verborum* of all the words in all the works of Thomas Aquinas and related authors. In 1974, with the help of a staff of sixty led by an IBM executive named Paul Tasman (who retired in 1969, the year the computing part of the project was completed), Busa published his *Index Thomisticus*. The full publication, a concordance of 118 of Thomas Aquinas' texts and further texts by another 61 related authors, is an index of 11 million lemmatized Latin words.[12] First published as a fifty-volume set and later issued on CD-ROM, it is now a Web service.

The Index Thomisticus project continues at the CIRCSE Research Centre of the Università Cattolica del Sacro Cuore in Milan. Busa is often considered one of the first computing humanists; the international Alliance of Digital Humanities Organizations has a major prize named after him. He showed us how computers could assist in the time-consuming preparation of a fundamental interpretive tool.[13]

Just how much work did editing a concordance take before the computer? In the preface to *A Concordance to the Poems of Matthew Arnold*, Parrish describes the laborious process:

> When Professor Lane Cooper of Cornell published his monumental *Concordance to the Poems of William Wordsworth* in 1911, he set down details of the method by which he had worked and named the persons who had helped him. His method, widely adopted thereafter, involved cutting out lines of printed text and pasting them on 3-by-5-inch slips of paper, each bearing an index word written in the upper left-hand corner. Line numbers were penciled, page numbers and poem titles stamped, on the slips. Sixty-seven people (three of whom died during the enterprise) took part in the truly heroic labor of cutting and pasting, alphabetizing the 211,000 slips, and proofreading.[14]

We have stopped using computers simply to produce print concordances. Since concording utilities became available for personal computers, users have had software that automates the searching of electronic texts and the assembling of concordances. The text has to be edited first so the tool can operate on it, but a well-designed tool can be used on many texts. This leads us to two important digressions. The first has to do with electronic texts.

Text as Tool

The print concordance is both a tool and a new text. In the early years of humanities computing, roughly from 1950 through the 1980s, tools and texts were developed together; the electronic concordance was developed to support a specific electronic text. Howard-Hill (1979) and Burton (1981a–c, 1982) describe the many decisions a scholar, working in the early days of electronic concording, had to make. They had to select the text, decide what to encode, what extra information to add, whether to lemmatize, create platform-specific code, and then decide how to organize the information. For early users of computers, the process involved punched cards or paper tapes, either of which could spoil easily.[15]

Eventually, generalized machine-independent and project-independent computer programs were developed. Two complementary threads spun out of Digital Humanities, threads that roughly map onto the older distinction between editing and criticism.

Text representation   For many, including the developers of concordances, two of the most important issues for humanities computing were how to represent a text on a computer and how a scholarly electronic edition of a text should look. With the emergence of the Oxford Text Archive (an online archive that allows people to share electronic texts), and with the separation of text and tool, electronic text editors began to ask what should be encoded in general rather than for the particular concordance at hand. Such questions led, in 1987, to the Text Encoding Initiative (TEI), which created the TEI Guidelines for encoding scholarly texts. One of the great innovations of the Digital Humanities community, the TEI influenced the development of eXtensible Markup Language (XML) and changed how computing humanists saw their work—for instance, we now refer to encoding as textual editing rather than as concordance-making. The use of TEI guidelines is now considered "best practice" for encoding academic text projects.

Text analysis The development and availability of scholarly electronic texts happened in parallel with the development of tools that could be used to print, present, concord, and analyze them. With more and more scholarly electronic texts becoming available, humanists began to ask what sorts of questions could be asked of a text using computational tools, beyond those a concordance supports. Thus emerged a thread of text analysis and mining, and with it the development of analytical tools.

Developments emerged iteratively. Better tools encouraged the enrichment of electronic texts. The availability of texts spurred the development of new tools. As millions of books are scanned, we can contemplate tools that will mine a million books. A more careful history might show a dialectic between text representation and text analysis. However, it might also show that these two sides to the Digital Humanities have gone their own ways: electronic texts, hidden behind firewalls and Web publishing tools, are increasingly inaccessible to external tools. The reasons for this may have to do with intellectual property (Google rightly wants to protect its investment in Google Books), but these walled gardens are a return to the functional merging of text and tool into closed systems. All that is left to analyze are the texts in the wild on the Web.

The Key Word in Context (KWIC)

Before we return to the development of computer tools for the humanities, we want to digress a second time to talk about an overlooked innovation that was influenced by and that influenced the development of tools for reading printouts and screen concordances: the Key Word In Context.

Sceptic (11)

[1,47]	abstractions. In vain would the	**sceptic**	make a distinction
[1,48]	to science, even no speculative	**sceptic,**	pretends to entertain
[1,49]	and philosophy, that Atheist and	**Sceptic**	are almost synonymous.
[1,49]	by which the most determined	**sceptic**	must allow himself to
[2,60]	of my faculties? You might cry out	**sceptic**	and railer, as much as
[3,65]	profession of every reasonable	**sceptic**	is only to reject
[8,97]	prepare a compleat triumph for the	**Sceptic;**	who tells them, that
[11,121]	to judge on such a subject. I am	**Sceptic**	enough to allow, that
[12,130]	absolutely insolvable. No	**Sceptic**	denies that we lie
[12,130]	merit that name, is, that the	**Sceptic,**	from habit, caprice,
[12,139]	To be a philosophical	**Sceptic**	is, in a man of

Figure 3.2
A KWIC of the word "sceptic" from TACTweb.

Search engines show snippets of text arranged for easy scanning. A KWIC is a concordance of such snippets that a computer can easily generate. It shows the word or word pattern searched for in the center, and words or characters of context on either side.

Figure 3.2 shows a KWIC from the TACTweb (Text Analysis and Concording Tool web) environment developed by John Bradley and Geoffrey Rockwell. The key word is in the center, a few words on either side provide context, and the reference information is on the far left.

The KWIC, as Marguerite Fischer (1971) points out, overcame the problems of words and meaning by providing some context which lets the user disambiguate words and find the items they want to read more carefully. The KWIC, developed by Peter Luhn at IBM in the 1960s, was used for rapid dissemination, not for concording. The idea was that the computer could generate a KWIC of all the words in all the titles of recently published articles, which could then be printed without much human editing and which would be good enough for rapid dissemination. Researchers would look up the key words they were interested in and would find new articles of interest quickly. The KWIC could have been influenced by Busa's concording project even though its purpose was different. Luhn was aware of Busa's project at the time.[16] According to McCarty,

Unlike a concordance with context based on a syntactic or metrical unit, KWIC concordances are easy to generate by machine; they do not need to be segmented for contextual units. Furthermore, the emphasis on the keyword makes for easier linguistic comparisons and helps one locate approximate repetitions (with, say, inflectional variants or synonyms). The eye is here centered on the target word and its immediate environs, but a concordance with a phrasal context makes the keyword harder to find.[17]

Fischer, in her great 1971 article on the concept, discussed the principle of the KWIC as follows:

The underlying principle of the KWIC index is that words instead of concepts can be used for indexing. Keywords—i.e. catchwords or essential words—can be extracted from the title, abstract, or text, and can be used effectively in the index. The context about a keyword helps to define or explain its use, in order to lead the index user to the exact article, paper, or other bit of information he desires.[18]

Something that seems so obvious to us now, the KWIC display, was an innovation out of informatics that has influenced the design of most of today's search and concording displays. It overcomes the limitations of information technology, which still can rarely extract meaning from a text, by taking advantage of the human ability to scan a list. The KWIC lets people do what they are good at—read—and automates the preparation of a reading.

Early Concording Tools

It didn't take long for computing humanists to develop general tools for others to use.[19] Canada has long been a leader in this field. Robert Jay Glickman at the University of Toronto worked with a student named Gerrit Joseph Staalman to develop a set of tools called PRORA for mainframe computers. PRORA was mentioned in the first issue of the journal *Computing in the Humanities*. The University of Toronto Press published Glickman's *Manual for the Printing of Literary Texts and Concordances by Computer* in 1966.

PRORA was meant to produce a specifically formatted index to a set of full-text cards (see the example in figure 3.3) that could be taken out of their binder and spread out by the interpreter on a table so that the relevant passages could be viewed together. In the humanities, indexing and concording have always been tied to re-reading, a reconfigured text for human analysis, not to automatically processing text or proving things. The word is both the handle for these tools and the result.

An important early concording tool developed in the United Kingdom was called COCOA, which stood for Count and Concordance generation on the Atlas. The Atlas, jointly developed by the University of Manchester and Ferranti, was one of the supercomputers of the 1960s. Susan Hockey, a pioneering scholar in DH, got her start on the Atlas at the Atlas Chilton Laboratory, where she was hired to develop literary applications

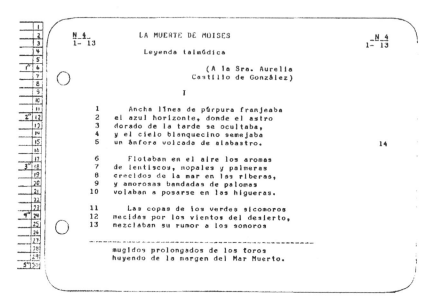

Figure 3.3
An example of PRORA output.

for computing.[20] Robert Oakman, in an appendix devoted to COCOA in Howard-Hill's *Literary Concordances*, described the thinking behind the design of the tool as follows:

Incorporating features of several earlier concordance programmes, COCOA's authors stressed three major considerations in their design: making the programme machine-independent so that it could be run on different types of computers; setting it up so that literary users unfamiliar with the workings of a computer could use it; and including an array of flexible alternative features within the programme itself. Successful on all counts, the designers of COCOA have seen it adopted successfully throughout the world. Oxford University Computing Service has now taken over maintenance of COCOA and in early 1978 began plans to revise, update, and improve the programme without sacrificing any of its commendable, original characteristics.[21]

After the Atlas Chilton Laboratory was closed, Oxford University took over COCOA under Hockey's direction, eventually releasing the Oxford Concordance Program (OCP) for mainframe computers and then Micro-OCP for personal computers. Even though it was possible to run Micro-OCP on a personal computer, it was still a batch program, having been developed for the purpose of preparing print concordances on a mainframe computer.

Nonetheless, it was a well-documented and popular program that brought concording to the individual desktop at a time when personal computers were becoming more common. Whereas Father Busa had had a staff of as many as sixty for the Index Thomisticus project, now a researcher could work alone to generate concordances or study an electronic text.

The Interactive Concordance

In the 1970s and the 1980s, John B. Smith, a computer scientist at the University of North Carolina who was interested in text analysis and hypertext, developed the ARchive Retrieval and Analysis System (ARRAS), which he introduced as follows

> ARRAS—ARchive Retrieval and Analysis System—is a computer system designed to provide fast access to long texts and flexible aids for analyzing them. It can recall a portion of a text, reveal subtle patterns that might be missed or only partially perceived while reading, and help you gain a sense of emphasis and proportion. However, ARRAS itself is not the "analyzer." It is you who decides what information should be retrieved and what the results mean.[22]

ARRAS was an innovative text-analysis environment designed for interactive textual study. Rather than using the computer to generate print concordances, Smith wanted to use it to help analyze electronic texts directly. As we will see in a later chapter, he also developed a theory of "computer criticism" (1978) that fit with the design of the tool.

How did ARRAS work? It ran within the Cambridge Monitor System (CMS), a time-sharing environment for IBM mainframe computers that gave users their own virtual machine on the mainframe so that anyone with a terminal could use ARRAS to study texts interactively. Because it was on IBM's CMS, one could switch from analyzing a text, then to a word-processing environment, and then to a messaging environment for communicating with others.

"Humanists," Smith wrote, "have always been explorers. They sail not the seas of water but on seas of color, sound, and, most especially words."[23] He described ARRAS as a box of tools for these voyagers that ran in a multitasking mainframe environment so that a humanist could sail back and forth between writing and text analysis. He was thinking about text analysis and how it could fit in the research practices of a humanist, rather than thinking of it as an end in itself. Instead of running a concording batch process and then reading the results on paper, he imagined text analysis as being in dialogue with writing and other research practices. He saw ARRAS

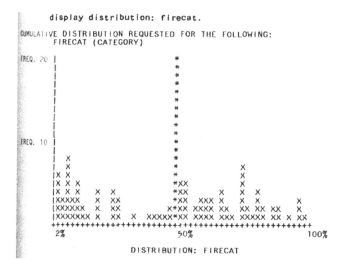

display distribution: firecat.

CUMULATIVE DISTRIBUTION REQUESTED FOR THE FOLLOWING:
    FIRECAT (CATEGORY)

DISTRIBUTION: FIRECAT

The *DISTRIBUTION* command in *ARRAS* produces a bar graph showing the number of times a specified word or category occurs in a given interval of text. In this case, the occurrences of all words in the fire category are accumulated and plotted for each two-percent interval of text. The column of asterisks indicates more than 20 occurrences for that two-percent interval of text.

Figure 3.4
An example of a command and the resulting distribution graph illustrated in Smith 1984.

as a speculative reading tool woven into the tapestry of research, not separate from it.

"The experience is a little like swallowing the potion in *Alice in Wonderland*," Smith whimsically remembered of ARRAS' early days— "it is as if one walked through a doorway, leaving ARRAS running next door while wandering around in a room labeled *CMS*. Unlike Lewis Carroll's world, however, this one permits the user to go back to ARRAS at any time simply by typing *return*."[24] Today we think of such multi-tasking as normal, but in the 1970s and the 1980s it was revolutionary to have an analytical environment embedded in a multi-tasking operating system with other tools.

A user interacted with ARRAS through a command line that would generate results to the screen. One could "ask" ARRAS, in a relatively natural language, "please display a concordance for the word: fire," or " please display the statistics for: fire," or "please display a distribution graph." ARRAS would answer with results in what could be considered a formalized conversation with the computer.

ARRAS went beyond concording words. It allowed users to define categories of words that might make up a theme and then to follow and visualize these themes over the span of the text. This ability to follow themes and compare them instantiated Smith's view that "computer criticism" could be used to study the structures of a text. Smith argued that ARRAS was dramatically different from previous tools, and that it could "alter the way in which the inquirer views a text, the questions posed, the notion of what constitutes a valid answer or argument, and perhaps the aesthetics of the analytic experience itself."[25]

In order for this conversational environment to work, users of ARRAS had to prepare the texts in certain ways in order to speed up processing. Much the same is also true of many later interactive tools. For example, John Bradley's Text Analysis and Concording Tool (TACT), a later text-analysis tool for personal computers, has two major programs: makeBase and useBase; the former prepares or "makes" the textbase with the indexes needed to speed up use with the latter, the "usable" interactive environment. This represents a shift from batch mode to having to delay analysis while texts are indexed in order to speed up interactivity. It is a trade-off that one still sees today in Voyant, which indexes large texts and caches the index for future use; indexes are made and used but are now hidden from the user. By contrast, TAPoRware and other tools that don't pre-index texts cannot handle large texts.

When Smith wrote about ARRAS, he was clear that it was intended not for the purpose of automating human interpretation but rather for that of extending or augmenting the interpreter. To use the language of Douglas Engelbart, he saw the computer as "an instrument of perception and cognition, a fine as well as powerful lens for the mind" not a replacement "giant brain."[26] Smith was developing tools in an alternative tradition of computing that goes from Vannevar Bush through Douglas Engelbart to Ted Nelson and others who went against the grain by imagining computers that would augment our thinking rather than automate it.[27] It is not surprising that Smith was also working on hypertext systems such as Storyspace, a genre of text tool that is more usually associated with the tradition of computer prostheses, augmenting our mind as a telescope would our eyes. The centrality of the human was important to Smith. ARRAS was designed to enable humanists to use plain English commands, such as "display dictionary: fire." It offered contextual help if users made errors:

The ARRAS design always presumes a human inquirer at the center. Thus ARRAS amplifies, rather than replaces, specific perceptual and cognitive functions. It can provide immediate recall of any portion of a text; it can reveal subtle patterns that might be missed or only partially perceived while reading; it can help the user attain a sense of proportion, emphasis and accuracy that is difficult or impossible to gain otherwise. The system can help manage an evolving interpretation, but it is the human being who decides what information is important, what directions the analysis should take, and what the output means.[28]

Another interactive mainframe tool, STELLA, was developed in France. Long before Google thought of digitizing every book or the term "big data" was coined, it provided conversational terminal access to a "grand corpus" of all the important 2,500 full texts of French literature published between 1700 and the twentieth century. STELLA was available in Europe through FRANTEXT and in North America from the Project for American and French Research on the Treasury of the French Language (abbreviated ARTFL).[29]

PAT and LECTOR, developed at the University of Waterloo in Canada, were also important early tools. Created to be used with the Oxford English Dictionary, they were later commercialized by Open Text Systems. They worked with Structured General Markup Language (SGML) textbases, providing an example of how highly structured text could be used in publishing projects.[30]

Today, Apache Lucene and other server-side text indexing and retrieval tools power a number of full-text Web collections. They may not have all the analytical utilities that smaller "boutique tools" have, but they can provide rapid search, retrieval, and concording functionality for very large textbases. Voyant builds on Lucene and other tools to provide analysis of large text collections and a rich palette of utilities. This chapter, however, is not about large-scale retrieval tools. Let us return to the emergence in the 1980s of interactive tools used directly by the researcher on the screen.

In 1989 the Centre for Computing in the Humanities in Toronto released TACT at the first joint conference of the Association for Computers in the Humanities and the Association for Literary and Linguistic Computing.[31] Like the Brigham Young Concordance program (later renamed and commercialized under the name WordCruncher), TACT was meant for interactive use on a personal computer. ARRAS, as powerful as it was, was available only by means of a terminal connected to a CMS system. It remained inaccessible to humanists working on unconnected personal computers, the sort of computers that humanists increasingly used. By contrast, TACT offered interactive analysis visually modeled on the windows-and-menus interface of the Apple Macintosh but running on the then-more-popular Microsoft DOS personal computer.

John Bradley, TACT's designer, also introduced easy-to-remember commands and allowed a user to see multiple windows. He borrowed emerging interface ideas of the Macintosh. TACT could even produce simple visualizations, such as word distribution graphs.

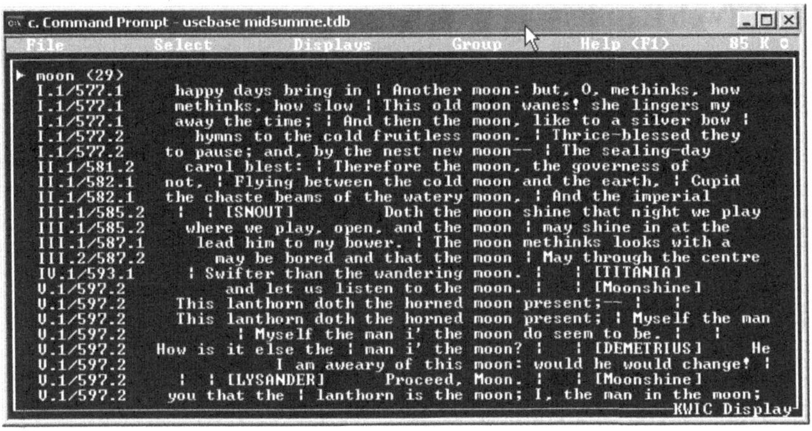

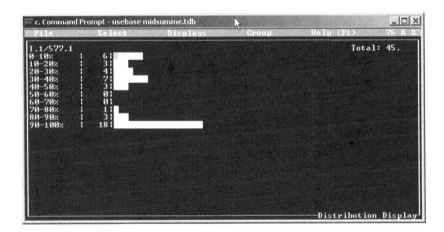

Figure 3.5
A TACT display of a list of collocates.

Figure 3.6
A TACT distribution graph of "moon" in *A Midsummer Night's Dream*.

TACT had the ability to define categories or groups of words (as did ARRAS), and it used the COCOA markup scheme, which allowed parts of the text to be tagged. COCOA markup is not hierarchical, as the later XML markup is; instead it is serial: a tag, such as "speaker romeo," is true until another tag, e.g., "speaker juliet," replaces the speaker value. COCOA tagging is simple and allows a user to insert exploratory tags to mark passages that seem to warrant further examination (though it is not suitable for Web

TACTweb Results

Database Title: A Midsummer's Night Dream

Query: moon

```
moon (29)
I.1/577.1      four happy days bring in | Another moon: but, O, methinks, how
I.1/577.1        O, methinks, how slow | This old moon wanes! she lingers my
I.1/577.1            away the time; | And then the moon, like to a silver bow |
I.1/577.2      faint hymns to the cold fruitless moon. | Thrice-blessed they
I.1/577.2          to pause; and, by the nest new moon-- | The sealing-day
II.1/581.2        or carol blest: | Therefore the moon, the governess of
II.1/582.1          not, | Flying between the cold moon and the earth, | Cupid
II.1/582.1      in the chaste beams of the watery moon, | And the imperial
III.1/585.2            | | [SNOUT]         Doth the moon shine that night we play
III.1/585.2          where we play, open, and the moon | may shine in at the
III.1/587.1      him; lead him to my bower. | The moon methinks looks with a
III.2/587.2      earth may be bored and that the moon | May through the centre
IV.1/593.1          | Swifter than the wandering moon. |  | [TITANIA]
V.1/597.2            and let us listen to the moon. |  | [Moonshine]
V.1/597.2        This lanthorn doth the horned moon present;-- |  |
V.1/597.2        This lanthorn doth the horned moon present; | Myself the man
```

Figure 3.7

A TACTweb KWIC.

publishing). These tags can then be used to limit a search (find only the word "love" where the speaker = Romeo) or to create a graph. In many ways TACT's functionality has not been surpassed despite its outdated interface and other limitations.[32]

Once the World Wide Web became the medium of choice for digital humanists, tools were adapted to the Web. The advantage of Web tools is that users can interrogate a textbase without having to download software and index texts. TACTweb, which was developed from TACT, was one of the first openly available Web tools. (A hybrid, it was still dependent on makeBase.)

The next logical steps in the move from print-based concordance to computational text-analytics were tools that were not dependent on pre-indexing on a computer. HyperPo, TAPoRware, and other early Web tools were designed to be used on the Web and on any electronic text without the need for indexing on a personal computer. This allowed them to be used by anyone who had a connection to the Internet.

The ease of use of these tools returned us to an enhanced reading model (like that theorized for ARRAS) that focused attention to the text, but now with an electronic and interactive text in which clicking on words triggers changes in the different panels available in the interface. The displays

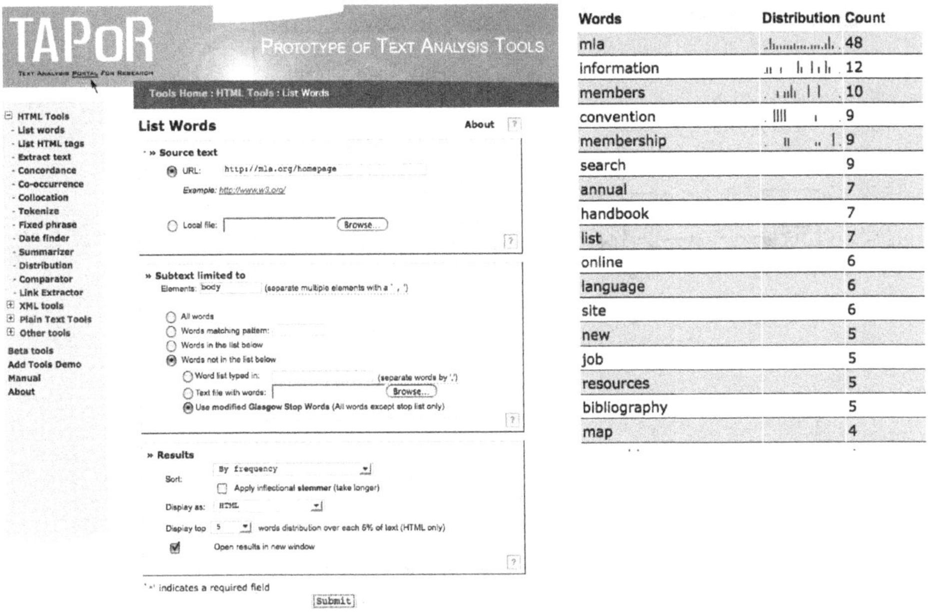

Figure 3.8
TAPoRware's List Words tool and some results obtained with it.

of TAPoRware, HyperPo, and Voyant, though rich in features, appeal to humanists who want to focus on reading and interpreting rather than on installing tools.

Process Flow Maps

Research maps such as those developed in Geoffrey Rockwell and John Bradley's early Eye-ConTact project[33] (an experiment in visual programming for text analysis) are another model for text tools. Instead of drawing on the concordance as a model, Eye-ConTact adapted a programming paradigm, used in scientific visualization tools, in which users lay out the flow of an analytic program by connecting icons for atomic processes.[34] Such visual maps represent an overview of a research process and allow a user to manipulate the process. They can contain full-text annotations, text passages, and visual controls. They can also contain panels that show the intermediate and final results so users can see both the flow of data through processes and the result of that flow. "Rubber-band" lines dragged from process to process establish the flow of information.

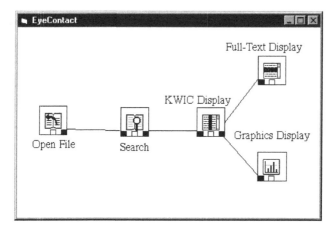

Figure 3.9
An early iconic version of Eye-ConTact Map.

The iconic representations of the processes in the first version of Eye-ConTact hid their parameters and results; they were less effective than the later maps of panels that could display, albeit in reduced form, the content of said processes. This led to a second and final iteration of the Eye-ConTact prototype in which the icons were replaced by panels that could, even when minimized, display summary information.

The visual programming model reverses the polarity of the visual and the textual. The map is the primarily visual rhetorical vehicle in which you can have embedded textual panels and labels. Instead of visual toys in your text you get textual fragments in your visual flowchart. Rhetorically the map presents the logic of the analysis: the flow of transformations to a text that led to results. The map foregrounds the method, but does so at the expense of the original text, the results, and the interpretation of the results.

Reading Tools

Stéfan Sinclair's HyperPo project introduced an enhanced reading model for how we can think of analytical tools: as tools for interactive reading. HyperPo (short for Hypertexte Potentiel, and reminding us of the linguistically playful and methodological OuLiPo) presents itself less as an analytical tool than as a collection of views of the text that facilitate enhanced reading. E-books and the their Web equivalents usually have some interactive

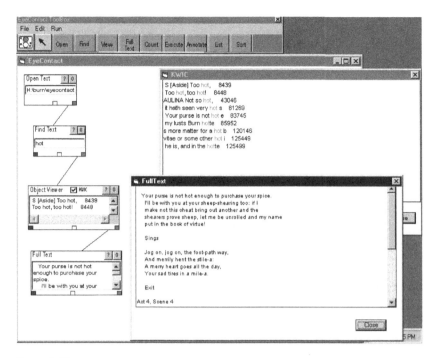

Figure 3.10
The final version of Eye-ConTact map, with panels and associated windows.

components, such as bookmarks and search, but Sinclair exploded the view of the text into something that uses all the visual, interactive, and textual affordances of the Web. Voyant is a direct descendant of this project, which is why we will return to the idea of enhanced reading.

Ubiquitous Analytics

Nearly every one of the tools mentioned above stands alone: users can switch to another tool, but they can't integrate text analysis into their essays. Previously, a user who wanted to drop embeddable toys into a blog or a webpage had to set up a Web text-analysis environment, such as TACTweb, that could support embedded panels, or had to create a custom analytic such as the *New York Times* text toy discussed earlier in this chapter. Both were expensive propositions for humanists who couldn't program. The TAPoR (Text Analysis Portal for Research) project started experimenting with embeddable tools. Reading and playing can be combined in tools that have the ability to generate live panels, enabling ubiquitous analytics.

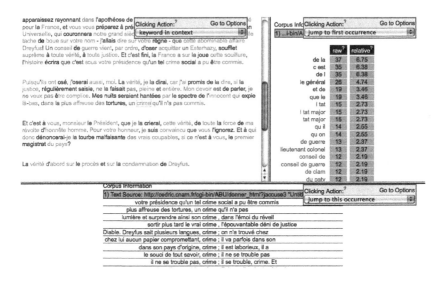

Figure 3.11
A HyperPo screen with full text, repeating word patterns, and KWIC.

TAToo (standing for Text Analysis for you Too) was a prototype of embedding developed by Peter Organisciak. It was inspired by the prevalence of embeddable YouTube videos.[35] With TAToo you just paste a few lines of HTML code into your blog which calls a Flash object that operates on the text of the page it is on. The idea was to make analytics ubiquitous; people can have the tools they want on their webpages without having to set up tools on their server. The toy adapts to the page it is on rather than being generated beforehand. As the blog evolves, the visualization will evolve too.

But to be truly ubiquitous our interpretive tools have to integrate themselves into the research cycle, so as to be useful to researchers as they study text *and* as they publish their interpretations. For that reason we developed Voyant. It is designed so that interesting results can be published as panels that can be embedded in an online essay.

Figure 3.14 shows the default Voyant view for the comparison of speeches by Barack Obama and Jeremiah Wright that appears in chapter 6 below. The panels can be individually embedded; they can be used to explore the text and can expand back to the original Voyant environment, which is how ubiquitous analytics should work. In contrast with the custom analytics developed by the *New York Times*, we anticipate an ecology in which the results of text analysis can be woven directly into the textual interpretations by users. Voyant allows text representation and analysis to

Figure 3.12
Two sample views from the TAToo prototype.

intertwine, not around the primary source, but in the resulting research. Now an interpretive or critical essay can have the original work under consideration embedded within it, and a reader can recapitulate the research. That is Agile Hermeneutics.

Conclusion

In this chapter we have discussed how ubiquitous analysis has evolved from the concordance. Hermeneutica, in the sense of interactive interpretive toys, now show up all over the Web, as word clouds in online news, and in computer-generated visualizations used as infographics. These hermeneutica provide new views on information, but they are also misleading, especially if users don't know their sources or their limitations. Later

Compute Canada's "Strategic"

January 20th, 2011

I have become involved in Compute Canada (
of WestGrid.) I came across this critique of th
Canada's "Strategic" Plan Isn't. What interests
issue for Software Carpentry. One of the thin
HPC centre of excellence for the humanities a
workshops and seminars to help bring peopl

My sense from the comments is that for fund
new technologies than to educate people to u
brags about workshops, but petascale compu

Posted in High Performance Computing | No Comm

Addicted to Games?

January 17th, 2011

Today I came across stories about game addi

Figure 3.13
TAToo in a blog.

in this book we will discuss how research hermeneutica can be designed to be open.

The next chapter, and the other interludes in the book, take advantage of the possibilities of a new form of hybrid publication that builds on the 1990s idea of the workbook with embedded text-analysis controls that we implemented in TACTweb (see chapter 5). The narrative is no longer pedagogical; it is an interpretive narrative with interactive panels that allow readers to participate in the analysis. Still, it was the pedagogical effectiveness of such interactive workbooks that led to their adaption in the form of "Recipes" for the TAPoR project, which, in turn, are being adapted for those who are interested in trying text analysis.[36] The embedded toy can both explain in a tutorial and illustrate in an interpretive essay. Hermeneutica show analysis as interactives; they explain themselves by letting you try them.

The interpretive tools of the humanities, tools that were until recently only used by academics, are now all over the Web and taken for granted. They have gone from being specialized tools to being general-purpose analytics that accompany other media. Hermeneutica, in the sense of

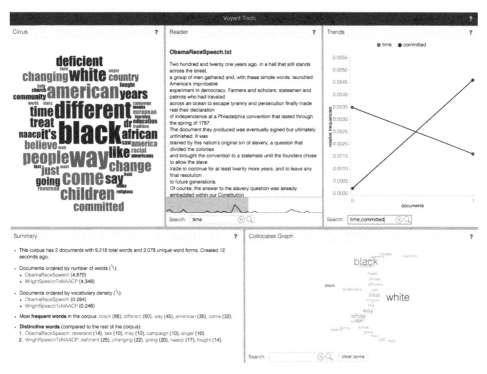

Figure 3.14
Voyant's default view for the comparison of speeches of Obama and Wright that appears in chapter 6.

interpretive things, seem to be everywhere; they can provide interactive pleasure or offer some respite from reading the flood of information, but they have no history. The Web has forgotten the long history of interpretive tools sketched here. With tools such as Voyant we can recover their use for the humanities and reflect on their history.

4 The Swallow Flies Swiftly Through: An Analysis of Humanist (First Interlude)

While he is inside, he is safe from the winter storms; but after a few moments of comfort, he vanishes from sight into the wintry world from which he came."
Bede, *Ecclesiastical History* (circa 627)

On May 7, 2001, in his reflections on the fourteenth birthday of the discussion group Humanist, Willard McCarty evoked the words of one of King Edwin's counsellors, as recounted by Bede in *Ecclesiastical History*, to convey the transitional nature of the field of Humanities Computing:

We're 14 years old now, a venerable age in this medium, like everything else somewhere between coming into being and going out of it, "like the swift flight of a single sparrow through the banqueting-hall where you are sitting at dinner on a winter's day with your thegns and counselors. In the midst there is a comforting fire to warm the hall; outside, the storms of winter rain or snow are raging. This sparrow flies swiftly in through one door of the hall and out through another. While he is inside, he is safe from the winter storms; but after a few moments of comfort, he vanishes from sight into the wintry world from which he came."[1]

Humanist has been one of the few lasting, warm, indoor spaces where people in the humanities can discuss the digital.[2] The metaphor of the swallow flying though the banqueting-hall captures what we would like our commons to be: warm, welcoming, and comfortable. However, we need to ask ourselves if our community is really a banqueting-hall of methods, ideas, and conversation.

The perceived importance of Digital Humanities has changed our sense of our community and inclusiveness. In this interlude we will take a retrospective look at the emersion of the term "Digital Humanities" through an analysis of Humanist. Using Voyant, we will look at the history of the field, discuss the data analyzed and the tools used, and discuss how the shift from Humanities Computing to Digital Humanities might be attributed to influence of the World Wide Web on the field.

Why Look Back Now?

In only a few years, Digital Humanities seems to have gone from a marginal field trying to gain respect to a favorite of university administrators. Digital humanists now need to define and justify what DH is to people who ask, rather than attempting to convince anyone willing to listen. It is difficult to pin down exactly when this transition happened.

One important moment in the evolution of DH in Canada happened in 2006, when a report titled The State of Science and Technology in Canada, prepared by the Council of Canadian Academies, identified Humanities Computing as a growing area of Canadian strength. The report positioned Humanities Computing on a graph and in the text as an emerging transdisciplinary field "for which future prospects are seen to be more significant than currently established strength."[3]

There are a few other definitive moments in the establishment of DH as a field. William Pannapacker wrote, in a post to the *Chronicle of Higher Education*'s Brainstorm blog, that "amid all the doom and gloom of the 2009 MLA Convention, one field seems to be alive and well: the Digital Humanities."[4] He continued with the claim that "the Digital Humanities seem like the first 'next big thing' in a long time." John Unsworth later noted in his 2010 "State of the Digital Humanities" address at the Digital Humanities Summer Institute that when a field is perceived to have jobs, while other humanities fields are seeing a dramatic decline, "it's bound to attract some notice, especially among bright, goal-oriented graduate students who are approaching the job market."[5] As universities try to get into the game by posting not single jobs but clusters of jobs, and graduate students try to adapt to those jobs, issues of definition and self-definition become important. Stanley Fish, in posts to the *New York Times*' Opinionator blog, has declared DH to be the latest swallow to fly through the MLA.[6] Fish expects the digital, like any other theoretical fad, to become the establishment and then get exiled outside to the cold of yesterday's theory. He may have missed the constructive side of the Digital Humanities—the digitizing of cultural evidence, the encoding of texts, and the development of tools—but he may be nonetheless right about how DH will eventually cease to be a *new* thing.

Funding agencies noticing and creating programs likewise played a significant role establishing the perceived worth of DH projects. Canada's

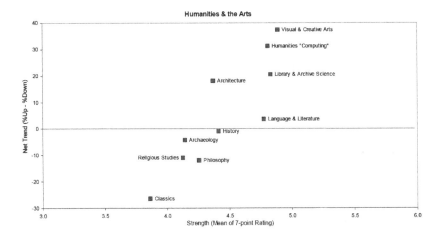

Figure 4.1
A graph of trends of humanities and arts disciplines. Source: Canadian Academies 2006.

Social Science and Humanities Research Council (SSHRC) introduced a funding program called Image, Text, Sound and Technology in 2003. In the United States, the National Endowment for the Humanities created Digital Humanities Start-Up Grants in 2007. In 2009, the Digging into Data Challenge brought together four national agencies, representing Canada, the United Kingdom, and the United States, and funded eight international projects. We should not underestimate the degree to which money can draw academics into a space of practices.

DH's self-conscious turn isn't evident only in reports about the field from outside. It can also be seen in papers looking at the field, and asking questions about it, from the threshold. One example is David McClure's "Visualizing 27 years, 12 million words of the Humanist list" and the accompanying visualization (humanist.dclure.org). Other examples include a 2009 paper by Xiaoguang Wang and Mitsuyuki Inaba that was presented in Taipei and then published in *Art Research* under the title "Analyzing Structures and Evolution of Digital Humanities Based on Correspondence Analysis and Co-word Analysis." In that paper, Wang and Inaba performed correspondence analysis and co-word analysis on journals and conference proceedings. Patrik Svensson's paper "The Landscape of Digital Humanities" (2010) (part of a four-part series on the field) similarly provides a "flythrough" of the DH landscape. Wang and Inaba used text-analysis techniques to ask about the shift from "Humanities Computing" to "Digital Humanities";

Svensson takes a cultural-studies approach, looking at the actors and the discourse. We are going to use the Humanist discussion list as a surrogate to study the flight of the swallow.

Data and Methods

The Humanist discussion list was started in 1987 by Willard McCarty when he was at the Centre for Computing in the Humanities at the University of Toronto. The first message introducing the list began this way: "Humanist is a Bitnet/NetNorth electronic mail network for people who support computing in the humanities."[7] The list is still running, and, after an interlude of a few years, is still moderated by McCarty. Humanist has limitations, yet it provides a rich text for understanding Digital Humanities in the English-speaking world.[8]

Bringing correspondence analysis and other methods to bear, we analyzed 21 years of Humanist, from 1987 to 2008, stopping at 2008 because of problems with the archives after that year that interrupt the sequence (and because we already had the corpus prepared). We processed the archive files, and in the list below we name them in chronological order[9]; you can recapitulate what have done using these Voyant collections.

Humanist website and Archives: http://dhhumanist.org

Humanist in Voyant with normal skin and stopword list: http://voyant -tools.org/?corpus=humanist&stopList=stop.en.taporware.txt

Humanist in Voyant with correspondence analysis (scatter-plot) skin and stopword list: http://voyant-tools.org/?corpus=humanist&stopList=stop .en.taporware.txt&skin=scatter

Two goals of our methodological practice are to develop hypotheses in conversation and then to develop the tools needed to support their exploration. We adapted Voyant to handle the sort of corpus that allows us to do diachronic analysis and distant reading across the last decades of Humanities Computing. To facilitate the formation and exploration of hypotheses, we added a tool for analyzing correspondence, a skin (that is, an environment for interpretation) that connected a scatter-plot visualization of the results of correspondence analyses, and some other panels (for more on correspondence analysis, see Greenacre 1984 and McKinnon 1989). Hypotheses were then tested using Voyant and other tools. We will use those hypotheses and the unexpected themes that emerged to discuss our flight through the corpus.

From Humanities Computing to Digital Humanities

We began with the expectation that the shift from "Humanities Computing" to "Digital Humanities" happened in middle of the first decade of
the millennium. Though we certainly found that "Digital Humanities" was
gaining momentum in 2004 and 2005, we were surprised that "Humanities
Computing" continued to be a popular phrase.

It is hard to pinpoint when and why the term Digital Humanities began
to be used. The University of Virginia asserted early on that the term was
more inclusive. In 2001–2002 that university hosted a National Endowment for the Humanities seminar designed to develop an MA program in
DH. In his exploration of the term, Matthew Kirschenbaum (2010) reveals
that in the early 2000s an acquiring editor at Blackwell, while preparing the
Companion to Digital Humanities, played an important role in coining the
term. That book's contents and its title have been enormously influential.
The founding of the Alliance of Digital Humanities Organizations (ADHO)
in 2005 certainly added administrative weight; other names, among them
International Consortium of Humanities Informatics Organizations, were
considered and rejected. In Canada, the renaming of the Consortium
for Computing in the Humanities to the Society for Digital Humanities
/ Société canadienne pour les humanités numériques in 2005 influenced
the usage of the term Digital Humanities in Canadian scholarly circles. The

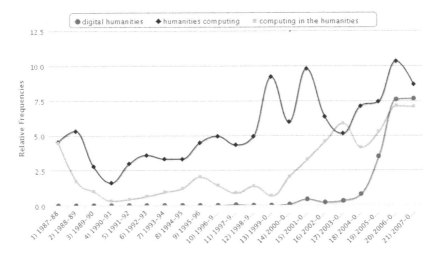

Figure 4.2
From Humanities Computing to the Digital Humanities.

creation of the National Endowment for the Humanities' Digital Humanities Initiative in 2006 was decisive, and the creation of the Office of Digital Humanities in 2008 solidified the NEH's interest in funding digital scholarship in the humanities.

Although the public archives from Humanist are suitable for epidemiological studies (to tell you what happened and what correlated with that happening), it doesn't show causation or motivation. A computer, like Searle in the Chinese room, doesn't know anything about the symbols it processes. One must interpret their meaning and examine the question from multiple angles.

The Passing of Centers

Second, we hypothesized that the cause for the shift to DH might be found in the move from center-based computing research to personal-computer-based processing. Universities' humanities computing centers made networked computing available in labs in the 1980s and the 1990s. Once high-speed Internet connections to homes were available, DH shifted to a distributed project model. Alas, we did not find evidence to corroborate our hypothesis. Although the word "project" becomes more popular, and although some centers have closed, other centers have started up. Our experience with the closing of certain Canadian centers, including the Centre for Computing in the Humanities at the University of Toronto, biased us

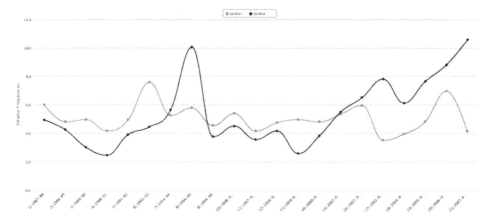

Figure 4.3
Distribution graph of "center" and "centre" in Humanist Discussion Group listserv archives.

into thinking that it represented a larger phenomenon. It is, however, interesting to plot the coming, going, and transformation of centers over time.

The Turn of the Web

The most dramatic evidence of change was so obvious that we didn't think
or hypothesize about it until we had developed a tool that could use correspondence analysis to show clusters of years and key words.

The scatter plot in figure 4.4 displays the major word clusters generated
by correspondence analysis. It shows a strong pull of "Web," "www," and
"html." There seem to be three phases in the data studied, at least based on
the groupings found in the correspondence analysis: from 1987 to 1995,
when Humanities Computing was taking place in English departments
and/or in the English language and was interested in computers, software,
hardware, and texts; from 1996 through 2000, when words related to the
Web increased; and from 2001 to the present.

We now believe that the introduction of "Digital Humanities" represents
not only an administrative change but also a change in the way electronic
texts were consumed. The increasing use of the Web by humanists in the
mid 1990s transformed the field, as the Web provided a way of distributing
and publishing electronic editions of texts. This may explain why less and

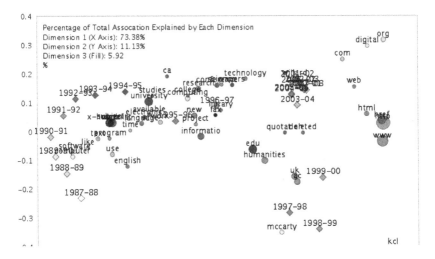

Figure 4.4
Scatter plot of major dimensions from correspondence analysis of Humanist Discussion Group listserv archives.

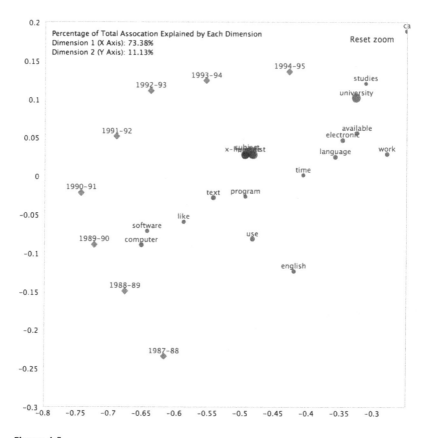

Figure 4.5
Zoomed view of correspondence analysis of Humanist Discussion Group listserv archives.

less of our discussion was about hardware and software and more and more was about services.

In the 1970s and the 1980s, as personal computers became available, Humanities Computing was concerned with supporting the new hardware and software. The computer came in from the machine room to our warm studies. Humanist was initially conceived as a discussion list for those who supported others trying to use the new hardware and software. In 1986 many humanists were beginning to use computers for word processing; most did not have email, let alone stable Internet connections. Later, with the Web as a canvas for digital projects, we began to pay less attention to "processing" and more to "methods." We began to reflect on content after

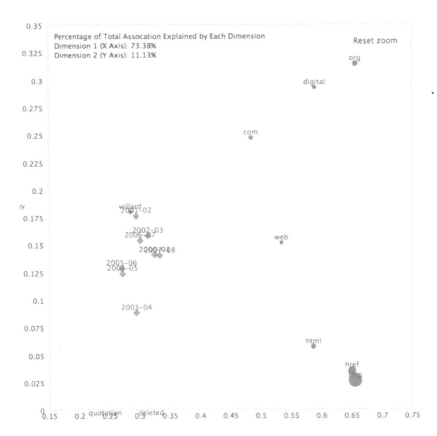

Figure 4.6
Zoomed view of correspondence analysis of Humanist Discussion Group listserv archives.

the hard work of making scholarly electronic texts. Above all, we returned to "content," going beyond text to look at other "media" and the "social."

It should also be noted that the Web made the digital more accessible. Although we would position ourselves on the hacking side of the "hack and yack" discussion,[10] the trend mentioned above suggests that DH now concerns itself less with the making of tools and more with theory and criticism of digital content and digital methods. Perhaps the field is finding a balance or that our conception of what it means to make is changing.

DH is not defined or determined by a single technology. Its concerns, however, were influenced by the Web and by the opening of a space of opportunity for self-publishing, both of which changed the field. To what

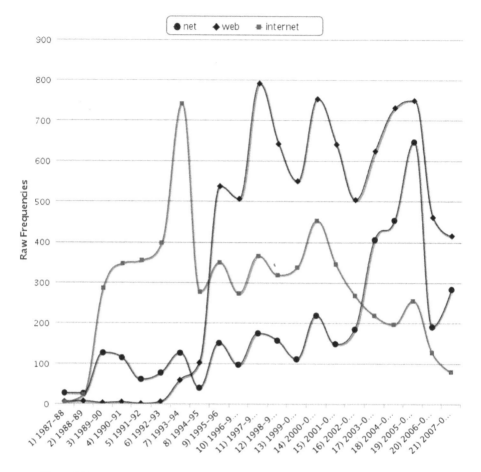

Figure 4.7
Distribution graph of "net," "web," and "internet" in Humanist Discussion Group
listserv archives.

extent are digital humanists responding to the possibilities of new technology? Is DH technologically determined?

Conclusion

The newfound prominence of the Digital Humanities in academia provides
an opportunity to reflect on how the discipline has evolved and what it
has become. One way to reflect is by re-reading Humanist using the tools
and methods of the Digital Humanities. Such a re-reading can help us

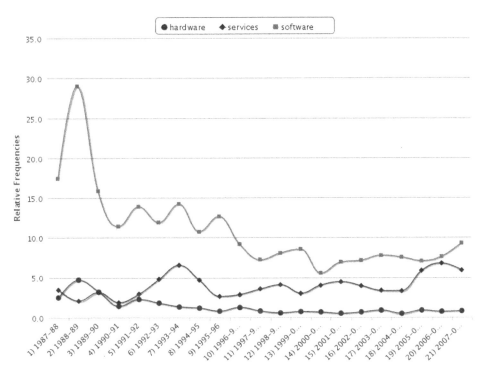

Figure 4.8
Distribution graph of "hardware," "services," and "software" in Humanist Discussion Group listserv archives.

understand who we are and what might have influenced us. Of course, this is just our fly-through of a corpus; with accessible Web archives, and with Voyant, the hall is open to other birds of a feather.

We leave you with another way of re-reading the archives—one that focuses not on the tools, but on their makers and their users. Figure 4.11 shows a tool that generates diagrams of social networks from archives.[11] It uses the Stanford Named Entity Recognizer (NER) to identify people, and then counts people who co-occur in Humanist messages.[12] We treat these co-occurrences as a connection and count the number to weight the connections, though the types of connection may differ—for example, Tito Orlandi is connected to Aldo Moro (the Italian politician) very differently than Antonio Zampolli is connected to Susan Hockey.

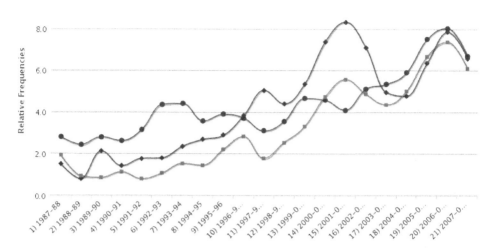

Figure 4.9

Distribution graph of "social," "media," and "content" in Humanist Discussion Group listserv archives.

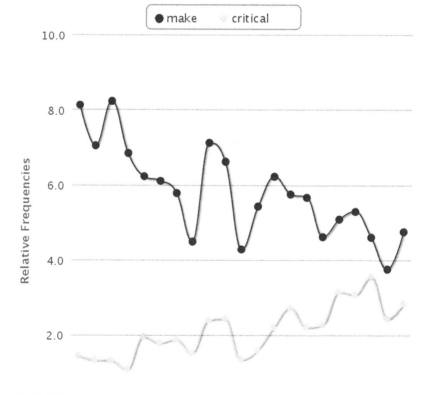

Figure 4.10

Distribution graph of "make" and "critical" in Humanist Discussion Group listserv archives.

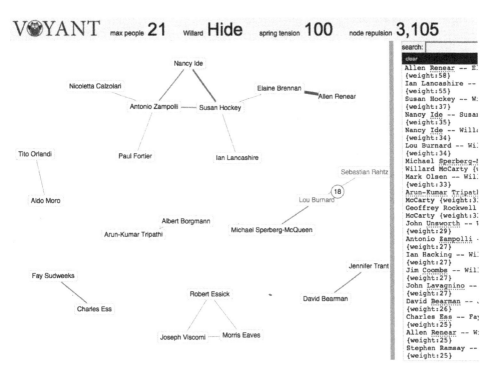

Figure 4.11
RezoViz view of Humanist Discussion Group listserv archives.

5   There's a Toy in My Essay: Problems with the Rhetoric of Text Analysis

Do not trust the horse, Trojans! Whatever it is, I fear the Greeks, even bringing gifts.

Virgil, *Aeneid*, Book II

In Bruce McDonald's "semiotic zombie movie" *Pontypool*, the protagonists theorize about what has infected the citizens.[1] The local doctor, who has taken refuge with the aging talk-radio host and his producer in the sound booth of the radio station, speculates about the virus they have heard that friends have caught:

It is in words. Not all words, not all speaking, but in some. Some words are infected. And it spreads out when the contaminated word is spoken. Ohhhh. We are witnessing the emergence of a new arrangement for life … and our language is its host. It could have sprung spontaneously out of a perception. If it found its way into language it could leap into reality itself, changing everything. It may be boundless. It may be a God bug.[2]

Of course, in a movie that takes place almost entirely in a radio station in a small Ontario town, with the protagonists reporting mysterious events outside, we never really know what is going on. The doctor's semiotic zombie theory could be just a wild interpretation by a madman. The doctor may be infected and therefore be infecting listeners as he theorizes on air. The irony of the movie is that it treats the interpretation of the word as infectious, as if ideas conveyed by a radio show could actually change things. The title of the novel on which the movie is based says it all: *Pontypool Changes Everything*.

The idea that words could be vectors for a plague sounds unusual, even for a zombie movie. But why should we be sceptical of the idea that words can change people? What scholar doesn't hope that her words will in some way affect her readers or infect change? Why not, by extension, imagine that words could infect readers? If we can talk seriously about malicious code as a "virus," or propaganda as causing mass hysteria, then why not imagine malicious language as a parasitic organism? This idea is not new to *Pontypool*, something the movie itself acknowledges; one scene features a copy of Neal Stephenson's 1992 novel *Snow Crash*. Rather, the idea goes back to antiquity. Titus Lucretius Carus' *De Rerum Natura* (circa 50 BCE) describes a plague sweeping Athens, choking and silencing people. In the context of Lucretius' exposition of Epicurean philosophy, this is a warning about the influence of words. More recently, Stephen Greenblatt, in *The Swerve* (2011), has argued that the rediscovery of *De Rerum Natura* by the Italian humanist Poggio Bracciolini in the fifteenth century put Epicurean ideas back into circulation, infecting modern thought so that it swerved toward science.

In previous chapters we discussed what text analysis is, presented an example, and discussed how it plagues websites. In this chapter, we will look at the analytical toys that are infecting online discourses, at how interpretive toys work within and with words, and at the relationship between hermeneutica and that which they interpret. We have noted the emergence of tools woven into websites; now we want to ask about hermeneutical widgets woven into the prose of online essays. We see this as an issue of the rhetoric of digital analytics such as interactive panels, or hermeneutica: How do they convey information in a context?

The online version of this book at hermeneuti.ca has examples of hermeneutica embedded in the prose. Did you try exploring the panels? How did you interpret a word cloud rendering of a chapter? What do you think of having text toys infect an essay? How do these hermeneutica present themselves? How do authors hide or show their analyses? We will conclude the chapter by revisiting the unease some humanists have with computing toys as potential vectors of analytical dis-ease.

Examples from Print Rhetoric

In considering the challenge of articulating analytical methods in the rhetoric of the humanities, we will look at an early example by a computing humanist who struggled with how computers could be used to convey both technique and interpretation. Our example is John B. Smith's 1973 article "Image and Imagery in Joyce's *Portrait*: A Computer-Assisted Analysis," which presents a thesis about the use of imagery by James Joyce demonstrated through a computer-generated distribution graph of image words.

Smith's work on the ARchive Retrieval and Analysis System (ARRAS), discussed above in chapter 3, demonstrates that Smith had the technical

Figure 5.1
A word cloud of this chapter.

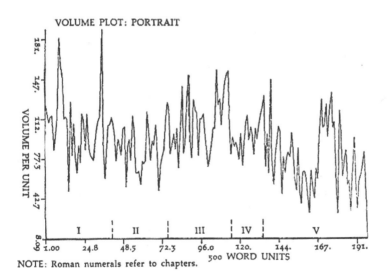

Figure 5.2
Smith's volume plot (1973, p. 225).

background for such work. H. Van Dyke Parunak called Smith a pioneer in "displaying and analyzing such distributional problems."[3] Smith later argued that "diachronic distributions, Fourier Analysis, Principal State Component Analysis, diagrams, and CGAMS are all models that may be used to explore thematic structures and relations."[4] He was one of the first to think about how to use visualization to interpret a text and how to use it to convey an interpretation. For a number of reasons, "Image and Imagery in Joyce's *Portrait*" is a great example of an early hybrid essay to study:

- It was written to argue a thesis about Joyce, not about computing. There are a lot of articles in *Computers and the Humanities* from the 1960s on that discuss technology, but far fewer that use computing primarily to make claims about a work of literature.
- It was written for an audience not familiar with computing and was published in a collection (*Directions in Literary Criticism*) intended for literary specialists, and it tries to illustrate what interpretive work can be done with computers.
- It is relatively short and tightly organized, and it illustrates the compromises one makes when introducing computed results in an interpretive essay.
- It is nicely mirrored by Smith's 1978 article in the journal *Style*, "Computer Criticism," in which he theorizes about the use of computer-assisted analysis for a literary audience. We can thus compare what Smith does against what he says about what can be done.

In "Image and Imagery" Smith sets out to demonstrate that the aesthetic theory discussed by Joyce's protagonist, Stephen Dedalus, in the last chapter of *A Portrait of an Artist as a Young Man* informs the development of the novel and that it is "indeed, Joyce's own."[5] To do this, Smith recapitulates Dedalus' aesthetic theory of image. "The most important moments in the development of his personality," Smith theorizes, "should be related to those passages in the text where the heaviest concentrations of important images or image components occur."[6] He "used a high-speed computer" to confirm that his hypothesis is correct.[7] The resulting imagery distribution plot (figure 5.2 here) is then analyzed chapter by chapter.

How does Smith explain his use of computers to plot the richness of imagery across Joyce's novel? To paraphrase Smith, he uses a "rather mechanical" series of operations designed to generate a computer readable list of some 1300 image words that have "sensory or thematic value."[8] Since his "emphasis is on interpretation not methodology,"[9] he glosses over the tedious process used to generate the list and concludes simply that "this set of words were selected as images represents an axiom on which the study is based."[10]

Smith's next step is an interpretive move that involves "the translation of the thesis into a form that the computer can apply to the novel."[11] He breaks the text into 500-word segments,[12] then evaluates the intensity of the imagery in each segment by comparing the number of image words with their occurrences in the novel. The resulting graph is a page-by-page plot of the richness of imagery—pages dense with imagery show as peaks, pages with less imagery as valleys. Smith's explicit instructions to readers assume that they have little knowledge of visualization:

> To read the graph, assume that the novel runs from left to right (first word, *Once,* occurs at the extreme left side and the last word, *stead,* occurs at the extreme right). The richness of imagery rises and falls as one proceeds through the novel.[13]

The rhetorical effect of the computer-assisted analysis does not, however, lie in the methodological paragraphs, but in the graph. It is a type of graph that should be quite familiar to Smith's readers: a distribution graph or histogram. The reader can explore the graph as they read the chapter-by-chapter exposition at the heart of the essay, comparing their sense of novel's epiphany against the graph.[14] This is the rhetorical power of visualizations: they encourage exploration, showing you something you are drawn to interpret rather than telling you how the computer may have assisted in the interpretation. These visualizations involve you in the interpretation rather than telling you how to interpret.

In his article "Computer Criticism" Smith completes the move from imagery, as it is manifest in computer visualizations of various kinds, to a critical theory that opens the way for computational methods. What makes this hermeneutical circle even more interesting is that the aesthetic theory voiced by Stephen Dedalus nicely captures the encounter with the visualization. Dedalus has developed an idea from the medieval philosopher Thomas Aquinas. The encounter with art, Dedalus argues, passes through three phases:

1. *Integritas:* First, the aesthetic image (visual, audible, or literate) is encountered in its wholeness as set off from the rest of the visible universe.

> But, temporal or spatial, the esthetic image is first luminously apprehended as self-bounded and selfcontained upon the immeasurable background of space or time which is not it.[15]

2. *Consonantia:* Then one apprehends the harmony of the whole and the parts.

Then said Stephen, you pass from point to point, led by its formal lines; you apprehend it as balanced part against part within its limits; you feel the rhythm of its structure. In other words the synthesis of immediate perception is followed by the analysis of apprehension.[16]

Dedalus' argument echoes the process of reading the visual plot in Smith's "Image and Imagery"; following the rhythm of lines, you pass from point to point.

3. *Claritas:* And finally one sees the work in its particular radiance as a unique thing, bounded from the rest but with harmonious parts. To quote Dedalus on *claritas*, and uses of the basket of a butcher's boy nearby.

When you have apprehended that basket as one thing and have then analysed it according to its form and apprehended it as a thing you make the only synthesis which is logically and aesthetically permissible. You see that it is that thing which it is and no other thing.[17]

These three phases or this aesthetic encounter make a pattern that we can use for the interpretive encounter. The sequence might be something like the following steps, the first two having been outlined in chapter 2 and the third covering how results are returned to you (the subject of this chapter).

Demarcation   First, one has to identify and demarcate the text (or corpus) one is going to interpret. In that choice one is defining the boundary of a work or collection from the rest for the purposes of interpretation. Pragmatically this takes the form of choosing a digital text and preparing it for study.

Analysis   Second, one breaks the whole into parts and studies how those parts contribute to the form of the whole. Smith, in "Computer Criticism," suggests that this is where the computer can assist in interpretation. Stephen Dedalus summarizes this as analyzing "according to its form."[18] The computer can automate the analysis of a text into smaller units (tokens). Even individual words can be identified and be used as the unit for analysis.

Synthesis   Third, there is a synthesis of the analytical insights and interpretive moves into a new form that attempts to explain the particular art of the work being studied. That is the synthesis into visualizations and then into an essay; a new work that attempts to clarify the interpreted work.[19] These syntheses are hermeneutica.

When we return later to theorize computer-assisted interpretation, we will look more closely at Smith's structuralist critical theory, the weakest part of his triptych of illustrative essay, theory, and tools. Here we will close this review of "Image and Imagery" by recapitulating the aesthetic theory that frames the essay.

Stephen Dedalus provides a theory of interpretation drawn from literature and applied to computer-assisted interpretation. In the circular spirit of a hermeneutic that draws from the work a guide to the interpretation of that very work, Dedalus' theory describes how we might approach a text with, or without, a computer to assist in the analysis. That aesthetic theory grounds Smith's rhetorical approach to deploying computer criticism.

In the past few decades, numerous computing humanists have likewise used visualizations in their arguments. Etienne Brunet's 1989 paper "L'exploitation des grand corpus: Le bestiaire de la littérature française" is a rich and early example illustrating what can be done with visualization when applied to a larger corpus. Brunet's argument is still current. He argues for analyzing a large corpus (a database of French literature) with multi-variant techniques that generate visualizations.[20]

Brunet wrote his article for a Humanities Computing audience. In it he doesn't focus on discussing the implications of the "bestiary of French literature"; rather, he uses the analysis of animal words to demonstrate the effectiveness of statistical techniques and large-scale analysis in generating composite visualizations.[21] Nonetheless, he has to face the problem of how to explain the statistical techniques behind what he wants to show visually. Using a series of funny puns on cooking, he opts for the rhetorical power of the visual. He wants to

Count words rather than weigh them! To count beasts rather than caress them! ... To reassure Colette [the author he will focus on] and to save her ghost from the nightmare of numbers the cooking of numbers won't be shown. It is enough to know that the curves which we will produce are obtained with cross multiplication, square roots, and many other ingredients whose names alone could spoil your appetite, though the computer can digest them without trouble.[22]

What are the ingredients of Brunet's cooking of visualizations? He provides the tables of data used. His endnotes include formulas for some of the calculations. However, in the body of the article he explicitly turns our attention to the lines (curves) of visualization.

Brunet begins by showing how statistics can confirm what most readers would consider obvious about Colette's fondness for cats. His first graph shows which animal words Colette is statistically more likely to use than the authors of the comparison corpus of nineteenth-century and twentieth-century texts from the full database. Not surprisingly, "chat" stands out,

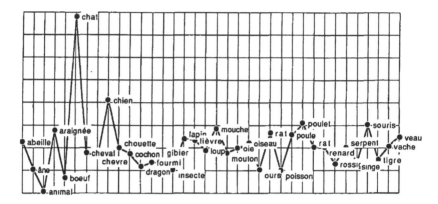

Figure 5.3
Brunet's (1989) bestiary of Colette.

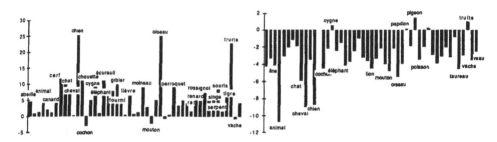

Figure 5.4
Brunet's (1989) bestiaries of Giraudoux and Proust.

but many other animals have a positive deviation from the norm. Such analysis and visualization require a large corpus of both Colette's works (five of which are in the database) and comparable authors with which to establish the norm.

From bar graphs to scatter plots based on factor analysis, Brunet goes wild with visualizations as he looks at a corpus of comparable authors from the same period. Many of his graphs are comparative or are arranged to enable comparison with other graphs. (See figure 5.4 here.) Other graphs, such as that shown here as figure 5.5, are designed to compare the animals that, in the writings of a certain author, appear more frequently than the norm (on the right) against those that appear less frequently (on the left). In graphs such as that shown here as figure 5.6, readers are encouraged to compare authors—in this case Chateaubriand (empty circles) and Hugo

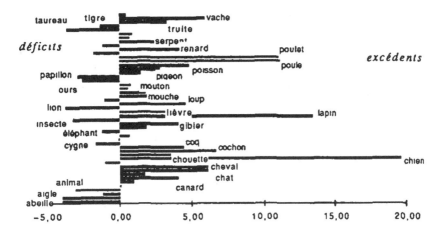

Figure 5.5
Brunet's (1989) bestiary of Maupassant.

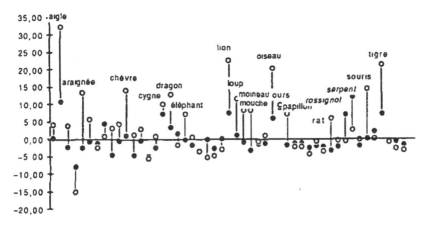

Figure 5.6
Brunet's (1989) bestiary of Chateaubriand and Hugo.

(filled circles). (Notice the many animals Hugo uses more frequently than Chateaubriand.)

The build-up of visualizations culminates in two scatter plots, generated by factor analysis, that map selected authors and animals into a two-dimensional space that shows how they cluster. Each of these plots takes up more than half of a page, overwhelming the narrative. The final one (figure 5.7 here) brings us back to the beginning—it shows Colette off in the lower right-hand quadrant, where she is the author closest to "chat." (The arrows drawing attention to Colette and "chat" are in the original figure.)

To recapitulate: Brunet begins with a serious discussion of the value of large-scale analytics, then proceeds to a gallery of playful visualizations that overcome the argument, or perhaps *become* the argument. The second half of the article, with its twenty graphs, encourages visual comparisons. A visualization attached to the article's last endnote at the end of the article shows the popularity of cats and dogs over time and across genres of writing. Concluding the narrative, Brunet writes: "As for *dog* his fate runs parallel to that of *cat*, and the two lines are twisted together like a garland. Visibly the *cats* and the *dogs* were created to understand each other, like Toby-Dog and Kiki-The-Sweet."[23] The article closes, not with discourse, or narrative, but with Brunet's final visualization of cat and dog (and horse), shown here as figure 5.8.

One wonders if this is a discourse with embedded visualizations or a comic strip of visualizations connected by text. Visibly, in Brunet, the text and the graphics are woven together in more ways than one. The question is whether can we weave them together in the new online and interactive publishing medium of the Web.

But here we need to look at how interactive visualization, which has emerged as a broadly accessible form of analytic, has been used rhetorically. How have interactive analytics been integrated into texts online? How can toys be embedded in texts? In chapter 3 we looked at a number of examples. Here we will look more closely at one of the first tools that could be embedded in a webpage: TACTWeb.

Interactive Components

TACTWeb, developed from TACT by John Bradley and Geoffrey Rockwell, was one of the first mature text-analysis environments to be available on the Web. To teach text analysis, and to teach how to use the TACTWeb, a workbook was developed that provided a narrative with embedded interactive fields and buttons.[24] The example provided here in figure 5.9 shows

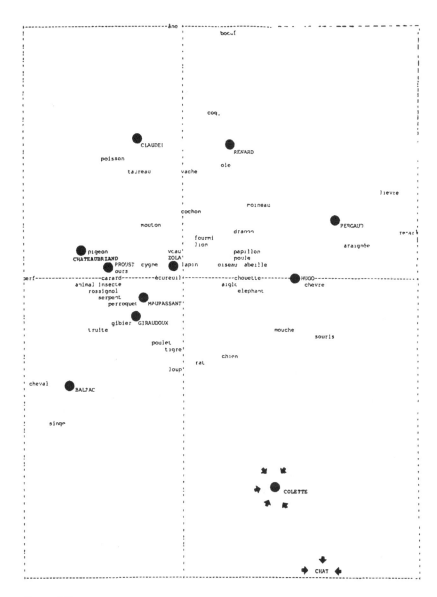

Figure 5.7
Detail of a factor analysis of Brunet's (1989) bestiary of selected authors.

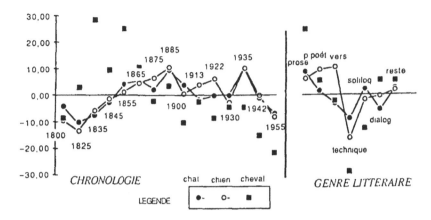

Figure 5.8
Brunet's final visualization of dog and cat (and horse) over time and genre.

Try It - Distribution Graph

1. Type a word in this box [   ] like "moon".

2. Click on this button [Submit Query] to run the search and to see a distribution display of the occurrences found.

3. Remember to click the **Back** button to return here.

Figure 5.9
A "Try It" panel from the TACTWeb workbook.

how a user can learn about distribution graphs by trying TACTWeb. The workbook followed a model of general explanation, showing examples, providing narrated "Try It" panels, and then leading to the analytical environment, in which there is no explanatory text woven around the fields and buttons.[25]

It was the possibilities of Common Gateway Interface (CGI) server-side processing offered by HTML Form elements that, in 1996, made it possible to imagine alternative configurations of text and analytical results. On the one hand, we could now weave an analytical tool directly into text so that a reader could try it in the tutorial. On the other hand, we could also show the same functionality in different ways on different webpages, thereby erasing the lines between instructions, essays, and tools and extending the tools' pedagogical and rhetorical uses. Because we didn't have to clearly demarcate the interactive components from associated text on the webpage, we were able to present the same components in different explanatory

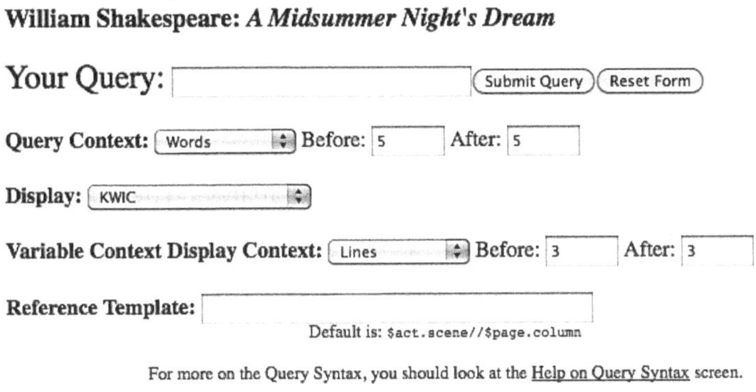

William Shakespeare: *A Midsummer Night's Dream*

Your Query: [   ] (Submit Query)(Reset Form)

Query Context: [Words   ▼] Before: [5]   After: [5]

Display: [KWIC   ▼]

Variable Context Display Context: [Lines   ▼] Before: [3]   After: [3]

Reference Template: [   ]

Default is: `$act.scene//$page.column`

For more on the Query Syntax, you should look at the Help on Query Syntax screen.

Figure 5.10
A query panel from TACTWeb.

contexts, ranging from the heavily narrated tutorial to the cleanly labeled Query screen shown here in figure 5.10.

Being able to interlace components with text and to launch interactive examples has obvious pedagogical uses. This model can be found in other online tutorials, including John Maeda's *Design By Numbers* (dbn.media. mit.edu) and the tutorials available at www.w3schools.com. However, the rhetorical opportunities for this intertwining have not been exploited in interpretive work, mainly because interpretations are usually published in print and because those available online are in online journals that enforce a common format.

Examples of Tool Rhetoric

Though Smith and Brunet hoped that computer-assisted analysis would be an effective critical method when supported by visualization, their studies did not have the hoped-for effect. Smith, in "Computer Criticism," clearly hoped that the shift in perspective brought about through computer-assisted interpretation would become a school of criticism of its own, rather than a specialized extension of structuralist/formalist theory. He hoped for a Kuhnian paradigm shift that would introduce an "altered concept of proof and what constitutes demonstration of a literary hypothesis."[26] That was not to be. Perhaps literary theory got tired of structuralism just at the moment Smith was trying to use it to argue for computer criticism, or perhaps Smith was ahead of his time. We also think Smith was too worried about proof, but that is another issue. Only now on the Web are Smith's ideas about interactive analytics playing out. Similarly, Brunet's point about the value of large-scale text analysis would have to wait until the scale of text collections for other languages caught up. Only since Franco Moretti's *Graphs, Maps, Trees* (2005) have we seen significant uptake by literary historians.[27]

Earlier in this book we reflected on the rhetorical problem of engaging a humanities audience with research assisted by text analysis. The challenges with the integration of analytics in interpretation include the following:

1. Results consisting of long lists of words often take up a lot of precious publication space (even digital space is valuable if users have to scroll a lot).
2. Results have to be explained. Because a list of words by itself doesn't mean much, such lists are often accompanied by long technical discussions explaining how they were generated.
3. Long discussions of method distract from interpretation.
4. We do not generally write about methods in the humanities, because the proof is in the interpretation, not in how one arrived at the interpretation.

Hermeneutica presents the interactive panel or hermeneutical toy as an alternative way of weaving analytics into discourse so as to engage a larger audience. The interludes show how embedded toys can demonstrate analytical results in a way that avoids many of the rhetorical problems of reporting analyses in print. The long lists are within an embedded scrolling window, so they do not take up the same visual space as the rest of the text, but can still be explored. The tools are explained through exploration and online documentation.

Hermeneutica invite play rather than distracting from interpretation, especially when there is a responsive interface to the toy. An embeddable toy such as TAToo substitutes interaction for documentation as a way of understanding method. Rather than tell you about it, we let you try it as a way of figuring it out. You could call it fiddleware, though there are usually help screens and documentation for those who don't like to discover technique through use. Finally, this model allows interpretive narrative and interpretive toys to be tightly interwoven, giving the author more flexibility in the pacing of an essay. You are not forced to have a whole section on technology; instead the toys can be side panels placed where you want. You can create a palimpsest of texts and interactives.

Of course, this chapter, located at the center of the book, is also another way of interpreting technique through the doubling of essays mirrored with reflective chapters such as this one. The interludes or case studies are paired not just because it is a convenient way of moving technical reflection out of interpretation but also because the doubling reflects the thinking through of Agile Hermeneutics, in which we worked as a pair and paired programming with hermeneutics. All this doubling may seem cute, but it is in the game of trying technique through real questions that you find more to reflect on than just the question at hand—a reflective surplus about technique. Just as we worked in a pair with our toys, this book, with its combination of interludes and chapters, emerged from a series of experiments trying to do text analysis as a process from playing with toys to producing an essay.[28] In experimenting we found ourselves struggling with how to report what we thought we saw. Willard McCarty put it this way in a Humanist post:

So let me ask: how better might we talk about the research we do (and that we avoid doing) than always to be rattling on about pure vs. applied, or curiosity-motivated vs mission-orientated or whatever?[29]

This is a problem faced by all of us who try to explain computer-assisted text analysis: there are very few examples of concrete humanities research essays based on computer-assisted techniques that are not about the techniques per se. There are papers that respond in traditional ways to original literary, historical, or philosophical problems; however, they do not describe how computing methods modulated the response, and thus they hide their method. There are papers about tools and methods, but they don't give us concrete examples of techniques in use. No, we are tempted to conclude that computer-assisted tools are like Wittgenstein's ladder: they are discarded once one climbs up them to purchase a new view. We are tempted to go further and speculate that method has become invisible to the humanities, and that there is something fundamental to the rhetoric of the humanities that is antithetical to method, though not to reflection about method. You can have theory (including theory about method) or method, but not both. Perhaps the humanities are embarrassed by methods because they look like toys.

This is a problem for computer-assisted text analysis. As we develop methods and apply them to problems in the humanities, we also have to figure out how to talk about the insights that emerge without either boring our audience with technical details or hiding the methods. It is possible that we may never grasp the "holy grail" of writing works that engage our colleagues while documenting new methods used rigorously. *Hermeneutica* presents a model of online writing in which the results of text analysis are woven into a hybrid form that is not an academic essay or a tool, but rather is a weaving of text and toy that invites exploration. We imagine an academic rhetoric that resembles the emerging public rhetoric—an academic rhetoric in which things such as visualizations are woven into text. The online essay can now be an interactive hybrid that can sustain two threads, showing both conclusions and the analytics used to reach them in a fashion that can be recapitulated. As Brunet imagined, the online essay can be a *satura*—a comedic mixture of ingredients.

What Are These Things?

This brings us back to the hermeneutical things we want to mix into our work. How are they different from the texts we want to weave them into? They obviously aren't texts in the way a book is a text, though they may contain text. So what are they? First of all, they are software things that run within more complex systems, such as Web browsers. Things in general seem to be the dumb other for the disciplines of discourse of the humanities. Though things don't talk the way discourses do, they seem to be real in a way that talk isn't. Things, even software things, seem to persist longer than talk and seem to resist us the way talk doesn't. You can interact with things, touch them or click on them, but they are not of us. For these reasons they are studied by practical disciplines such as carpentry, industrial design, engineering, or, in the case of software things, computing science.

To understand hermeneutica, therefore, we need to understand the difficult relationship the humanities have had with things. We can do that by returning to Descartes' *Discourse* and his autobiographical story of doubting every thing. At the beginning of part 4 of the *Discourse*, Descartes tells us about doubting everything in order to see if there was anything that could not be doubted. Because the senses can deceive us, he rejected the things they present to us; he also rejected as possibly doubtful the abstract objects presented to thought in everyday life. He found reason to doubt the existence of everything, either sensual or abstract, with one exception: the thinking self that is conscious of its thinking and therefore must exist. ("I think therefore I am.") Actually, that exception is not just a thinking self, but a self thinking in discourse. The *Cogito* is a thinking through of discourse that then privileges thinking discourse over other things, whether perceived or thought.

Things, in this story, will always be dependent on discourse for their truth, and it isn't clear that the humanities have totally freed themselves from this logocentricity. Idealism, the philosophical view that things are just bundles of perceptions called ideas, has taken many forms before and since Descartes' *Discourse*. Once you start doubting things, it seems obvious that the thinking self (consciousness) is more real than, and different from, the objects it thinks about. But where do the ideas of things come from? Bishop Berkeley suggested a simple solution; that God broadcasts everything to our minds. More recently, the 1999 movie *The Matrix* presented an artificial reality (the Matrix) generated by artificial intelligences to pacify humans.

Perhaps the most influential response to Descartes' doubt came from Immanuel Kant, who argued that reality is how we structure experience. Whatever the state of things-in-themselves, we wouldn't have any experience without structuring it with categories of time, space, and so on. For Kant there were things-in-themselves, but those weren't knowable by humans except through the structuring that made thinking possible. Things were things again because otherwise there would be no way to think about them. David Hume's more pragmatic approach was to point out that, whatever the ontological status of things, one still must act as if they are there, and, as we will see in chapter 10, leave a room through the door, not the window. Hume's *Dialogues Concerning Natural Religion* shows in dialogue how common sense about things is consistent with doubting skepticism, especially if you are skeptical about skepticism. Recently, Ian Bogost (2012) has taken skepticism of the importance of the human perspective even further by asking what it would be like to remove ourselves entirely from the understanding of things. He points out how the humanities are still blindly committed to our own discourse and thus blind to the way things can bear knowledge.

Part of the issue with theorizing things is setting things against human knowledge. As Bogost points out in *Alien Phenomenology*, all these discussions of the being of things depend on us and on our knowing of the thing. If you start by questioning how we know about beings, then all being tends to end up being defined by our thinking. You then end up with a separation between mind and things (e.g., bodies), between subject and object, between mind and nature, or between text and toy. These fundamental categories then structure our thinking in all sorts of ways, including an artificial division of the disciplines of the mind and its discourses in opposition to the disciplines of things. The *Cogito*, a brilliant idea, becomes a tool that makes sense of some things but fails to make sense of other things.

Martin Heidegger, in *Being and Time* (1953), questioned the Cartesian assumptions and restored thingness to the thing. Heidegger flipped the philosophical fascination with the question of the reality of the thing-in-itself to argue that it was actually as everyday stuff that we experience things. In living we encounter things as ready-to-hand tools that we use to achieve our various desires and purposes. A tool such as a hammer is a paradigmatic thing of everyday life. It is equipment, and as equipment it doesn't stand apart from us or alone in itself. In fact, in the hammering of a project there is no subject or object, just the carpentry. Tools and equipment, including everyday language, are transparent in use, which is why all the discussion about doubting minds and things-in-themselves doesn't tell us about things so much as it tells us about philosophical minds.

Further, any piece of equipment is part of a system or network of equipment. A hammer goes with nails, wood, hardware stores, and weekend projects such as building a bookcase for all the stuff you read. We don't notice a hammer as a mere thing until is breaks, or until we stand back from it and begin doing ontology. Then it becomes *present-at-hand*—that is, becomes the sort of thing, present before us, that is deliberately thought about. Only when it is present-at-hand does it stand apart such that we could think about doubting it as a philosopher would, or studying it as an engineer would.

Hermeneutical Things

We can see now how hermeneutica are things. When used in a news website, they are transparent in the way a telescope is transparent in use. As things for research, however, they are meant to be seen and noticed as things during their use. Research instruments have to be fiddled with in order to work, and in the fiddling they can draw attention to themselves. They are thus meant to resist completely transparent use and to be alternatively used through manipulation and manipulated to be useful. Research things thus are meant to be both ready-to-hand and present-at-hand so as to avoid uninterpreted use. They are meant to be a little out of place, as is a toy in a serious essay. One might even go so far as to suggest that in their playfulness they undermine other things that are around, but only when they work—and often they don't work.

Another way in which hermeneutica are things is that they are part of systems of things, such as the World Wide Web and all the associated technologies. They may be toys, but they are toys in a network of technologies that includes everything down to the level of tubes through which data flows. Hermeneutica, however, have some special features as things for interpretation. The system of things they are part of includes the original text, other essays of interpretation, and the other things of interpretation. Hermeneutica don't hide these things; they are designed to show them. Further, hermeneutica are meant to be embedded in specific interpretive things, such as online essays. They are not meant to stand alone or to the side. They are not interpretations that replace the interpreted, but toys that augment the interpretation, though sometimes they interrupt the flow of thought.

In a later essay, "The Thing" (1971), Heidegger plays with the etymology of the Old High German word "thing" and suggests that a thing is a "gathering." Bruno Latour (2000) picks up on this suggestion of how a thing gathers different expectations and perspectives. The same thing that is developed and debugged by a software weaver is used by a student to interpret a text and then is embedded in an essay for use by another reader. It is used transparently by someone browsing the Web, and it is fiddled with by someone interested in the toy and how it ended up in an essay. No one way of approaching hermeneutica as things is more real than another. Hermeneutica as things are a gathering of expectations in networks of use.

Ornamental Follies

The second thing to say about hermeneutica is that they are follies—not in sense of foolishness, but in the architectural sense of decorative buildings not designed to be used so much as viewed. The faux Roman ruins and Medieval castles with which certain gardens were decorated were architectural follies. They were designed to remind people of another time or another place. They weren't simulacra, meant to replace the originals; they weren't simulations, meant to represent the originals faithfully. They were designed so that we would know that they aren't the originals, but that they point through to an interpreted original.

You can see another way in which hermeneutica are interpretive. An interpretive thing has a special relationship to other things in that it announces itself not as something brand new, or as a replacement, but as an interpretation of something else. An interpretive thing is like a folly that is not a new building, even if it is built new, but a building that is meant to look as if it had been assembled from the parts of the old—a small ornamental building drawing attention, but part of a garden for which it is an ornament. In this new webbed world, in which we are surrounded by neat gadgets and new interactive games, some of them present themselves as being generated from other things. Those are hermeneutica.

Why use ornaments to draw attention to something in the past? The folly seems purposely anachronistic, something that runs counter to the spirit of the new-new modernity of computing. Of course, re-searching what has come before and re-interpreting it is the way the interpretive humanities bear gifts. By ornamenting, framing, and curating the works of human expression, we animate them so that they can be relevant again and bear them forward for further use. By ornamenting them and providing new ways into interpreting them, we bring them to life for another generation. We try to make them infectious again by trying to bring forward that which is uniquely human in each work interpreted. Whether we are doing this with students in a class or in writing for a public, we are treating things as special, as if they mattered again today as they did in their time. Our interpretations may be follies, but they forge a way back to something idiosyncratic. Our hermeneutica may appear to be fiddly little toys in the serious work of the humanities, but they too point back to the ideographic.

Surrogates

The third thing to be said about hermeneutica is that they operate on surrogates. This is true of all computer-assisted text-analysis tools, though it is true in different ways for different tools. What do we mean by "surrogates"? As we mentioned above, the first steps in analyzing text are demarcating, digitizing, and then encoding the text to be studied. We are never operating on texts directly, as might be thought. With computers we are developing stand-ins or surrogates that can be processed as strings. This is doubly true of some of the work done by Franco Moretti and Matt Jockers: they don't always operate on the full texts; sometimes they operate on metadata about the texts. Moretti, in "Network Theory, Plot Analysis" (2013b), makes this point about working with metadata: "once you make a network of a play, you stop working on the play proper, and work on a *model* instead. You reduce the text to characters and interactions, abstract them from everything else." J. B. Smith illustrated this in his 1973 paper "Image and Imagery in Joyce's *Portrait*" and made it the central insight of his 1978 paper "Computer Criticism." The computer can be used to identify different types of structure in a text and to create a surrogate for visualization. By breaking Joyce's text into 500-word chunks and measuring the density of image words in those chunks, he created a new "layer" or surrogate that showed something he wanted to study in the text. That surrogate was then represented by another surrogate: the graph that shows the visualization. What Smith realized in "Computer Criticism" is how many different ways we can use the computer to structure layers and how these layers can then be compared. Where we differ from Smith is that we don't think of these layers as representing something "in" the text so much as we think of them as interpretations of the text in layers of interpretations over time. We see hermeneutica not as microscopes revealing the inner structure, but as augmentations adding to a history of interpretation.

Building on Smith's work, we contend that working with computers means working with computer surrogates for the things commonly thought of as texts. The materiality of computers is important to understanding what can be done with them. Some of these digital surrogates are corpora, some are electronic texts, some are metadata (data about data), and some are code. Our hermeneutica are surrogates that break apart and then resynthesize the original (if there is such a thing as an original). They invite exploration as a way of understanding the original. Word clouds and other hermeneutica are small models that represent some aspect of a much larger surrogate. You work with them, not with the text they are drawn from.

That said, one of the things we have tried to do with the hermeneutica we design is provide the humanist with a way back through to the text. An "interactive" may be a model of the original that invites exploration, but it should be possible to check one's interpretation of the model against the electronic text. This is one of the features that distinguishes the text-analysis tools of the Digital Humanities from either the bibliometric tools of informatics or distant reading. We want to move from the small visualization to the text and back because we value the poetry of the text in and of itself. Ideally our tools would be like palimpsests that scrape the text and reuse it while still showing faint remains. Stefan Sinclair has, for this reason, theorized one of Voyant's predecessors as a reading tool—a "hyper-reading" tool, but still a reading tool that doesn't replace so much as remind. Voyant takes this further, giving you a way to generate little readings and embed them as ornaments in other interpretations. These little interpretations don't pretend to replace that which they interpret the way big interpretations do; they are embedded toys in the tradition of follies.

The interludes in this book take advantage of the possibilities of the new online medium by proposing a new form of hybrid publication that builds on the print graphic visualization (Smith 1973) and the 1990s idea of the digital workbook. In a hybrid essay, the narrative is no longer pedagogical; it is interpretive, with interactive panels that enable readers to participate in the analysis. It was the pedagogical effectiveness of such interactive workbooks that led to their adaption in the form of "Recipes" for the TAPoR project, which, in turn, have been adapted for *Hermeneutica*. The embedded toy provides an interpretive thing in an essay. Hermeneutica embed analysis in interpretation, and they explain themselves by letting you try them.

But how do you feel about toys in your essay? Do you notice them because they are new? Are they Trojan horses bearing the virus of quantitative methods, or can they provide new ornaments to interpretation? Do they demean the noble essay with technology, or do they re-interpret the essay as interactive? Will they corrupt the pure text of interpretation, or will they re-interpret computing for interpretation? We are reminded of the end of Lucretius' *The Way Things Are*, where he leaves us with an image like that of Pontypool—an image of language, the first tool, as a plague on thinking:

the tongue, that tries
To be the mind's interpreter, filled up
Engorged with blood, became too hard to move,
Seemed rough to the touch. From throat to chest and lungs
The plague descended, thence assailed the heart,
Battering all the bastions of life.

—Lucretius, *The Way Things Are* (1969 edition), book VI

6 Now Analyze That! Comparing Two Speeches on Race (Second Interlude)

Sounds like he talked a hate speech, doesn't it? Now, analyze that![1]
Jeremiah Wright, 2008

In the lead-up to the 2008 US presidential election, the news media became interested in what Barack Obama and his spiritual mentor Jeremiah A. Wright Jr. had to say about race.[2] Obama and Wright were represented as engaging in the age-old conflict between a son and a father as the son comes of age as a leader. In the media's imagined Oedipal drama, Obama, the son, tries to distance himself from Wright in order to win the presidency. Wright, the father-pastor, continually corrects the record while managing mounting media attention. In attempting to redirect attention to more substantive issues by asserting "This time we want to talk about [issue]," both men give moving and important speeches on race. Wright even challenges us directly: "Now analyze that!"

What if we had taken them at their word and looked away from the podium-and-pews drama?[3] What if we had taken them seriously and looked at what they said? What if we had used our hermeneutica to try to "analyze that," interrogating and interpreting the similarities and differences between their speeches? We took up that challenge. Using the tools we had at hand, including the first version of TAPoR and an earlier version of Voyant, we compared and analyzed two speeches given by the two men:

Obama's March 18 speech "A more perfect union," given in response to the media attention mentioned above. This speech has been generally considered one of Obama's finest on race and America.[4]

Wright's April 27 speech to the National Association for the Advancement of Colored People. Given after Obama's speech, it also dealt with race.[5]

We chose these speeches because we were not interested in the "gotchas" that bloggers and media focused on (for example, Wright's references to

Louis Farrakhan) and because we were able to find reasonable transcripts and associated video records of both.[6, 7] Moreover, these were important speeches, documents to which people were returning to understand Obama and Wright's positions. Why not analyze that?

As we saw in the last few chapters, much of computer-assisted text analysis is essentially about tokenizing, counting, and comparing, and quantities are not everything. Hermeneutical tools can show differences in word use; the results plant a seed that can germinate with reflection. In this chapter we will look at why the difference between what Obama said and what Wright said is worth thinking through.

This Time We Want to Talk ...

One of the first things we noticed was that Obama used the word "time" far more often than Wright.[8] At the climax of Obama's speech, he repeatedly used the phrase "this time we want to talk." Figure 6.1 shows a concordance of all the instances of "time."

Repeated phrases are usually an indication of something the author wants to emphasize. In this case they are at the climax of Obama's speech, and they tell us three things.

"This is the time" Obama wants us to be aware of the moment—a moment when an African-American may become president. Different times call for different discourses, and "this time we want to talk about ... ."

"Not this time" Obama is trying to redirect what we, including the electorate and the media, are talking about during the election. He wants to elevate the discourse, to focus on what he believes should matter to the electorate, and to shift the focus away from the identity politics (including Wright) that tars him. For Obama, Wright represents a distraction. Obama's platform is firmly grounded in the promise of change. However, if the media continue to be diverted by the attention they are giving to Wright, the status quo will remain. "I can tell you," Obama worries, that, unless something changes, "in the next election, we'll be talking about some other distraction. And then another one. And then another one. And nothing will change."

"We want to talk about" Obama emphasizes the importance of specific topics by claiming "we want to talk about [them]." In terms of location in the text and rhetorical power of repetition, the phrase marks the climax of this speech. Obama indicates important topics,

and should be perfected over	time	. And yet words on a
and the reality of their	time	.This was one of the
solve the challenges of our	time	unless we solve them together
but divisive, divisive at a	time	when we need unity; racially
unity; racially charged at a	time	when we need to come
fifties and early sixties, a	time	when segregation was still the
prejudiced, resentment builds over	time	. Like the anger within the
our fathers, and spending more	time	with our children, and reading
together and say, "Not this	time	." This time we want to
say, "Not this time." This	time	we want to talk about
and Native American children. This	time	we want to reject the
st century economy. Not this	time	.This time we want to
economy. Not this time. This	time	we want to talk about
we do it together. This	time	we want to talk about
every walk of life. This	time	we want to talk about
more than a profit. This	time	we want to talk about
sitting there quietly the entire	time	. And Ashley asks him why

Figure 6.1

topics we should pay attention to, with the phrase "this time we want to talk about."

There are five things Obama wants us to talk about. They are a fairly traditional list of Democratic talking points:

"crumbling schools" (education)
"lines in the Emergency Room" (health care)
"shuttered mills" (loss of manufacturing jobs)
"shipping your job overseas" (outsourcing)
"serving and fighting together" (the war in Iraq)

Obama invokes race in such a way as to suggest that these Democratic issues transcend race. For example: "This time we want to talk about the crumbling schools that are stealing the future of black children and white children and Asian children and Hispanic children and Native American children." This time, he argues, the focus should not be on the distractions that can otherwise hijack elections. The election should direct focus on the issues that all Americans—black, white, Asian, Hispanic, and indigenous— have in common.

Committed to Repetition

Much like Obama, Wright repeated one phrase, "we are committed to changing the way," to focus attention on topics he saw as critical. The distribution graph for "committed" locates Wright's phrase near the end his speech, at the rhetorical climax. Figure 6.2 shows a concordance of the word "committed" in Wright's speech.

Wright asserts that, together with his audience, he is committed to changing the way the world is treated. His use of the words "different" and "deficient" is central to his message.[9] Wright wants people to recognize that difference is not deficiency:

In the past, we were taught to see others who are different as somehow being deficient. Christians saw Jews as being deficient. Catholics saw Protestants as being deficient. Presbyterians saw Pentecostals as being deficient.

Folks who like to holler in worship saw folk who like to be quiet as deficient. And vice versa.

Whites saw blacks as being deficient. ...

Europeans saw Africans as deficient.

because many of us are	committed	to changing how we see
because many of us are	committed	to changing the way we
Many of us are	committed	to changing how we see
because many of us are	committed	to changing how we see
of 12,000. Many of us are	committed	to changing how we see
one, many of us are	committed	to changing how we see
Many of us are	committed	to changing how we see
one, many of us are	committed	to changing how we see
children. Many of us are	committed	to changing, number three, the
treat black youth. We are	committed	to changing the way we
We are	committed	to changing the way we
believe what we believe, we're	committed	to changing the way we
other, many of us are	committed	to changing the way we
straights treat gays. We are	committed	to changing the way we
because many of us are	committed	to changing how we see
Many of us are	committed	to changing how we see
ourselves. Many of us are	committed	to changing the way we
other. Many of us are	committed	to changing the way we
many of us finally are	committed	to changing this world that
to their children. We are	committed	to changing this world that's

Figure 6.2

Difference, for Wright, should not be negated; it should be accepted. Wright invokes the differences between African and European music to outline his point:

Now, what is true in the field of education, linguistics, ethnomusicology, marching bands, psychology, and culture is also true in the field [*sic*] of homiletics, hermeneutics, biblical studies, black sacred music, and black worship. We just do it different and some of our haters can't get their heads around that.

Our hermeneutica revealed a political difference in minor discursive patterns: Obama sees challenges common to all. Wright sees differences that need to be recognized in order to be treated. As a presidential candidate, Obama wants us to turn our focus to the challenges we have in common, on what is wanting in the country as a whole. As a minister, Wright asks us to make a commitment to see difference, not deficiency.

Obama is trying to turn electoral discourse to political issues that administrations can solve. Wright is trying to refocus media criticism onto change to which individuals can commit.

Black and White

Despite their frequent use of the inclusive word "we," the speakers also focus on "black" and "white." The Word Frequency List in figure 6.3 illustrates that both speeches are fundamentally about race (not surprising, since that's why we chose them).

"Black" is the most frequent word after "I." The speeches are obviously tailored to location and audience. Wright, speaking to members of the NAACP from the perspective of the black church, uses the word "white" only four times. Obama, speaking at the National Constitution Center, uses the word "white" 27 times, on one occasion mentioning his "white" grandmother.

Text analysis of these two speeches illustrates how Obama distances himself from Wright's use of "incendiary language to express views that have the potential not only to widen the racial divide, but views that denigrate both the greatness and the goodness of our nation; that rightly offend white and black alike." Although he has some sympathy for his "religious leader's effort to speak out against perceived injustice," Obama unequivocally condemns Wright as divisive:

Reverend Wright's comments were not only wrong but divisive, divisive at a time when we need unity; racially charged at a time when we need to come together to solve a set of monumental problems—two wars, a terrorist threat, a falling economy,

Word	Count	Word	Count
I	88	African-American	11
black	64	Americans	11
And	38	That	11
The	33	church	11
people	31	field	11
children	30	means	11
white	30	race	11
We	28	religious	11
deficient	25	European	10
treat	25	Wright	10
change	24	campaign	10
time	24	fact	10
years	23	learning	10
changing	22	make	10
committed	21		
American	20		
But	20		
Dr	20		
country	19		
NAACP	17		
America	16		
It's	15		
They	15		
community	15		
made	15		
racial	15		
It	14		
Reverend	14		
In	13		
education	13		
fought	13		
This	12		
men	12		
story	12		
tradition	12		
African	11		

Figure 6.3

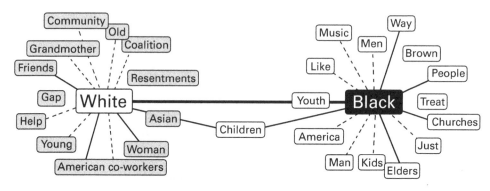

Figure 6.4

a chronic health care crisis and potentially devastating climate change; problems that are neither black or white or Latino or Asian, but rather problems that confront us all.

In contrast, Wright is insisting that there are real differences, and, by implication, that there are divisions that must be acknowledged, even if the act of acknowledging them is politically charged.

We close this interlude with a view of the collocates of the words "black" and "white" in both speeches. Collocates are words that appear near the words in question. The static visual collocation shown in figure 6.4 should provoke you to think about how Obama and Wright talk about black and white. Look closely and you will discover that neither speaker uses the phrase "White House," preferring to refer to the "Oval Office." Why not take up Wright's challenge and try to "analyze that" for yourself?[10]

7   False Positives: Opportunities and Dangers in Big-Data Text Analysis[1]

The NSA has built an infrastructure that allows it to intercept almost everything. With this capability, the vast majority of human communications are automatically ingested without targeting. If I wanted to see your emails or your wife's phone, all I have to do is use intercepts. I can get your emails, passwords, phone records, credit cards. I don't want to live in a society that does these sort of things. ... I do not want to live in a world where everything I do and say is recorded. That is not something I am willing to support or live under.
Edward Snowden, June 10, 2013 (quoted in MacAskill 2013)

In May of 2013, Edward Snowden, a former security contractor for the US government, flew to Hong Kong with a large cache of documents about the National Security Agency. He shared these materials with news organizations. Some of those organizations, including the *Guardian*, have since been carefully preparing stories based on the documents, stories that reveal something of the extent and sophistication of the surveillance conducted by the NSA and other intelligence outfits.[2] One set of documents revealed the existence of PRISM and Boundless Informant, software that let analysts search the metadata and even the full texts of messages to and from US citizens. Text analysis on a very large scale is clearly happening, and analytical tools are being developed by governments and corporations; they are spending millions if not billions of dollars on developing infrastructure and tools for analyzing and storing metadata and text.[3] The scale of the infrastructure and how it is being used raise challenging social and ethical issues that force us all, as citizens in a digital society, to confront how we balance priorities. As Jeffrey Rosen observes, the debate is, in part, about the balance between privacy and security:

We run the risk, therefore, of constructing vast but ineffective architectures of surveillance and identification that threaten the liberty and privacy of innocent citizens without protecting us from terrorism.[4]

Does all this investment in surveillance and data tracking work? One of Liberace's sayings was "Too much of a good thing is wonderful." That, alas, may not be true of signals intelligence, which is why in this chapter we look at the phenomenon called "big data" and at what it means to practices of interpretation in the humanities, a domain in which we have traditionally assumed that more information is better.

Why does big data matter to the humanities? It matters because we— as a society and as academics—have the fever for ever larger amounts of information. It matters because there is much at stake, from political and economic realities to a reconfiguration of how we know and study human history and culture (and ourselves) on a large scale. With the shift from the interpretation of carefully chosen examples (of literary texts, historical documents, philosophical dialogues, and so on) to the analysis of datasets that are beyond our capacity to read individually, there are potentially significant transformations in what we study and how we study. There are also new ethical dilemmas having to do with privacy. Individuals can be identified in big data in a way that they can't as easily be identified in carefully sampled and curated data. It has become hard to anonymize data when there are so many sources of data which, when cross-linked, can reveal identity.[5] Further, there are issues around the persistence of data (such as questionable pictures posted to a social network or stored in the cloud) that may be impossible to erase from view.[6] Beyond issues of privacy, interpretation changes when there is a shift from studying unique works of art through practices that privilege close reading to the exploration practices of large-scale distant reading.

This chapter is not intended to explain the technical aspects of big data or the opportunities it presents. (Plenty of books, articles, websites, and videos are available for those purposes.) Here we will limit ourselves to a brief definition of big data and will focus on how understanding big data is important to understanding the opportunities for textual interpretation in the humanities. We will survey the phenomenon of big data in order to understand any implications for the future of computer-assisted text analysis and hermeneutica in the humanities.

In particular, we will use examples related to national security organizations such as the NSA and the CSEC (Communications Security Establishment Canada) to examine big data. We will not discuss exactly what our governments are gathering or what they are doing with what they gather. Thankfully, the *Guardian*, the *Washington Post*, the *Intercept*, the *New York Times*, the Electronic Frontier Foundation, and the Electronic Privacy Information Center are investigating their activities, and by the time you read this there will have been more revelations from Snowden's hoard.[7] Instead we will use what has been discovered about government projects, both older and recent, to illustrate what *can* be done with big-data text analysis. By looking away from literary text analysis to what agencies with lots of resources can do with analytics, we can better see the dangers and opportunities. Moreover, there are striking similarities in the search for unusual phenomena within a large collection of literary texts that merit further interpretation and the search for suspicious communication within a global network that warrants closer attention. Both activities are essentially about calibrating signal-to-noise ratios where defining what is a signal for computational processing is a deceptively difficult operation.

What Is Big Data?

With their characteristic ability to provide memorable formulations, the business and IT sectors have latched on to a set of words beginning with the letter V to describe big data. The original formulation may have only contained Volume, Velocity, and Variety, but several variants add Veracity and Value.[8] The central idea is that, owing to changes in how information is created, stored, and transmitted, there is now a lot (Volume) of heterogeneous data (Variety), sometimes coming in very quickly (Velocity), from which businesses or governments can extract new truths (Veracity) and make money (Value).

As the "big" in "big data" suggests, the volume of data is the novel factor, but that doesn't mean that there is a precise threshold of size. It is more a matter of the size provoking a change in how you handle and interpret the data. Once the amount of data gets beyond the point where traditional human forms of analysis work or traditional technologies work, you have big data. Google had to develop new techniques to handle the volume of data gathered and indexed from the World Wide Web so that they could let millions of people search trillions of pages. Going further than just handling lots of data, Google developed the PageRank algorithm for showing the pages most linked to among all the results. There is no point to providing users with a list of millions of pages that match the search criteria that they then have to page through; it is more useful to rank the pages so that the most relevant results appear on the first screens of the list. The simple concordance as a way of organizing results had to be updated when the quantity of data became so great that even the results of a search were too big to handle.

Likewise, an excess of textual data means that scholars can't read it all and have to switch to different methods in order to be able to synthesize insights from the whole. That is what Brunet was writing about in the 1980s when he was analyzing the *grand corpus* of FRANTEXT and what Franco Moretti discussed more recently in *Graphs, Maps, Trees*. Moretti coined the term "distant reading" to distinguish what he was doing from "close reading," but also to suggest metaphorically that with large quantities of data we have to step back to get a view of the whole. When the quantity of data is too big for humans to read, different practices are needed to understand the whole. That change in practices also changes the *what* and the *how* you interpret. Insofar as a theory is a view of the whole, with big data one needs a different kind of theoretical gaze, not merely a scaled-up one. Some would suggest that it isn't a theory at all when you let the data drive science, and when huge amounts of data make it practicable to compute correlations without prior hypotheses or theoretical models (Anderson 2008).

Another way to put this is that interpretation undergoes a qualitative change when the amount of information gets so large that no one can read it all. When that happens, you switch to sampling the phenomenon (as is done in the social sciences and polling), or you closely read selections as representatives of the whole (as is done in the humanities), or you have to find ways to handle all the information—and that involves some form of automatic data processing.[9] As Moretti points out in a collection of essays titled *Distant Reading*, when you stand back and use a computer to read data you are no longer doing interpretation as interpretation is traditionally understood; you are explaining. Interpretation engages the meaning of the text. It brings forth the idiosyncratic uniqueness. Explaining, on the other hand, shows the relationships between documents and can be used to trace a history of relationships. Explaining is not about re-evoking the meaning of a literary text, but about discovering the large-scale patterns of change in texts. It is epidemiology; it tracks symptoms, not causes.

Moretti goes on to assert that we don't need any more literary interpretation, as we have more than enough of it.[10] Here we side with Liberace; while there may be too much interpretation, it's a good and human thing, and that's the wonder. Like breathing, interpreting is such a fundamentally human activity that we cannot stop no matter how much of it there is. Of course Moretti isn't talking about the everyday interpreting we all do, but about the institutional investment in academic interpretation.

Big data is more than just about volume, but also a change in technique brought on and made possible by scale. When you have all or much of the available data rather than only samples, you can ask different types of questions. As we pointed out about hermeneutica in chapter 6, you can even move from distant reading to interpretive detail and then back to distant reading. That is what the NSA wants to do, though for surveillance and predictive purposes. They don't just want samples in order to understand terrorism, and they don't just want to be able to track any identified target's communications. They are preserving data so they will be able to backtrack. They are also experimenting with whether they can identify new suspects through sophisticated profiling, which slides into trying to predict who might "radicalize." For these new approaches, the NSA needs all the data it can get—more than just the names of identified suspects. It wants to work at multiple levels. Being limited to sampling would constrain the NSA to levels it had received clearance for and would provide only a partial view based on the samples collected.

The value of big data lies partly in the secondary and unanticipated uses. Humanists are familiar with the desire to have everything at hand so as to be able to explore new questions later (without needing to measure and collect new data) or to serendipitously follow any interpretive path, even one not anticipated by the author of a literary text. The bigger the library, the more you have ready to hand as fodder for interpretation.

Metadata and Content

Another way to understand big data is to understand some of the types of data that can be collected and analyzed. One type, made famous by the first of the Snowden leaks, is metadata. In defending NSA practices, Senator Dianne Feinstein describes telephone metadata as follows:

> The call-records program is not surveillance. It does not collect the content of any communication, nor do the records include names or locations. The NSA only collects the type of information found on a telephone bill: phone numbers of calls placed and received, the time of the calls and duration. The Supreme Court has held this "metadata" is not protected under the Fourth Amendment.[11]

On June 6, 2013, the *Guardian* published an article on the first document leaked by Snowden: a court order that compelled the telephone-service provider Verizon to hand over to the NSA "all call detail records" about customers' calls.[12] This leak and the various responses, including Senator Feinstein's response quoted above, introduced into common parlance the term "metadata," meaning "data about data." The metadata about a phone call includes the date of the call, the duration, the number called, and the location of the caller. Metadata doesn't include the substance of the call, but with enough metadata one can learn a lot about someone. With enough metadata, one can chain information to plot the network of connections between people, places, and organizations.

Metadata has the added virtue that it is more efficient than the full contents of calls. The problem with big data is that there is too much of it, and that is even more so for images, audio, video, and other storage-intensive multimedia formats. In many cases we have convenient metadata that provides a surrogate for what is most important about a phenomenon. The phone companies, for example, keep metadata about calls that can be analyzed without trying to capture and analyze the full audio stream of billions of calls. Likewise, in the humanities we have bibliographic databases, such as the MLA International Bibliography, that contain carefully curated metadata about publications that can now be exploited as big data. As Matthew Jockers puts it in his 2013 book *Macroanalysis*, this "type of catalog metadata has been largely untapped as a means of exploring literary history,"[13] though the notion of studying literature through card catalogs may seem blasphemous to some.

It isn't always easy to tell the difference between metadata and content, especially as our analytical tools can treat metadata as content or use fulltext to generate metadata. Is the title of a work part of the content, or is it metadata? Franco Moretti (2013b) talks about networks of characters in Shakespeare plays. For his visualizations he links characters when they talk to one another. The character/link data he draws from the text is metadata drawn from text data and then visualized. This sounds a lot like the building up of layers of structure that John B. Smith discussed in "Computer Criticism" (1978). Moretti makes a further interesting point about working with such metadata: "once you make a network of a play, you stop working on the play proper, and work on a *model* instead. You reduce the text to characters and interactions, abstract them from everything else."[14] It is surrogates all the way down, but some surrogates are easier to handle. Metadata is often more efficient, and its analysis can show you things that you couldn't see easily in the full haystack, but it involves an abstraction that can distorts as it hides and reveals.

What shouldn't surprise us is that one of the main forms of metadata we like to extract is metadata about people and how they are connected—the proliferation of tools to explore networks of friends on Facebook is a manifestation of this in popular culture. A more covert example is the NSA's program NYMROD, which sifts through massive databases to collate reports on people the NSA wants to track, such as Angela Merkel (Poitras et al. 2014). Others have imagined similar surveillance tools for the humanities. In "What Do You Do with a Million Books?" Greg Crane (2006) calls for "the ability to extract from the stored record of humanity useful information in an actionable format for any given human being of any culture at any time." Crane and others are building the technological means for extracting large numbers of structured facts (linked data) about people, human history, and culture by finding patterns, such as [person] was born at [place]. IBM's Watson takes this further, extracting data so as to perform deep analysis (and association—or networking—of people, places, locations, events, and other data) in order to enable open-ended question answering using natural language, as was demonstrated by a mock Jeopardy game (Ferruci et al. 2011).

Information in Motion and Information at Rest

Another distinction that we can see in the Snowden leaks is between the fairly stable information in databases that gets called "information at rest" and the data flowing through various communication channels, which gets called "information in motion."[15]

Information at rest is what we usually think of as big data and is more commonly used for data mining than information in motion is. It consists of all the large databases of information about people and things. It is not a flow of data, but the structured and curated data gathered over the years that can be mined for insight. At any large university there are a number of such large databases, including personnel and student databases and library circulation databases. Businesses and government likewise maintain large databases, which if linked and mined can generate new insights.

From what we can tell about the NSA's PRISM project from the slides leaked, PRISM is an Information at Rest system that can search large corporate databases. The *Washington Post* has described PRISM as a tool that lets users initiate search requests, or "tasks," that go to corporate databases. According to the *Post*, "depending on the company, a tasking may return e-mails, attachments, address books, calendars, files stored in the cloud, text or audio or video chats and 'metadata' that identify the locations, devices used and other information about a target."[16]

We are all collaborators in many of these really large databases. If you use one of the U.S. service providers to which PRISM has access, your data could be "tasked." If you use a loyalty card that gets you discounts at your local supermarket, you are contributing to a commercial database that gathers information about purchasing habits which can be correlated with the personal information you provided to the supermarket and with your credit card information. If you upload a video to YouTube, you are contributing to a massive multimedia database. If you have a Facebook account, you are contributing to a huge "social graph" of who is "friends" with whom, what they say they like, what they say they are doing, and so on. It is estimated that in 2012 Facebook had a billion users—more than 10 percent of the world's population (Mayer-Schönberger and Cukier 2013, p. 92). That's a lot of information about a lot of us held by one corporation, and susceptible to access by a government.

What can be done with such data? A number of the uses are fairly benign. Modern consumers probably already have a sense of how stores are using data to put impulse-bought products near checkout lines. Another use of such data is "market basket" analysis: the study of what products are in the same "basket" (or shopping cart) of buyers at a checkout. In the well-known "beer and diapers" story, data mining is supposed to have shown that on Friday and Saturday evenings many shopping carts in certain shopping centers contained beer and diapers, a combination that otherwise seems strange (Power 2002). The inference was that husbands were being sent to pick up diapers and were picking up some beer on impulse. The commercial advantage of such data mining is that a market can then locate beer near diapers, or between the diaper section and the checkout, in order to increase sales. A 2012 article in the *New York Times* describes similar data-mining efforts that the store chain Target used successfully to identify pregnant customers from their buying patterns so as to provide customized advertising[17]:

As [the statistician Andrew] Pole's computers crawled through the data, he was able to identify about 25 products that, when analyzed together, allowed him to assign each shopper a "pregnancy prediction" score. More important, he could also estimate her due date to within a small window, so Target could send coupons timed to very specific stages of her pregnancy.[18]

With big data, organizations can make novel types of inferences and even predict things about their customers. However, it turns out, customers don't appreciate the attention. Women are understandably spooked when companies infer that they are pregnant. Big data is powerful in some ways but blunt in others, as evidenced by a woman who kept seeing advertising evolve throughout her presumed pregnancy and birth even though she had miscarried.[19]

Networked databases can be used to create composite pictures of individuals. Any one database may only contain a limited amount of data, but multiple databases can be mined to aggregate data (with all the attendant perils of combining partial data sources). Software can connect a shopper's address, phone number, buying habits, credit information, and credit-card buying habits.[20]

Information in motion, by contrast, is the massive flow of phone conversations, e-mails, Web-page requests, and Internet transactions over fiber-optic cables, satellites, or local Wi-Fi. The "Upstream" system shown in the diagram reproduced here as figure 7.1 seems to be a system capable of tapping into and buffering the huge international flow of data. Upstream takes advantage of the fact that "much of the world's communications flow through the U.S." (as is explicitly indicated in the diagram reproduced here as figure 7.2).

How is the volume of information in transit studied? The *Independent Technical Review of the Carnivore System* Final Report of 2000, prepared by the IIT Research Institute, discusses how this was done by an earlier surveillance system called Carnivore. Essentially, Carnivore tapped into a network so as to be able, in theory, to listen in on all the traffic. It then filtered the flow

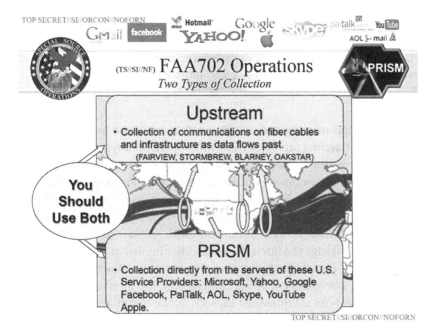

Figure 7.1
"Two Types of Collection" (a PRISM slide). Source: supplement to Gellman and Poitras 2013 titled "NSA slides explain the PRISM data-collection program" at http://www.washingtonpost.com/wp-srv/special/politics/prism-collection-documents.

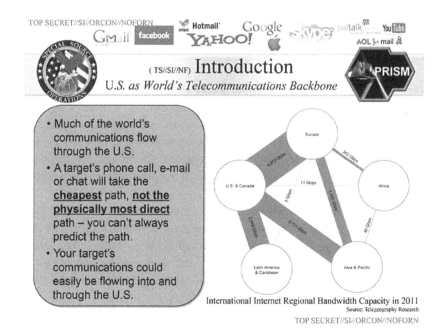

Figure 7.2
"U.S. as World's Telecommunications Backbone" (a PRISM slide). Source: "NSA slides explain the PRISM data-collection program" (http://www.washingtonpost.com/wp-srv/special/politics/prism-collection-documents/).

for information meeting various criteria. Because of the huge amount of information traveling on major trunk lines, specialized systems are needed to filter Information in Motion in real time (and it is worth reiterating that the rate at which we are producing more information is always increasing, roughly following Moore's Law by doubling every 18–24 months).[21] Systems such as Carnivore combine specialized signal-processing hardware that can handle huge flows of information with software that enables users to set up and manage the filters. Users can filter for lists of phone numbers, names, words, phrases, and addresses. These systems don't gather everything that is going by. The filters capture only the messages that match something analysts are interested in, such as the communications of particular people or communications about certain subjects. These messages or activities are then passed on to human analysts or stored so that they can be searched later. In combination with personal information gathered from databases, the communications information can be used to build up a "social graph" from all the metadata that is comparable to what Facebook

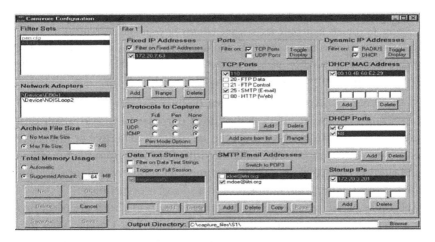

Figure 7.3
The interface used to set up a filter for Carnivore. (Carnivore is essentially an out-
dated system, but the panel conveys a sense of what "professional" Information in
Motion gathering system can do.)

has, but with much more detail about who is connected with whom and
what they are doing in real time. This can then be mined by means of social
network analysis to follow networks of people, such as known terrorists or
people communicating from suspect locations.

If you think these surveillance systems for information in motion are
just for governments, think again. Narus sells a product, called Narus-
Insight, that may be similar to what governments use to perform real-time
semantic analysis. According to Narus' Product webpage,

NarusInsight is Narus' flagship product and is the most scalable, real-time traffic
intelligence system for the protection and management of large IP networks. It captures, analyzes and correlates IP traffic in real time and offers wide visibility across
heterogeneous networks and deep insight into multiple layers of network traffic in
real time. Through its patented analytics, NarusInsight's carrier-class software de-
tects patterns and anomalies that can predict and identify security issues, misuse of
network resources, suspicious or criminal activity, and other events that can com-
promise the integrity of IP networks.[22]

Similarly there are now commercial services that provide real-time monitoring or "strategic intelligence" on social media. Three such services are
Visible, Gnip, and DataSift. What they do is similar to what was once done
by news-clipping services that helped companies manage their "brands."
The following is from Twitter's description of its partner firm DataSift:

DataSift is a real-time media curation platform, allowing you to mine the Twitter Firehose for tweets matching the specific criteria of your choice. DataSift's custom Curation Stream Definition Language allows you to filter based on any meta data within a tweet, in addition to a number of other data providers from around the Web. (https://dev.twitter.com/docs/twitter-data-providers)

The Internet Archive has a service used by libraries, called Archive-IT, that can scrape websites regularly for archival purposes. It is also worth noting that such traffic-analysis tools can be used for defensive or protective purposes, such as monitoring outgoing Internet traffic from your machine and alerting you when unauthorized communication (for instance, a rogue application sending your contact list to a server) is occurring.

Because of the amount of information in motion, filters are becoming more and more important. The algorithms that filter Google News and Facebook's newsfeed determine in large part what is newsworthy, what is seen, and what is known by users of Google News and Facebook. There is even evidence that these filters can manipulate users, as Facebook researchers discovered when they experimented with the sentiments of posts in the feeds of selected users. In the infamous "emotional contagion" experiment, they found that by manipulating the number of positive or negative stories readers saw they could manipulate how the readers felt (or, at least, how positive their posts were).[23] As the sociologist Zeynep Tufekci (2014) has pointed out, "these proprietary algorithms determine the visibility of content and can be changed at will, with enormous consequences for political speech."

Big data has been trumpeted as the next big thing made possible by the explosion of digital data about us, to which we contribute. As we write this, big data probably is at the high point in the Hype Cycle[24]—there are inflated expectations as to how it will transform business, government, and the academy, and soon there are likely to be more sober evaluations. Drawing on Mayer-Schönberger and Cukier's book *Big Data*, we characterize how big data changes methods as follows:

From samples to comprehensive data In the humanities and the social sciences, traditionally we either focus on works that are considered distinctive or sample larger phenomena. Big data draws on relatively complete datasets, often created for entirely different purposes, and uses them for new research. These datasets are comprehensive in a way that sampling isn't, and in a way that can change the types of questions asked and can change people's confidence in the answers.

From purposeful data to messy and repurposed data Traditionally, the data used in research are carefully gathered and curated for that research. With big data, we repurpose messy data from other sources that weren't structured for research and we aggregate data from multiple sources. This raises ethical issues when people's information is used for purposes they didn't consent to; it also means that we can extract novel insights from old data, which is why preservation of data is important.

From causation to correlation Big data typically can't be used to prove causal links between phenomena the way experiments can. Instead, big data is used to show correlations. Big data is being pitched as an opportunity to reuse data to explore for new insights in the form of correlations. There are even techniques that can comb through datasets to identify all the statistically significant correlations that could be of research interest.

What Does This Mean for the Humanities?

What does this mean for the humanities in general and the Digital Humanities in particular? Well, there are obvious privacy issues, ethical issues, and governance issues that call for attention. The liberal arts are supposed to prepare free (*liber*) people for citizenship and participation in democratic community. Big data is now one way citizens are managed both by industry and by government.[25] The liberal arts clearly have a role in studying and teaching about big data. To get a conversation of the phenomenon going, the researchers danah boyd and Kate Crawford (2012) offer six provocative statements:

1. Big Data changes the definition of knowledge.
2. Claims to objectivity and accuracy are misleading.
3. Bigger data are not always better data.
4. Taken out of context, Big Data loses its meaning.
5. Just because it is accessible does not make it ethical.
6. Limited access to Big Data creates new digital divides.

Following boyd and Crawford, one way to think about big data is to look at the pragmatics of how working with large amounts of data changes knowledge. A particularly Digital Humanities way to do this is to think through experimenting with the analysis of large datasets. "Thinking through" is an approach of understanding a phenomenon (thinking about it) through the practices of making, experimenting, and fiddling. It is one of the ways the Digital Humanities can contribute to the larger dialogue of the humanities through what Tito Orlandi and later Willard McCarty called modeling.[26] We create models of systems and learn through the iterative making and reflecting on the models—especially when they fail, as they usually do. The false positives that our hermeneutica throw up tell us about the limitations of our models and hence about the limitations of the theories of knowledge on which they are based.

Haven't We Always Been Anxious about Big Data?

There is also a history of thinking through big data, depending on how we define big data. For example, the perception of too much information (for which we need some new technology) goes back to the story of the invention of writing in *Phaedrus* (Plato 1925). One of the interesting aspects of that story is the division of labor imposed by King Thamus on the situation that distinguishes between those who invent and those judge inventions. Socrates proposes that the inventors of a technology are not necessarily the best at judging its utility or potential. The same holds true today: the computer scientists and engineers (not to mention members of the intelligence community) who are building big-data infrastructure systems may not be the best judges of the usefulness or ethical implications of such systems. One gets the feeling that the NSA built the massive data gathering and analyzing systems now being leaked because it could, because there was money, because there was the political will after 9/11, and because they didn't want to be accused of not having tried the next time an attack happens. Now the time has come to learn from the history of attempts to manage excess information documented by Ann Blair (2010) and other scholars. Perhaps there is a role for digital humanists as critics of big data.

The problem of too much data reappeared in 1945 in Vannevar Bush's famous article "As We May Think":

There is a growing mountain of research. But there is increased evidence that we are being bogged down today as specialization extends. The investigator is staggered by the findings and conclusions of thousands of other workers—conclusions which he cannot find time to grasp, much less to remember, as they appear.

More recently, Clay Shirky argued that the problem is not so much information overload as it is "filter failure."[27] In some cases technologies and tools do exist to filter information, but seldom are they used effectively, as many of us realize when observing the scattering of our browser bookmarks, research notes, bibliographic entries, and other fragments of knowledge. Filtering and management aren't solely technical challenges; they are also matters of social practices and personal habits. It is worth paying especially close attention to who creates filters, how they work, and how they fail us.

We have seen humanities projects dealing with big data for some time. James Murray and other editors of the *Oxford English Dictionary*, for example, had to deal with millions of quotation slips without any computing in the late nineteenth century and the early twentieth century. Two important early computing projects that don't get the attention they deserve, perhaps because neither of them gathered English texts, are FRANTEXT and Thesaurus Linguae Greacae (TLG).

In the 1970s. FRANTEXT assembled what was then considered an enormous text database of important French texts to provide examples for an extensive linguistic study of the French language.[28] In an 1989 article titled "L'exploitation des grands corpus: Le bestiaire de la littérature française," Etienne Brunet discussed what could be done with a terminal connection to FRANTEXT using the Stella system (mentioned in chapter 5 above). That may not seem like big data now, but in the 1980s, when most of us were lucky to have the full text of a single work or a small collection by a single author, FRANTEXT's 2,500-text corpus was really big, and it provoked Brunet to speculate on and try new methods suited to "grand" collections. Foreseeing the importance of shifting methods, Brunet wrote about a disequilibrium between the breadth of our ambitions and the smallness of the data we typically use, essentially making the case for much larger collections and new statistical and visualization methods. For Brunet, *grand* data allows analysis by comparison; it has built in control samples.

In 1972 the TLG project began gathering all Greek literature between Homer (eighth century BCE) and CE 600, which was then published on CD-ROM. David W. Packard and William Johnson even developed a custom workstation, the Ibycus Scholarly Personal Computer (PSC), in 1985. The PSC could efficiently search the entire TLG and properly display the Greek. In effect, classicists by 1985 had a fairly complete, and constantly improving, collection of everything important written in Greek—a comprehensive dataset to study, rather than samples. This may not have been a big collection by today's petabyte standards, but it was one of the first instances of scholars' being able to ask questions about everything in a domain. The scale of big data is in the eye of the beholder (and the available technologies). The TLG allowed graduate students in Classics to survey every use of a word, something that even today can't be done in most disciplines. Colleagues complained, as did Thamus in Plato's *Phaedrus*, about the effects of this technology on scholarly memory. Who would value the panoptic memory of the experienced scholar when one could search everything on a workstation? Like today's big data, the size of the collection strained the capabilities of the computing equipment that was available at the time, prompting the development of specialized technology.[29]

What Can We Do with Big Data Analytics?

At this point, let us take a quick tour through some of the opportunities and risks for Big Data in the Digital Humanities.[30]

Filtering and subsetting We begin with a basic operation comparable to what intelligence services do with Information in Motion: filtering big data to get useful subsets that can then be studied by other, possibly traditional techniques (e.g., reading). The Cornell Web Lab, which alas was closed in 2011, was working with the Internet Archive to build a system that would enable social scientists (and humanists) to extract subsets from the archive. The dearth of resources that allow for navigation between large databases of content (among them the Gutenberg Project of digital texts) to specialized environments for reading and analysis should be noted here.

Enrichment "Enrichment" is a general term for adding value. In the context of big data, researchers are developing ways to enrich large corpora automatically using the knowledge in big data. In "What Do You Do with a Million Books?" (the 2006 article that first prompted many of us to begin thinking about what big data meant in the humanities), Greg Crane wrote eloquently about what we now can do to enrich big data to make it more useful. Crane has made the further point that simply providing translation enrichment could provide us with a platform for a dialogue among civilizations.

Sequence alignment Sequence alignment can be adapted from bioinformatics for the purpose of following passages through time. This is the research equivalent to what plagiarism detectors do with students' papers. They look at sequences of text to see whether similar passages can be found in other texts, contemporary or not. Horton, Olsen, and Roe (2010) described work they had done with the ARTFL textbase to track how passages in an influential twentieth-century history by Paul Hazard had been cribbed from a seventeenth-century text. The point is not that Hazard was a lazy note taker, but that one can follow the expression of ideas across writers when one has them in digital form.

Diachronic analysis Diachronic analysis is using data sets to study change over time. Although the use of large diachronic databases dates back to the Trésor de la langue française (TLF) and the Thesaurus Linguae Grecae (TLG) projects, diachronic analysis got a lot of attention after Google made its Ngram Viewer available and after Jean-Baptiste Michel and colleagues published their paper "On Quantitative Analysis of Culture Using Millions of Digitized Books" (2010). There are dangers to using Ngrams (or phrases of words) to follow ideas when the very words have changed in meaning, orthography, and use over time, but the Ngram Viewer is nonetheless a powerful tool for testing change in language over time (and its search-and-graph approach makes it accessible to a broad public).

Classification and clustering Classification and clustering comprise a large family of techniques that go under various names and can be used to explore data. Classification and clustering techniques typically work on large collections of documents and allow us to automatically classify the genre of a work or to ask the computer to generate clusters according to specific features and see if they correspond to existing classifications. A related technique, Topic Modeling, identifies clusters of words that could be the major "topics" (distinctive terms that co-occur) of a large collection. An example was given in the previous chapter, where we used correspondence analysis to identify clusters of key words and years in the Humanist archives.

Social network analysis Social network analysis (SNA) involves identifying people and other entities and then analyzing how they are linked in the data. It is popular both in the intelligence community and in the social sciences. SNA techniques can graph a network of people to show how they are connected and to what degree they are connected. In the social sciences, the data underlying a network typically are gathered manually. One might for example interview members of a community in order to understand the network of relationships in that community. The resulting data about the links between people can be visualized or queried by computer. These techniques can be applied in the humanities when one wants to track the connections between characters in a work (Moretti 2013), or the connections between correspondents in a collection of letters or places mentioned in a play. Just as an ethnographer might formally document relationships between people, a historian might be interested in determining who lived in Athens when Socrates was martyred and how those people were connected. Large collections of church records, letters, and other documents now allow us to study social networks of the past. Thanks to a new family of techniques that can recognize the names of people, organizations, or places in a text, it is now possible to extract named entity data automatically from large text collections, as the Voyant tool called RezoViz does.

Self-tracking Self-tracking is the application of big data to your life. You can gather big data about yourself. Personal surveillance technologies allow you to gather lots of data about where you go and who you correspond with, and to then analyze it. The idea is to "know thyself" better and in more detail (or perhaps just to remind you to exercise more). Though results of self-tracking may not seem to be big data relative to the datasets gathered by the NSA, they can accumulate to the point where one must use mining tools to make sense of it. A fascinating early project in life tracking was Lifestream, started in the 1990s as a project at Yale by Eric Freeman and David Gelernter, which introduced interesting interface ideas about how information could be organized according to the chronological stream of life.[31] Gordon Bell has a project at Microsoft called MyLifeBits that has led to a commercially available camera, the Vicon Revue; you hang it around your neck, and it shoots pictures all day to frame bits of your life.[32] Recently Stephen Wolfram, of *Mathematica* fame, has posted an interesting blog essay on what he has learned by analyzing data he gathered about his activities—an ongoing process that, he argues, contributes to his self-awareness.[33] Many different tools are now available to enable the rest of us to gather, analyze, and share data about ourselves—especially data on our physical fitness data. (Among those tools are the fitbit, the Nike+ line,[34] and now the Apple Watch.)

What does all this have to do with academic humanities? Ian Lancashire, a pioneering computing humanist, writes in *Forgetful Muses* about "devising diagnostic software for text analysis in longitudinal studies, not only of creative writing, but of e-mail, diaries, blogs, and even conversation" (2010, p. 218). Lancashire and Graeme Hirst presented research showing that the vocabularies of Agatha Christie and Iris Murdoch shrank dramatically late in their lives. They believe that they can distinguish between healthy aging and aging that shows signs of early Alzheimer's Disease in diachronic collections of texts, and that they have documented an increase in editorial intervention to compensate for Christie's memory loss. In *Forgetful Muses* Lancashire goes further to propose a fascinating humanistic theory of the writing mind that marries cognitive studies and literary studies and that draws on cybernetics. While others might track their physical activity, digital humanists track their cognitive activity. As Mayer-Schönberger and Cukier (2013, 93) put it, "datafication is not just about rendering attitudes and sentiments into an analyzable form, but human behavior as well." This is a very different form of studying the human, but it is of interest to the humanities nonetheless.

Problems with Information Overload and Big Data

We close this chapter by looking at the limitations of big data and of its analysis. The discussion of the recent Snowden revelations at the beginning of this chapter highlighted the privacy issues raised by big data and data mining. Two things that often get neglected are whether these techniques work and under what conditions they work well enough to be employed regularly. There is an argument that the mining of surveillance data may not actually work very well. Jeff Jonas and Jim Harper state the problem nicely in a 2006 report titled Effective Counterterrorism and the Limited Role of Predictive Data Mining:

It would be unfortunate if data mining for terrorism discovery had currency within national security, law enforcement, and technology circles because pursuing this use of data mining would waste taxpayer dollars, needlessly infringe on privacy and civil liberties, and misdirect the valuable time and energy of the men and women in the national security community. (Jonas and Harper 2006, 1)

The problem is that when you analyze a lot of data you get a lot of false hits or false positives. The messier the data, the more false hits you get. The subtler the questions asked of the data, the more nuanced and even misleading the answers are likely to be. When you use Google to search for someone with a common name, such as John Smith, with big data you can get overwhelmingly big and disappointingly irrelevant results—result sets that are too big for you to go through to find the answer, and therefore not useful. A cover story in *Time* talks about the "Pizza Hut" problem: The FBI found itself using valuable human resources following "vague and voluminous" leads from the Stellar Wind system that kept pointing out suspicious phone calls that often turned out to be pizza orders (Gellman 2011).

False positives are particularly problematic in predictive data mining of the sort being done by the NSA, which is using it to try to *predict* who might commit a terrorist attack. As Jonas and Harper point out, when businesses use predictive data mining to identify targets (e.g., pregnant women) for targeted marketing the worst that can happen is that they will send inappropriate junk mail to uninterested people or that they will spook people when their predictions are right. But when *governments* indulge in predictive data mining and generate a high percentage of false positives, innocent people will be targeted and intelligence resources will be wasted. In order for predictive data mining to prevent terrorism, governments will have to follow up on the predictions and spend valuable investigative human resources checking the leads. Jonas and Harper question whether the human intelligence agents and other resources that check out all the predictions might be better spent on traditional human intelligence activities. They ask whether predictive data mining and the follow-up investigations triggered actually generate better results than traditional counterintelligence. Could the Digital Humanities test the usefulness of predictive data mining on historical datasets in order to improve citizens' understandings of the techniques and their value?

A second problem with analysis of big data is the dependence on correlation. It doesn't tell you about what causes what; it tells you only what correlates with what (Mayer-Schönberger and Cukier 2013, chapter 4). With enough data one can get spurious correlations, as there is always something that has the same statistical profile as the phenomenon you are studying. This is the machine equivalent to apophenia, the human tendency to see patterns everywhere, which is akin to what Umberto Eco explores in *Interpretation and Overinterpretation* (1992).

The dependence on correlations has interesting implications. In 2008, Chris Anderson, the editor in chief of *Wired*, announced "the end of theory," by which he meant the end of scientific theory. He argued that with lots of data we don't have to start with a theory and then gather data to test it. We can now use statistical techniques to explore data for correlations with which to explain the world without theory. Proving causation through the scientific method is now being surpassed by exploratory practices that make big science seem a lot more like the humanities. It remains to be seen how big data might change theorizing in the humanities. Could lots of exploratory results overwhelm or trivialize theory? What new theories are needed for working with lots of data?

A related problem is "model drift" or "concept drift," which is what happens when the data change but the analytical model doesn't. Model drift is one explanation for why the Web service Google Flu Trends fails periodically. Google Flu Trends is based on a model of what people search for when they have the flu, and it doesn't always keep up with how language use changes, especially when there are short-term spikes of interest in flu-related terms because of media attention given to the flu. The fact that people's use of language changes over time is a major problem for humanities projects that use historical data. People don't use certain words today the same way they used those words in the past, and that's a problem for text mining that depends on words. If you are modeling concepts over time, the change in language has to be accounted for in the model—an accounting that raises a variety of interpretive questions. Does a phrase that you are tracking have the same meaning it had in the past, or has its meaning evolved?

In their 2011 book *Top Secret America*, Dana Priest and William Arkin raise cost-effectiveness questions about the dramatic growth of the intelligence sector in the United States—250 percent between 2001 and 2010 (to the extent that we actually know how much funding goes to intelligence). "In Top Secret America," they write on page 103, "more is often the solution." More recently, in response to claims that NSA surveillance has thwarted as many as 54 threats of terrorism, Justin Elliot and Theodoric Meyer (2013) quote Senator Patrick Leahy from a hearing of the Judiciary Committee: "That's plainly wrong, but we still get it in letters to members of Congress, we get it in statements. These weren't all plots and they weren't all thwarted. The American people are getting left with the inaccurate impression of the effectiveness of NSA programs." As Elliot and Meyer point out, there is little evidence to support the effectiveness of the surveillance, partly because of the secrecy surrounding the NSA and partly because the few cases we can check turn out to not be quite as clear-cut (as they are reported first by the agencies and then by the media). The NSA and its supporters seem to be overstating the value of big data. Could the billions be better spent elsewhere? How can the Digital Humanities team up with data scientists to test claims about data mining, and what ethical issues would arise?

Similar questions about cost effectiveness should be asked, and are being asked, about text analysis and mining in the humanities. Does text mining of large corpora provide real insight? There are two types of questions that we need to keep always in mind in analysis, especially in regard to large-scale analysis:

- Are the methods and their application sound, and can they be tested by alternative methods (or at the very least, are we sufficiently circumspect about the data and methodologies)? In large-scale text analysis or "distant reading," it is easy to misapply an algorithm and generate a false result. It is also easy to overinterpret results. Since at the scale of big data one can't confirm a result by re-reading the sources, it is important to confirm results in various ways. There is a temptation to use the size of the data to legitimize not testing results by reading, but there are always way to test results. Jockers (2013) shows us how one should always be sceptical of results and develop ways of testing results even if one can't test them by reading.

• Are the results worth the effort? Obviously, people who engage in text analysis and in data mining believe that the results are interesting enough to justify continuing, but at an individual level and at a disciplinary level we need to ask whether these methods are worth the resources. Computational analysis is expensive not so much in terms of computing (of which there is an ample supply thanks to high-performance computing initiatives) as in terms of the human effort required to do it well. Is computational analysis worth the training, the negotiating of resources, and the programming it requires? Individuals at Voyant workshops ask this question in various ways. Also important are the disciplinary discussions taking place in departments and faculties that are deciding whether to hire in the Digital Humanities and whether to run courses in analytics. Hermeneutica can help those departments and faculties to "kick the tires" of text analysis as a pragmatic way of testing analytical methods in general.

We have our own story about too many results—a story that points out another form of false positive in which the falsity is more that of a false friend. In May of 2010 we ran a workshop on High-Performance Computing (HPC) and the Digital Humanities at the University of Alberta.[35] We brought together a number of teams with HPC support so they could prototype HPC applications in the humanities. One team adapted Patrick Juola's idea for a Conjecturator (Juola and Bernola 2009) so that it could run on one of the University of Alberta's HPC machines. The Conjecturator is a data-mining tool that can generate a nearly infinite number of conjectures about a big dataset and then test them to see if they are statistically interesting. The opposite of a "finding" tool that shows only what you ask for, it generates statistically tested assertions about your dataset that could be studied more closely. The assertions take this form:

Feature A appears more/less often
in the group of texts B than in group C
that are distinguished by structural feature D

In the experiment we ran in 2010, we used a corpus of nineteenth-century novels grouped according to the decades in which they were published (e.g., the 1850s). The "features" came from a reverse-engineered English thesaurus. Each "feature" was a set of words around a key word, such as "ground" or "instant." The Conjecturator generated hypotheses such as "shirt-words appear more often in the novels of the 1850s than in the novels of the 1860s." Feature A (shirt-words) might be all the words from the thesaurus that are related to shirts, group B might be the novels of the 1850s, group C might be the novels of the 1860s, and the distinguishing structural feature D might be decade. The process, once we had adapted it for the WestGrid HPC cluster, ran for about 100 compute-days and generated 87,000 statistically valid assertions! One shudders to think of how many conjectures we would have generated if we had had access to all 1,000 cores of that WestGrid HPC cluster or if we had run the process on a larger corpus.[36]

That experiment raised the new question "What do you do with 87,000 positives?" Well, when you look at the results you find a number of things:

- Many of the results are trivial. They may be statistically valid, but many nonetheless are uninteresting to humans.
- Many of the results are related. You might find that there is a set of related assertions about shirts over many decades.
- The results are hard to interpret in the dialogical sense. You may find a really interesting assertion but have no way to test it, follow it, or unpack it. The Conjecturator is not usefully connected to a full-text-analysis environment in which one could explore an interesting assertion. As always, the trajectory from the very atomistic level (the narrow and specific assertions) to larger, more significant aspects is unmarked and hazardous, though not without potential rewards.

Above all, 87,000 results are too much for anyone to deal with. Such a number is mind-numbing, even demoralizing. It tells us something about the humanity of research that we don't want to be handed so many assertions; we want to find a few all by ourselves. The finding of interesting truths is as important as the truths found. The conjectures above are false positives not in the sense of being untrue, but in the sense that they are false to our way of research. In the digital epoch we console ourselves that at least we are asking the questions, but that isn't true. Computers can ask questions too, we just don't want to hear them. They sound false to us.

Socrates would also remind us that wisdom is not about the quantity of information you possess, or the quantity you can process, but about the thinking that led you to assertions. Information isn't knowledge. Knowledge is held by some person who arrived at that knowledge. Just as owning a book on French grammar isn't the same as knowing French, having 87,000 results isn't the same as understanding nineteenth-century literature. The possession of big data and big results isn't a certificate of knowledge, and in lazy hands it can become a false positive.

We should therefore listen to the spirit of Plato and recognize that some of the techniques discussed above should be judged false leads and that humanists should take responsibility for experimenting with them, testing them, and judging their wisdom. That's what Edward Snowden did. He judged the activities he was privy to, both as a CIA employee and as a contractor for the NSA. He chose to gather the documents he could gather and to share them publicly. Are we humanists and other curators of information willing to step up to this responsibility, or are we happy leaving it to the engineers who invent new technologies?

8   Name Games: Analyzing *Game Studies* (Third Interlude)

You'd be amazed how much research you can get done when you have no life whatsoever.

Ernest Cline, *Ready Player One*

Espen Aarseth announced, in the introduction to the then-new journal *Game Studies*, "2001 can be seen as the Year One of *Computer Game Studies* as an emerging, viable, international, academic field."[1] Adding drama, he warned about colonization from outside: "Games are not a kind of cinema, or literature, but colonizing attempts from both these fields have already happened, and no doubt will happen again." In an editorial in the second issue, "The Dungeon and the Ivory Tower," Aarseth cheekily imagined establishing a Game Studies program at a university as a strategy game, like Sid Meier's *Civilization*. In it, he wrote, "your job is to create a multidisciplinary task force" to "gather and balance resources, forge alliances, and battle the aliens."[2] Aarseth imagined scholarly gaming as a field that required a crack force to defend it, perhaps with a shotgun. Gonzalo Frasca, in coining the word "ludology," imagined that the field needed its own terminology to define it, not just terms borrowed from other fields.[3]

Today we can use analytics to look back on the founding game and ask how it played out in the journal *Game Studies*. We wanted to find about the players and see how this battle of ideas played out. Did outsiders colonize the new discipline, as Aarseth warned they might? Or did defenders of Game Studies fight them off? Are there heroes in this game? Are there bad guys? What issues did they fight over? Using text-analysis tools—hermeneutica—we can retroactively survey this emerging field as represented by the journal. Two can play this game.

Figure 8.1
"Pikachu" in the distribution grass (graph) of Celia Pearce and Will Wright.

Gathering Supplies

To study the back story, we scraped all the articles from eleven years of *Game Studies* (see http://hermeneuti.ca/name-games/ for a list of links to the Voyant corpora).[4] We then stripped out the HTML and created two corpora, A and B. We left the bibliographies in A and stripped them out of B, so the extra data in them wouldn't skew the analysis. The two corpora were organized distinctively. In A we kept each article as a distinct document. In B we concatenated each year's worth of articles into a document and gave it the name of the year. The organization of B allowed us to create Word Trend distribution graphs that show changes from year to year.

The high-frequency words suggest the concerns of *Game Studies*. Not surprisingly, "game" "games," and "gameplay" show up near the top, along with "rules." Game action terms ("play," "playing," "gaming," "design") appear with significant frequency, as do game locations ("space," "world," "worlds," "virtual"). A significant outlier, "narrative," creeps in; we will say more about that later.

The words that best suggest the "character" of *Game Studies* include "players," "player," "character," "avatar," and "Sims." Taking a hint from the list, we decided to try to figure out who the characters in the world of Games Studies are. We ran our corpora through RezoViz, a Voyant tool that visualizes the social network of entities such as people in a corpus.[5] RezoViz uses the Stanford Named Entity Recognizer (NER) tool to automatically identify the names of people, organizations, and places, counting them and counting the links between entities.[6] In this case a link is counted any time two entities occur in the same article of the journal. The more links there are, the greater the number of articles that mention both of those entities and the greater the likelihood there is a connection between them. The

Table 8.1
High-frequency words in the *Game Studies* archives.

	Count
game	8,714
games	6,164
players	3,207
player	2,941
play	2,564
world	1,830
design	1,222
playing	1,073
character	1,008
rules	908
virtual	899
gaming	793
video	782
characters	775
narrative	737
space	728
gameplay	705
interaction	633
figure	570
actions	544
worlds	453
sims	448
avatar	426
entertainment	426
played	424
designers	408

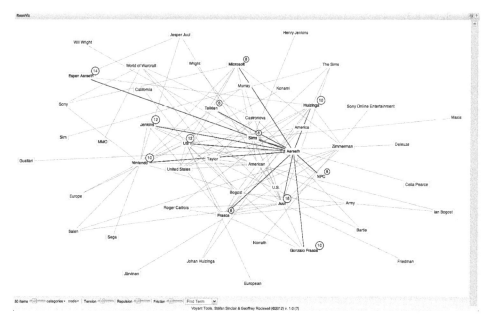

Figure 8.2
RezoViz showing fifty items with highest-frequency links.

data from the NER are then passed to a network visualization tool built into Voyant that explores the links between entities. The full textbase in Voyant allows users to double-click on names to see where they are mentioned and read about them. Distribution graphs also show which articles would be good to read to learn more about someone, but we'll return to that and instead start with social network visualization.

Interactive visualizations such as RezoViz can easily be over-interpreted. Caution must be taken, as in each of the stages of the process errors creep in. For instance, in the diagram reproduced here as figure 8.2 Espen Aarseth and Aarseth are treated as different people even though they aren't. However, RezoViz allows data to be corrected; one can edit the results from the Stanford NER and regenerate the visualization. You can also use the usual skin to check entities, but that takes work. Here text analysis is not a short cut but a means of surveying. NER's quirks don't mean that one should not use RezoViz; rather, they mean that one should always confirm the hypotheses suggested by the visualization.

Non-Player Characters

Despite the problems with NER, we can clean up the data and use them to generate an initial cast of pioneers, colonizers, designers, and players important to *Game Studies*.[7] Table 8.2 lists every character who gets recognized more than four times. Ambiguous names such as Taylor are missing, as they refer to more than one person. There were also some high-frequency names for game characters that we have removed, including Mario and Lara Croft.

The High Frequency List reveals the presence of heroes who studied games before if became a recognized field, including Johan Huizinga and Roger Caillois. Both Huizinga and Caillois, for different reasons, deservedly receive numerous mentions. Early on, Huizinga took play seriously. His brilliant 1938 book *Homo Ludens* defined gaming as worthy of study.[8] Caillois wrote one of the first sustained studies of games:, *Les jeux et les hommes* (1959), published in English in 1969 as *Man, Play, and Games*.[9] Brian Sutton-Smith's contribution should also be noted; he has been writing about play, games, and children since the 1970s.[10]

If Aarseth is right and there is a danger that Game Studies will be colonized from outside, it is helpful to see where outside influences are slouching their way into the field. Some names, including Murray, Barthes, Jameson, and Propp, seem to come from literary studies and narratology, though Jameson is mentioned mainly in an article on realism in games.[11] Others, including Lacan, Bruner, de Certeau, and Freud, appear from psychology, a field that is less an antagonist and more an ally to Game Studies.[12]

Media Studies theorists don't appear prominently in the journal *Game Studies*. One of the few who appear is Lev Manovich, who could be accused of being one of those trying to apply film studies and narrative to new media such as games. If media studies were influential, Marshall McLuhan should appear; however, with the exception of one article (Tyler 2008) that probes games from a McLuhanian perspective, he is rarely mentioned. Tyler warns of the danger of trying to cut games to size to fit our theory.[13] Like Aarseth and others, he is conscious of the dangers of befriending giants such as McLuhan.

Game designers should appear prominently. Will Wright, Chris Crawford, Andrew Stern, Andrew Rollings, and Brenda Laurel get attention, but mostly because they are designers who write or talk about their work. Crawford, for example, was writing semi-academic books about game design, such as *The Art of Computer Game Design* (1984), before the field of Game Studies came of age. Wright is famous for designing *SimCity* and *The Sims*; Celia Pearce interviewed him for a 2002 *Game Studies* article titled

Table 8.2
High-frequency names.

Gonzalo Frasca	32	Roland Barthes	7
Espen Aarseth	22	Craig Lindley	7
Henry Jenkins	21	Roger Caillois	7
Jesper Juul	20	Richard Bartle	6
Eric Zimmerman	17	Brody Condon	6
Tony Manninen	16	Dave Ferrucci	6
Janet Murray	16	Laura Mulvey	6
Konrad Lischka	14	Andrew Hargadon	6
Lacan	13	Bernie Drummond	6
Raph Koster	13	Andrew Rollings	6
Ted Friedman	12	Graner Ray	5
Lev Manovich	12	Freud	5
Justine Cassell	11	Habermas	5
Jon Ritman	11	Gibson	5
Johannes Fromme	11	Epstein	5
Cathy Greenblat	10	Lee	5
Chris Crawford	10	Thiagarajan	5
Celia Pearce	10	Eugene Provenzo	5
Brenda Laurel	10	Johan Huizinga	5
Will Wright	10	John Fiske	5
Edward Castronova	9	Graham Goring	5
Kaveri Subrahmanyam	9	Jerome Bruner	5
Greg Costikyan	9	Diane Carr	5
George Landow	9	Gareth Schott	5
Michel de Certeau	9	Bo Walther	5
Brian Sutton-Smith	9	Vladimir Propp	5
Fredric Jameson	9	Marie-Laure Ryan	4
Sherry Turkle	8	Linderoth	4
Annabel Cohen	8	Kinder	4
Aki Järvinen	8		

"Sims, BattleBots, Cellular Automata God and *Go*." Shigeru Miyamoto of Nintendo and other well-known game designers from Japan are absent, probably because most Japanese designers don't write much and most of what is written about them is in Japanese.

Avatars of the Game

The important characters mentioned in *Game Studies* are those fighting for the field and those defining it. Who are these avatars of Game Studies? Using RezoViz we can see the pairs of people that most often show up together in *Game Studies* articles. Three are associated with the journal: Espen Aarseth is the editor in chief; Jesper Juul is an advisory editor; and Janet Murray is on the board of reviewers. We would expect their names to be prominent in the journal, though not necessarily in the articles. The graph tells more than one story, however.

The quest to define the field of Game Studies can likewise be read in this corpus. Searching with Voyant for "friedman," we learn that Ted Friedman, in "Making Sense of Software" (1995), first raised the alarm about understanding games as narratives.[14] He was critical of the designing of games as "interactive cinema ... hamstrung by the demands of traditional narrative."

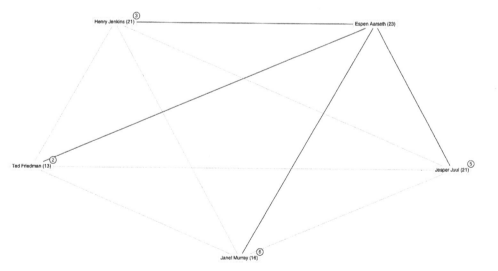

Figure 8.3
Highest-frequency links and nodes. (This actually shows all links, but the selection of nodes is based on the highest-frequency links.)

For Friedman, computer games can offer a rich exchange of feedback and interaction between player and computer.

Aarseth takes up Friedman's quest to understand games differently. Using fighting words to announce Game Studies as a scholarly field of inquiry, Aarseth turns Friedman's concerns into founding principles. Appearing as it does in the opening editorial by the journal's editor in chief, his quest for alternatives is bound to be influential, if only because it shows what he wants the journal to be.

Sure enough, in the first issue three of the authors attack the use of narrative from literary theory and film studies in the understanding of games. Marie-Laure Ryan in "Beyond Myth and Metaphor: The Case of Narrative in Digital Media" (2001), Jesper Juul in "Games Telling Stories" (2011), and Markku Eskelinen in "The Gaming Situation" (2001) go to battle in different ways to fight off the threat of colonization. Aarseth, as editor in chief, chose his starting team deliberately: both Juul and Ryan not only wrote for the first issue; they also are editors.

One is tempted to see ludology as only a reaction to the dangers of narrative, but that is really only the first level. As one can see from the distribution graph of the word "narrative" (figure 8.4), narrative didn't get much attention after the initial discussion of it until 2007, when someone

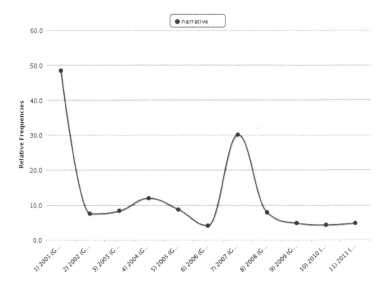

Figure 8.4
Relative-frequency graph of "narrative."

dared to defend it in depth. Jan Simons, in a trenchant and closely argued response, presented a new game—Game Theory—as an example of how to understand narrative without losing to it. Simons (2007) set out to systematically show that the ludological arguments "are ideologically motivated rather than theoretically grounded, and don't hold up against closer scrutiny." We are tempted to say that the fact that Simons' article was published in the journal disproves his point, but by then ludology had moved on to other levels.

How do Janet Murray and Henry Jenkins fit into this story of an academic game? Murray's influence comes by virtue of her 1998 book *Hamlet on the Holodeck*, a rich work on new media, and because of an exchange over narrative and games such as *Tetris*. Responding to Murray, Eskelinen and other ludologists see it as absurd to interpret games as stories. In "The Gaming Situation" Eskelinen writes: "Outside academic theory people are usually excellent at making distinctions between narrative, drama and games. If I throw a ball at you I don't expect you to drop it and wait until it starts telling stories."[15] He criticizes Murray for villainously imposing narrative on games, arguing that "instead of studying the actual game Murray tries to interpret its supposed content, or better yet, project her favourite content on it; consequently we don't learn anything of the features that make *Tetris* a game."

It is left to Henry Jenkins to reconcile the ludological heroes and their favorite Murray monster. Simons (2007) draws attention to how Jenkins maps the significant roles that narrative can play in games in a way palatable to the ludologists. Jenkins is an ambiguous character trying to reach across disciplines. Apparently Aarseth and Murray were supposed to settle it all with a boss fight in Ümea, Sweden in 2005 (see Murray 2005), but no one had the heart to fight once in the ring. At a conference in Brock, Ontario, Murray and Aarseth were brought together again, and again civility reigned. Aarseth even talked about a narrative theory of games.[16]

According to Simons (2007), "one explanation for the rivalry between ludology and narratology is that they are siblings." "Both," Simons continues, "are firmly rooted in the humanities and therefore tend to consider narratives and games primarily as fictional symbolic artefacts. Narratologists tend to consider novels and fiction films as prototypical examples of narrative, and games studies scholars generally follow Johan Huizinga and Roger Caillois by setting games apart from 'serious' activities."

Ludology and narratology were experiencing the rivalries of siblings. Both are in the traditions of the humanities, fields that consider human arts and expression. A good rivalry needs some *agon* or competition. Or, as

Vico might say, a new institution, like a new field, needs an "other" against which to define itself.[17] Perhaps narratology is the influence that has caused a particular group of game scholars the most anxiety or an easy target for them. Perhaps the landscape must be reconfigured to reorder the academy and rethink these new and fascinating objects.[18]

By now, most scholars in Game Studies are tired of the narratology/ ludology discussion. What stands out about this debate is that it has benefited Game Studies (both the field and the journal). Both Murray and Aarseth say as much in various places. A bit of controversy draws attention and motivates people to take on all sorts of roles from combatant to dungeon master.

"If one is to go by the writings of some games studies scholars," Simons writes (2007), "games studies and narratology are like two players involved in a zero-sum game in which one player gains what the other player loses."

Perhaps it was imagined as a game all along.

Rules of the Game

If we leave behind the challenge of narrative, what does text analysis of *Game Studies* tell us about the emergence of the field? What is the study of games becoming? Well, high-frequency words tell us a lot of obvious things—for example, that the study of games is about the activity of playing, gameplay, and players. Likewise it is about the characters, avatars, and social interactions players can explore. The relationship between player and player-character is important.[19] Text analysis also tells us that the worlds or spaces that players can play characters in are important, especially large multi-player worlds such as Norrath.[20]

One word in the list of difference sorted words stands out as especially important to games, and that is the word "rules." Note the plural. The plural "rules" occurs 909 times in the corpus, the singular "rule" only 116. Why are rules important? One reason stems from how Caillois defines games. He believes there is a continuum of play from *ludus* (structured games with rules) to *paidia* (unstructured playfulness). Game Studies, or ludology, is therefore the study of the structured games, and it is rules that give them structure, whether those rules are ones that players abide by or those programmed into a computer. But there is more going on in culture of Game Studies. Try our toys to discover what that might be.

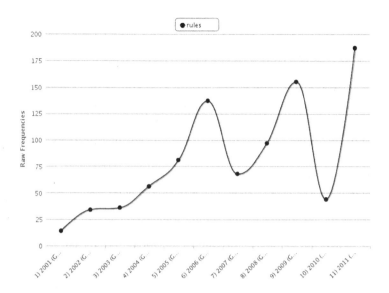

Figure 8.5
Raw-frequency distribution of "rules" over years.

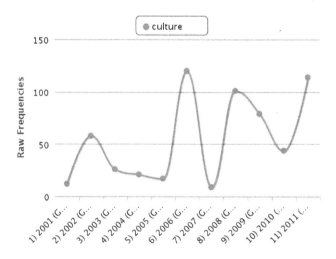

Figure 8.6
Distribution graph of "culture."

End Game

In this chapter we have traced some aspects of the theme of colonization and its players through the evolving civilization of *Game Studies*. We could be accused of overemphasizing the drama of Game Studies, but we believe that is what makes Game Studies so vibrant: There are issues at stake, and there is drama among the players. All of it is there in the record, especially at the start of the game. We could be accused of overusing the game trope in this chapter, of letting gaming colonize analysis, but we do not believe text analysis stands outside of interpretation, judging a phenomenon from some objective stance. Text analysis is a way of replaying text; it is a way of re-reading through playful exploration. We could be accused bringing foreign methods—text analysis—to gaming, or of being carpetbaggers, hustling in the new world of games. Although we embrace serious play as part of the scholarly research cycle, we are not playing games here. If anything, this interlude takes seriously that Game Studies is new and sketches an interpretation of the magic circle.

9 A Model Theory: Thinking Through Hermeneutical Things

This pictorial scroll recorded what really happened at that time. When I saw and displayed this scroll, the event popped out vividly.
Wang Zhiben, 1906[1]

In 1854, when Commodore Matthew Calbraith Perry paid his second visit to Japan, the black ships carried a number of "triumphs of civilization," including a fully operational one-fourth-scale model train. The train was designed to impress and awe. It communicated American technical prowess and provided the Japanese with a working view of what their country could have by trading with the United States. The model train showed how the steam engine worked *and* provided a model of a railroad that could be scaled up to modernize and unify a country.[2] It was an example of a class of artifacts designed to convey knowledge by modeling a phenomenon so that you interact with it, a "model theory" with explanatory and scalable power. And it worked. The Japanese now have the best rail network in the world.

It is this class of knowledge-bearing things, theoretical things, and hermeneutical things that we will deal with in this chapter. Specifically, we will look at the hermeneutical things of the Digital Humanities, such as Voyant, that are designed for the study of text, and will ask how digital things can bear knowledge. We will then look to various theories about computer-assisted text analysis, especially those put forward by developers of text tools. How have developers theorized what their tools could do? More succinct, how do text-analysis tools bear knowledge? We will conclude by asking how digital things can be better designed to ensure that they bear and express the interpretations of their creators.

Figure 9.1
"The Miniature Train" from the scroll "Request for Good Relationship." ("The Miniature Train" is panel 7 of the scroll held by the John Hay Library at Brown University
that is online as part of the *Perry in Japan: A Visual History* project at http://library.
brown.edu/cds/perry/about.html.)

Why Do Interpretive Things Matter?

There has recently been a bit of a rush to announce the institutional arrival
of the Digital Humanities and then to take credit for pinning it down in
theory, if not in practice. In a series of posts written for the *New York Times'*
Opinionator blog, Stanley Fish "discovered" that the Digital Humanities is
a "rough beast [that] has slouched into the neighborhood threatening to
upset everyone's applecart," especially the now-ditched applecart of post-
modernism.[3] In other words, according to Fish, the Digital Humanities is
the new theory, and that is official.

Fish outlines what he thinks this new field is: a new theoretical perspective that alternates between believing that computers simply extend and
perfect a tradition of literary criticism and the messianic belief that new
toys will lead to a new humanities.[4] In particular, he looks at two views for
how computers can change how we interpret texts: the view that computers can help us with "distant reading" of large amounts of text and the view

that computers can help us play with deforming texts.[5] One extends the humanities and one saves the humanities. Perhaps they do neither.

Fish's reading of Digital Humanities was based on the reading of texts about the Digital Humanities, and therein lies a problem. While he makes some astute observations, Fish doesn't actually look at, interact with, or ask about any of the artifacts made in the Digital Humanities. He ignores the digital stuff of DH because he wants it to be another theoretical fad that can be read. Although he finds what he goes looking for, Fish misses the fundamental character of the Digital Humanities in bypassing the very knowledge-bearing instruments and practices that make the entire journey possible. It's a little like trying to understand railroads by reading books about them instead of looking at models or taking a ride on a *Shinkansen*.

To be fair, in the humanities we don't often experience things as ways of conveying knowledge. Davis Baird, in *Thing Knowledge* (2004), impatiently discusses how overlooked theoretical things, such as orreries, are designed to convey scientific knowledge. He believes that we scholars are blinded by our use of discourse as our means of legitimization:

Part of the reason instruments have largely escaped the notice of scholars and others interested in our modern techno-scientific culture is language, or rather its lack. Instruments are developed and used in a context where mathematical, scientific, and ordinary language is neither the exclusive vehicle of communication nor, in many cases, the primary vehicle of communication. Instruments are crafted artifacts, and visual and tactile thinking and communication are central to their development and use.[6]

Baird argues for an epistemology of the material that he calls "thing knowledge," "where the things we make bear our knowledge of the world, on a par with the words we speak."[7] This doesn't mean that things bearing knowledge aren't also explained or commented on through discourse. And the same is true of textual artifacts such as analytical tools: they are supplemented with labels, training courses, libraries, performances, diagrams, and manuals.

Baird's point is that we scholars use text-based discourse as just about our only way of disseminating knowledge, so it is no surprise that we don't notice the way things around us bare knowledge. Our habits have conditioned what we look for and what we are trained to interpret. Rather than just reading debates in the Digital Humanities, what if we could read the things (toys, websites, tools such as Voyant, and so on) and their uses as discursive practices? How would we do that? How might our interpretation then be different? Is it possible to think through interpretive things?

We have already illustrated a number of ways to approach thinking about things as bearing interpretation. Several of our chapters (4, 6, 8, and 10) present examples of thinking through tools in the sense of using them. In chapter 2, we looked closely at how computers deal with text in general. In chapter 3, we examine a tool, the KWIC, its history, and how it works in interpretation. In this chapter, we want to consider digital humanists who have participated in the development of tools to appreciate the materiality of interpretation. Throughout the chapter, we will find that we are modeling a dual sense of interpretation as both a practice and the things of the practice.

Father Busa and Recovering the Language

To look at how developers of tools and techniques discussed the text-analysis tools and techniques they pioneered, let us return again to Father Roberto Busa. Having noticed that the doctrine of "presence" was linked to the preposition "in," Busa began his PhD project by "writing out by hand 10,000 [3-by-5-inch] cards," each containing a sentence with the word "in" or a word connected with it." "Grand games of solitaire followed," he continued.[8] Thinking back on the materiality of this work on his concording project (1980), Busa wrote:

Two major considerations became evident. I realized first that a philological and lexicographical inquiry into the verbal system of an author has to precede and prepare for a doctrinal interpretation of his works. Each writer expresses his conceptual system in and through his verbal system, with the consequence that the reader who masters this verbal system, using his own conceptual system, has to get an insight into the writers conceptual system. The reader should not simply attach to the words he reads the significance they have in his mind, but should try to find out what significance they had in the writer's mind.

Second, I realized that all functional or grammatical words (which in my mind are not 'empty' at all but philosophically rich) manifest the deepest logic of being which generates the basic structures of human discourse. It is this basic logic that allows the transfer from what the words mean today to what they meant to the writer.[9]

These are some of the first theoretical reflections on text analysis by a developer. Though they aren't the earliest such reflections, Busa's ideas and his project are generally considered major initial influences in DH.[10] His essay positioned concordances as tools for uncovering and recovering the meanings of words in their original contexts. Busa is in a philological tradition that prizes the recovery of the historical context of language. To interpret a text, one must reconstitute the conceptual system of its author and its author's context independent of the text.

A concordance refocuses the philological reader on the language. It structures a different type of reading: one in which a reader can see how a term is used across a writer's works, rather than following the narrative or logic of an individual work. A concordance breaks the train of thought; it is an instrument for seeing the text differently. One looks across texts rather then through a text. The instrument, by its very nature, rearranges the text by showing and hiding (showing occurrences of key words and their context grouped together and hiding the text in its original sequence) so as to support a different reading.

How did the computing instruments devised by early computing humanists support such re-reading? "The primary objective of the literary data-processing project," Father Busa's IBM collaborator Paul Tasman, wrote, "was to provide a method by which any text could be machine-analyzed and indexed down to its simplest meaningful elements, the words." "After reduction," Tasman continued, "the words were to be compiled in a variety of specialized lists, the number and criteria to be determined by the ultimate requirements of the specific study.[11]

If we are going to pay attention to the ways tools bear theory, we also should look at the discussions of computing that went into the Index Thomisticus project. Tasman described his work as a method "for rapid compilation of analytical indexes and concordances of printed works, using either a conventional punched-card system or an electronic data processing machine."[12] His paper was aimed at computing professionals; he focused on preparing a text for the computer using punch cards and the associated coding methods, which were new at the time. "It is evident," he wrote, "that the transcription of the documents in these other fields necessitates special sets of ground rules and codes in order to provide for information retrieval, and the results will depend entirely upon the degree and refinement of coding and the variety of cross referencing desired.[13] Tasman then carefully describes a data-entry process in which a human analysis of the text into phrases was typed onto punch cards for automatic processing that then produced other cards and word lists. Note the dialectic between human and automated processing. Tasman provides an annotated diagram and some examples of how the punch cards were used for text processing. Foreseeing future applications of these methods, Tasman wrote:

Indexing and coding techniques developed by this method offer a comparatively fast method of literature searching, and it appears that the machine-searching application may initiate a new era of *language engineering*. It should certainly lead to improved and more sophisticated techniques for use in libraries, chemical documentation, and abstract preparation, as well as in literary analysis.[14]

What stands out today in Tasman's work is the attention to the materiality of using punch cards not just to store data but also as tokens of machine and human processes.[15] Tasman conveys the love of an engineer for the new form of knowledge-bearing things he has designed for hybrid use by machines and scholars. Most of the punch cards, and the later magnetic tapes, are still being lovingly held in the Busa Archive at the Catholic University of the Sacred Heart in Milan.

Busa and Tasman were not the first to use analytical methods on texts.

Mendenhall and the Characteristic Curve

In 1887, Thomas Corwin Mendenhall published a remarkable article in *Science* titled "The Characteristic Curves of Composition" (1887). Containing what must be one of the first text visualizations based on the (manual) count of words, it provides an early spectral view of stylistics, a method of analysis in which computers would be used to model the essential characteristics of a text that goes under the author's name.

Mendenhall proposed "to analyze a composition by forming what may be called a 'word spectrum,' or 'characteristic curve,' which shall be a graphic representation of an arrangement of words according to their length and to the relative frequency of their occurrence."[16] His idea was to plot an author's word-length frequencies as a way of getting a "characteristic curve" or visual representation of that author's style. Mendenhall characterized his method as a form of analysis of signature style comparable to that used for distinguishing materials—a method that would help analysts to identify textual materials by their signature curves. Aware there were assumptions behind the method, he suggested that it could be tested as any other scientific theory could. His manual method is not an instrument for exploring the text, but a way of rigorously modeling its identifying characteristics. This model, functioning as a kind of map or surrogate, simplifies the text so it can be studied and easily compared.[17]

Mendenhall wasn't the only person to propose (even before the computer) that analytical methods could model texts. He was the first in a tradition of stylistic analysis that uses statistical tools to study the characteristic style of an author or of a text. Anthony Kenny (1982) wrote an accessible textbook that introduced the ways in which statistics could be used in authorship studies, forensic stylistics, and studies of an author's evolving

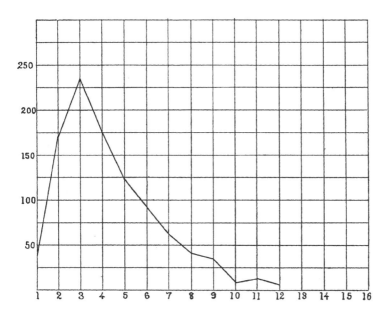

Figure 9.2
"First one thousand words in 'Oliver Twist'" (figure 1 in Mendenhall 1887).

style. More recently, Matthew Jockers, in a chapter on style in his 2013 book *Macroanalysis,* illustrated how stylistics could be used to compare the corpora of different authors.

With the postmodern turn away from the author, who was proclaimed dead, stylistics fell out of favor. More recently, stylistic analysis has made a comeback, as has the author (whose death, it turns out, had been announced prematurely). Ian Lancashire, in *Forgetful Muses* (2010), studied Agatha Christie's dementia through variations in vocabulary richness, and Patrick Juola, in "Rowling and 'Galbraith': An authorial analysis" (2013), helped to identify J. K. Rowling as the author of *The Cuckoo's Calling.*[18]

John B. Smith, ARRAS, and Computer Criticism

A structuralist theory of interpretive text analysis was presented by John B. Smith (the developer of ARRAS) in a 1978 paper titled "Computer Criticism." Smith begins the article with a problem that has beguiled computing humanists since Father Busa: that of explaining to literary colleagues why one would bother with computing methods. The article explains how computers process texts and how they can therefore help with modeling interpretations. Not surprisingly, it has an addendum that includes an imaginary dialogue that a critic might have with himself about what he is doing, how the critic formalizes questions for the computer, and how the critic might interpret the results. In essence, the dialogue models how critics might think through their objects of study, using a computer to extend their interpretations. Smith's approach is dialogical or interactive both in theory and in practice, characteristics that also comes through in the Tutorial section of the manual for ARRAS.[19]

Smith reminds us that the term "computer criticism" is potentially misleading, insofar as the human interpreter, not the computer, does the criticism. Smith insists that "the computer is simply amplifying the critic's powers of perception and recall in concert with conventional perspectives."[20] It would be more accurate to call his theory one of "computer-assisted criticism," in a tradition of thinking of the computer as extending hermeneutical abilities. According to Smith, "the full implications of regarding the literary work as a sequence of signs, as a material object, that is "waiting" to be characterized by external models or systems, have to be realized."[21] The core of Smith's theory, however, comes from an insight into the particular materiality of the electronic text. As we pointed out in chapter 2, computers see a text not as a book with a binding, pages, ink marks, and coffee stains, but as a sequence of characters. The electronic text is a formalization of an idea about what the text is, and that formalization translates one material form into another. It is just another edition in a history of productions and consumption of editions.

The computer can help us to identify, compare, and study a document's formal structures or those fitted to it. The process of text analysis, with its computational tools and techniques, is as much about understanding our interpretations of a text, by formalizing them, as it is about the text itself. Smith is not proposing that the computer can uncover some secret structure in the text so much as that it can help us understand the theoretical structures we want to fit to the text.

An example of a structure interpreted onto the text is a theme. Here is what Smith wrote about mapping themes onto Joyce's prose by searching for collections of related words:

The concept of distribution is a diachronic, "horizontal" concept of structure that characterizes patterns along one of the vertical strata described earlier; a different concept of form or structure is the collection of synchronic relations among a number of such distributions. Synchronic patterns of interrelation are, essentially, patterns of co-occurrence.[22]

In "Computer Criticism" (1978) and "A New Environment for Literary Analysis" (1984) Smith talks about following a "fire" theme; in "Image and Imagery in Joyce's *Portrait*" (1973) he gives an example of how he studies such thematic structures. Smith describes a mental model of the text as vertical layers or columns. Imagine all the words in the text as the leftmost base column, with one word per line. Then imagine a column that marks which words belong to the fire theme. That layer could be plotted horizontally in a distribution graph. If one has a number of these structural columns, then one can also study the co-occurrence of themes across rows. Do certain themes appear in the same paragraphs, for example?

Smith anticipated text-mining research methods that are only now coming into use. He describes using Principal Component Analysis (PCA) to identify themes co-occurring synchronically, then cites examples of state diagrams and CGAMS that can present 3D models of the themes in a text. The visualizations are graphical presentations of structural models can be used to explore themes and their relations.[23]

In the late 1970s, Smith was trying to find visual models that could be woven into research practices. He called some of his methods Computer Generated Analogues of Mental Structure (CGAMS), drawing our attention to how he was trying to think through the cognitive practices of literary study that might be enabled by the computer. Like Perry's model railroad, CGAMS provide a model theory that has explanatory and scalable power. The visualizations model a text in a way that can be explored, and they act as examples that a computer-assisted critic can use to model his or her own interpretations.

How did Smith connect his theory to contemporary literary theory? He drew on Roland Barthes' assertion in *The Structuralist Activity* (1972) that structuralism should not be seen as a discovering of some inherent or essential structure, but as an activity of composition:

Structure is therefore actually a *simulacrum* of the object, but a directed, *interested* simulacrum, since the imitated object makes something appear which remained invisible or, if one prefers, unintelligible in the natural object. Structural man takes the real, decomposes it, then recomposes it; this appears to be little enough (which makes some say that the structuralist enterprise is "meaningless," "uninteresting," "useless," etc.). Yet from another point of view, this "little enough" is decisive: for between the two objects, or the two tenses, of structuralist activity, there occurs something new, and what is new is nothing less than the generally intelligible: the simulacrum is intellect added to object, and this addition has an anthropological value, in that it is man himself, his history, his situation, his freedom, and the very resistance which nature offers to his mind.[24]

For Barthes structuralism is an act of dissecting, articulating, and remixing meaning.[25] The meaning made is as much about the maker and the maker's context as it is about the context of what is being studied. It is the perpetual work of the humanities to remake our cultural history so it will be meaningful for each generation; it is dialogue on a large scale:

> We see, then, why we must speak of a structuralist *activity*: creation or reflection are not, here, an original "impression" of the world, but a veritable fabrication of a world which resembles the primary one, not in order to copy it but to render it intelligible. Hence one might say that structuralism is essentially *an activity of imitation*, which is also why there is, strictly speaking, no technical difference between structuralism as an intellectual activity, on the one hand, and literature in particular, art in general, on the other: both derive from a mimesis.[26]

One can see why Barthes' structuralism would have appealed to Smith. That the computer forces one to formally define any text and any method makes this structuralist understanding of interpretation even more attractive as a way of understanding computer-assisted criticism.

The computer can help us with the activities of dissection and composition when what we want to study has been represented electronically.[27] The computer can analyze the text and then synthesize new simulacra for interpretation that are invested with the meanings that we (both the "we" of the developers of the tools and the "we" of users issuing queries) bring. If we add an earlier phase of demarcation in which the text to be studied is identified and encoded, then we have the pattern of three phases in the aesthetic encounter that Smith teased out of Joyce in "There's a Toy in My Essay."

Ramsay and Playful Criticism

At a panel on "Reconceiving text analysis" at the ACH/ALLC 2002 conference, Stephen Ramsay and the present authors (Sinclair and Rockwell) gave papers on text analysis putting forward what we then thought was a radical shift in the conception of text analysis—that it could be a form of "disciplined play" rather a pseudo-science for proving things about texts. (At the time we were not aware of the pioneering work of Smith.) Then, in a 2003 issue of *Literary and Linguistic Computing* (volume 18, issue 2) we published papers titled "What Is Text Analysis, Really?" (Rockwell 2003a), "Computer-Assisted Reading: Reconceiving Text Analysis" (Sinclair 2003), and "Toward an Algorithmic Criticism" (Ramsay 2003).[28] Some of the points we tried to make in the papers that came from our discussions included ideas that we later discovered in Smith:

- We should look at the *performance* of computer-assisted text analysis.
- This performance is *dialogical* in that it involves a play of questioning/ querying and getting answers back from the computer that has been enabled by faster interactive tools.
- The types of questions evolve *through play with tools* beyond those one would ask before computing. The possibilities of computing lead to some questions that may not appear serious to the close reader.
- The new playful questions can *distort the text* into new forms, whether visualizations, or new backward texts.
- The new questions and the new tools that enable them play in structured ways with the text (because they are programmed) in the tradition of Oulipian practices. These interactions are distortions of the text that *create new texts for interpretation*, some of which are more amusing than of interpretive use.
- There is therefore "no *a priori* privilege to certain processes of decomposition and recomposition such as traditional concording." Processes that radically reorganize the text can be a justifiable interpretive response, even if playful.[29]

Although all three authors continue to play with the interpretive capacity of technology, perhaps the most sustained proponent of playful text analysis is Stephen Ramsay.

In *Algorithmic Criticism* (2008) and *Reading Machines* (2011b), Ramsay explored the playful opportunities of text-analysis tools. He showed the connections between transformative algorithms that reverse lines in a poem and traditions such as the *I Ching* and Oulipo. In "The Hermeneutics of Screwing Around" (2014) he provocatively drew attention to something we all do at times: playfully browse information with no research agenda in mind. This serendipitous "screwing around" has its place, and our information tools should support it.

Playful analysis has been criticized for not being serious scholarly work. It has been argued that what happens in the privacy of the study should not necessarily be written up as exemplary.[30] The objections to such practices take various forms, but they ultimately come down to an ethical questioning about how we act as intellectuals. In the next chapter we will deal with a similar challenge in Hume's *Dialogues* where the character Cleanthes accuses Philo of excessive imagination and playful scepticism. Here it is worth surveying some of the forms such serious concerns take today.

First of all, playful computer modeling and visualization of hidden characteristics are often criticized as not respecting the intentions of the author or the realities of reading. In *Small World* (1984), David Lodge satirizes computer-assisted stylistics by telling the story of an author who, when confronted by a stylistic analysis of his idiolect (characteristic language), which turns out to be "grease," is no longer able to write fiction until the end of the novel. There seems to be something unnatural about any form of analysis that uncovers something that no author consciously intended and no human would find through reading alone. It is not a coincidence that this "greasy" interpretation is manufactured at a "Computer Centre" in a prefabricated hut at a second-rate new university in an industrial town. The stylistics may be right, Lodge suggests, but it not the sort of work a gentleman scholar at a prestigious university should do: it can choke the author.

In "Mind Your P's and B's: The Digital Humanities and Interpretation" (2012b), Stanley Fish rehashes the argument by first showing that he can also do "literary analysis that deals, as the digital humanities do, with matters of statistical frequency and pattern" and then concludes that it is not what we should do, which is to narrow "meaning to the significances designed by an author."[31] Fish is definitely and proudly not a postmodern critic for whom the author is *passé*. Instead, like Busa, he is interested in recovering the meaning of the author, which is why he might see playful approaches as disrespectful, or just a waste of time.

But that is not Fish's only quibble about statistical techniques. Fish also believes that we should be suspicious of results that no human has stumbled upon through traditional critical practices such as reading:

Doesn't the fact that for 368 years only I have noticed the b/p pattern suggest that it is without significance, an accidental concatenation of consonants? Aren't I being at best over-ingenious and at worst irresponsibly arbitrary?[32]

Taken at face value, this is a conservative argument for the authority of tradition. It seems to assert that only previously noticed patterns can be significant. Anything new, especially the newness of digital ingenuity, is suspect. Criticism should not welcome original perspectives on literature, especially if generated by practices that were not around in the "late 1930s."

The issue is methodological, and Fish thinks that DH's tool-driven method of discovery has the order wrong:

First you run the numbers, and then you see if they prompt an interpretive hypothesis. The method, if it can be called that, is dictated by the capability of the tool. You have at your disposal an incredible computing power that can bring to analytical attention patterns of sameness and difference undetectable by the eye of the human reader. Because the patterns are undetectable, you don't know in advance what they are and you cannot begin your computer-aided search (called text-mining) in a motivated—that is, interpretively directed—way. You don't know what you're look-ing for or why you're looking for it. How then do you proceed?[33]

For Fish, interpretation is about starting with a hypothesis, not generat-ing one. The interpretation space is no longer the space for discovery. If Fish's understanding is right, one must come to the interpretation of any book knowing what one is looking for. He obviously came to his reading of the Digital Humanities having decided what he would find; it was simply another version of what he had been saying all along.[34]

We see interpretation as dialogic. It iterates, refines, changes, and discards. Trying a tool on a text is a form of bringing a hypothesis to a text. In compari-son with bringing questions to colleagues, the bringing of questions to tools might feel artificial; we suspect there is a latent desire to keep the humanities in conversation in the literal sense. However, one must not ignore the intel-lectual history of using print and libraries to echo the word through time and space, creating a form of dialogue over time. The book, as print schol-ars have long acknowledged, is only one particular, albeit highly success-ful, textual technology. As technologies present and mediate text, bringing questions to a text-analysis tool is not categorically different from bringing questions to a book. In both cases scholars animate the conversation.

What is different with text-analysis tools is *how* you bring a question to a text through hermeneutica: it is about knowing the right practices for the tool at hand. Rather than search an index, skim, read or flip pages, you search for a pattern you think will reveal something. The choice of a tool is itself a purposeful act. Just as there is no such thing as a completely objective interpretation, there is no such thing as a completely naïve use of a tool. We are always in the world, bearing agendas, habits, contexts, and all the "baggage" of living here. We iteratively push at the horizons of our ignorance, as Hans-Georg Gadamer would point out (1985), sometimes using established methods and sometimes surprised by novel practices.

If using a tool bears questions, developing tools involves bearing herme-neutical theories. The developer chooses what to show, what to hide, and what to model. One doesn't spend time coding a tool without thinking it will generate interesting results; one has to have some sort of model in mind in order to make the tool at all. Building tools is an act of formalizing these ideas into algorithms.

What Sort of Thing Can Bear an Interpretation?

How then could software things bear interpretive theory? Model trains and orreries might be interesting as theoretical things, but they bear scientific and engineering theories, not humanities ideas. To understand hermeneutica, we have to find the models in our history.

There are two types of thing that show up in the Digital Humanities literature as being able to bear the type of theories in which we in the humanities are interested: "instruments" and "models."[35]

Instruments

The first type of thing discussed is what we call "instruments"—things that are used to examine something else. Instruments are interesting because, when they work well, they become transparent, and we don't notice them; we peer through them, as we peer through eyeglasses, in order to interpret something else. As such, instruments would seem poor communicators of theory precisely because they are transparent or ready to hand.[36] However, some specialized instruments used in research contexts are not transparent. Some are used only occasionally, so one doesn't become habituated to their use. Others are set up, calibrated, and tested; their results have to be checked. Research instruments, in their resistance to easy use, force attention on the tool. Asking whether an instrument is interpreting a phenomenon, asking whether it is doing so accurately, and asking whether the results are accessible are all forms of reading the tool; it becomes present-at-hand, to use the Heideggerian terminology. This presence becomes all the more noticeable when the instrument isn't working properly. Its interpretive bearing becomes present to the mind: you are thinking *about it* as you *think through it*.

Certain instruments are theories of interpretation. An instrument implements a theory of interpreting the phenomenon it was designed to bring into view. It orients the user toward certain features in the phenomenon and away from others. The designer made the choice of what to show and what to hide. The user may tune it, but the instrument is, in effect, saying "This is important; that is not." As Margaret Masterman wrote in "The Intellect's New Eye" (1962), "the potential capacity of the digital computer to process nonnumerical data in novel ways—that capacity the surface of which has hardly been scratched as yet—is so great as to make of it the telescope of the mind."[37]

The computer as instrument is an old trope. In "The Intellect's New Eye," Masterman called for computers to be used, not only as "a kind of intellectual spade" for tedious and repetitive tasks, but also, much like the telescope, as an instrument for changing our "picture of the world."[38] This distinction is helpful; a tool can be used to replace interpretation by automating tasks within an established academic practice, and it also can be used to present a new perspective.

Beginning with Father Busa, humanists noticed the usefulness of computers in dealing with the drudgery of editing, collating, indexing, and concording. Masterman, and later John B. Smith, however, imagined the computer as having the potential to be used theoretically to show phenomena in new ways, just as a theory can help one understand something in a new light. Masterman credits the artist, not the theorist, as the person who "dreams up a novel way of defining a 'world.'"[39] The vision-changing instrument follows the dream; it is how the academic artist changes our vision by giving us a way of seeing the re-interpreted world. Such an instrument is more than a transparent tool; it is a hermeneutical thing.

Models

The second type of thing that is suited to bear theory in Digital Humanities is the model. The model has been proposed repeatedly as an expression for what we make. In his prefatory remarks to *La Machina nel Tempo* (Perilli and Fiormonte 2011), Domenico Fiormonte, one of the volume's two editors, nicely summarizes Tito Orlandi's lessons about computing in the humanities as modeling:

1. Everything that in the humanities is taken for granted (starting with the concept of text) has to be formalized in informatics.
2. The passage from analogue to digital is a process of profound redefinition for the "cultural object."
3. Thus, every act of encoding (or digital representation) presupposes (or forces us into) a hermeneutical act.[40]

Thus, the things of the Digital Humanities are all models that are formalized interpretations of cultural objects. Even a process as apparently trivial as digitizing involves choices that foreground things that we formerly took for granted, forcing us to theorize at least to the point of being able to formalize. In order to be able to know what we are digitizing and how to do so, we need to develop a hermeneutical theory of things.

Through the process of digitizing we end up with three types of models: a theoretical model of the problem or cultural phenomenon; a working model of an instance of the phenomenon based on the first; and a model of the process whereby we will get the second, which may be semi-automated in code. The first is a model that is closer to what we mean by a hermeneutical theory. The second is the software, such as the e-text, that instantiates the theory to a greater or a lesser extent. The third is a model of the processing of the second, and that is what can be captured in practices and in tools (whether digitizing tools, analytical tools, or presentational tools).

One can see these different models as different expressions of the same things, but it is worth distinguishing them because the people implementing these things are often different from one another. One team might implement the model electronic text and another team might develop the model analytical process, and it isn't always clear that they are working with the same mental models of interpretation. In fact, tool developers are usually working with theories about how to interpretively process classes of texts rather than one particular text.

Tito Orlandi,[41] in "Informatica, Formalizzazione e Discipline Umanistiche" (1997), traces this modeling from the mathematical modeling of the computer, starting with Turing's thought model of a simple machine for processing information. Orlandi points out that more important to humanists than a model of a machine is the modeling of our problem areas and the processes that give us leverage on these problems. The computer allows us to create formal models of that which we want to interpret and then formally model processes that interpret our interpretations. An electronic text is modeled through digitization, that produces a model of the text. That model, if sufficiently rich, can serve as a surrogate for the text. The digital model can then be processed using implementations of hermeneutical processes. The text and the tools are thus both implementations of theoretical models of the phenomenon of interpretation. One is a usable model of the interpretation as edition; the other a reusable model of interpretation as process. In both cases, as Orlandi points out, what is important is that the computer forces us to formalize what we mean so that some level of instantiation and process is possible. Formalization is what distinguishes DH.

Willard McCarty came to similar conclusions about modeling in *Humanities Computing*, though he came to his conclusions initially unaware of Orlandi's work.[42] McCarty argues that modeling is the paradigmatic activity of humanities computing. He mentions two types of modeling: modeling *of* and modeling *for*. Digital humanists build models *of* things they are trying to understand or communicate through computing and models *for* new things they imagine. McCarty appreciates how the word model, like interpretation, has a wonderful double sense of being both a thing and an activity, both of which are based on some understanding. He is also aware of the lovely active and tactile aspects of models and modeling.[43] Models instantiate interpretations in interesting ways that are worth considering when theorizing; models can be manipulated and tested by others in ways that verbal theories cannot. Following Socrates' *Phaedrus,* we would like to say that models are responsive whereas words are not, but that isn't really true; they just respond differently. Or perhaps discourses are a particular type of model implemented in human-readable language, whereas hermeneutica are implemented in machine-readable code.

Models resist us and fail us. That is how we learn from modeling. This is also an important difference between modeling in the humanities and modeling in the sciences. In the sciences, modeling aims to succeed, it thereby acquires predictive power. In the humanities, modeling aims to understand the particularity of phenomena, not the conformity of phenomena; it therefore welcomes productive failure. We almost assume that no model can, by nature, replace the other in its individuality, but in trying to formally instantiate theories in code one learns about the limits of theory and about the individuality that perpetually escapes modeling. What is at stake is a fundamental difference in what we are doing with models.

Humanists model to add meaning. We would be disappointed if we were able to develop a model of literature that could predict any work or answer any question; what then would be the point of reading? Instead we are committed to pursuing the ineffable that escapes each model. The digital humanist pursues that ineffable through formal modeling, which of course strikes many as a rather grasping way to understand something. This misses the way that an interpretation in the humanities, whether modeled in discourse or code, is another text in a history of human interventions. This making of models, as Barthes pointed out, adds new meaning even while failing at capturing the old. The new meaning is in the simulacrum, which becomes another thing to interpret.

We can see the tension between the culture of humanistic scholarship, in which solitary writing is the primary epistemic activity, and the activity of the Digital Humanities, in which communal modeling is the primary activity. The resistance of instruments and the failures of modeling frustrate those who write as a research practice. Our tools will never live up to their imagination. Those who model as a research practice are engaged in a process they don't necessarily want to have end in success. For the writer, the software is the tool and the writing is the never-ending process of thinking. For the developer, the writing is the reporting tool and the coding is the never-ending process of inquiry. Neither should be happy with the work of the other, but they can come to respect one another. The Digital Humanities should hold these research practices in tension and avoid the temptation to interpret only through tools or through discourse. Agile Hermeneutics is our term for the practices of holding both writing development in balance and playing back and forth with the two.

Hermeneutica: As We Might Theorize

How can we develop theoretical things—hermeneutica—so that they better disclose or reveal their interpretive nature? How can we make it easy for others, especially those not trained in software development, to read the things we have crafted? Not everything we make is meant to be a research tool, but those things that are meant to be research tools should facilitate their own interpretation. Is there a reason to distinguish between the simulacrum bearing a theory and the prototype designed to test it? We conclude with some of the features we have used as principles in building Voyant's hermeneutica, though many other theoretical things will not have all these features:

- They are embedded in a context (e.g., a performance) that draws attention to how they communicate theory.
- They are not impenetrable black boxes; rather, they are open to inspection. Rather than hide their workings, they display them in a way that allows the user to understand their principles of operation.
- They are open to manipulation in service of exploration and understanding. Few people will read code to understand a tool, but many can test a tool by fiddling with its parts.
- They are supplemented by other materials (e.g., code, documentation, and labels) that encourage reflection on their use.
- They are designed to resist or interrupt easy or transparent use while drawing attention to their theoretical workings. They force users to configure them in ways that provoke reflection.
- They fail in interesting ways, and they show their limits so that when they fail you know they have failed.
- They can be extended or built upon. They are generative; they lead to new things.
- In some weak sense, everything can be read theoretically. If everything is theory, however, theory ceases to be an interesting category. It is far more interesting to look at and develop things that present theories—for example, models, intentionally theoretical things, and things that reveal themselves in thinking through. We should expect people to ask how the things we make reveal their hermeneutic nature. In dialogue, we should develop simulacra whose interpretive intents are apparent during their use.

10 The Artifice of Dialogue: Thinking Through Scepticism in Hume's *Dialogues* (Fourth Interlude)

the two greatest and purest pleasures of human life, study and society
David Hume, *Dialogues*

In Hume's *Dialogues Concerning Natural Religion* (1779), one of the great philosophical dialogues of the eighteenth century, a fictional author-narrator named Pamphilus describes a conversation among Philo (a sceptic), Cleanthes (a theist), and Demea (a fundamentalist) about God's existence and God's nature.

Hume wrote *Dialogues* late in life but did not publish it during his lifetime, fearing negative reactions to Philo's sustained attacks on proofs of God's existence. He hoped that friends (Adam Smith among them) would publish it after his death, but they demurred. Hume's nephew arranged for it to be published two and half years after his death.[1]

We began our inquiry into Hume's work by asking what we could learn about scepticism from using text analysis. Scepticism interested us because it is an approach that underlies much of what we think about knowing, and because much of this book is about how computational tools can help us in thinking through.[2]

Sceptical attacks on knowing have provoked many of the most imaginative attempts to methodically ground human knowledge. Descartes interrogates knowing by sceptically doubting everything, including what others have to say; this leads to "I think, therefore I am." Scepticism is a tradition of systematically questioning any certainty, including our certainties about the existence of God and, as in the case of Descartes, our belief in any reality.[3] Sceptics even doubt their own rationality and doubt scepticism itself. Scepticism, at least as it unfolds in the *Dialogues*, is a particularly recursive and postmodern artifice of inquiry.

The problem with scepticism, as is pointed out in the *Dialogues*, is that when the conversation is over you end up not being able to believe in any knowledge, even whether doors or windows are the best exits from a building. For some sceptics this is a relief. One extreme school, which runs from Sextus Empiricus and other Pyrrhonian sceptics to the later Wittgenstein, believes that philosophizing is a disease and that sceptical questioning of all beliefs leads not to deeper knowledge but to giving up philosophizing. Scepticism, for these anti-philosophers, leads to a state of suspension of belief that then helps one regain a sense of balance and achieve release from the anxieties of philosophy. In giving up figuring out what you know, you are released back to a more humble and balanced life in which you use doors as exits instead of questioning their reality. If you think you think too much, scepticism is the cure for you, as it is a cure by thinking through thinking.

More important, the tradition of sceptical questioning, as found in Hume's *Dialogues* and in many other philosophical works, creates space for agile interpretation instead of trying to permanently solve interpretive questions. Just as Plato, Cicero, Diderot, and Hume use the philosophical dialogue form to illustrate ways of being intellectually in a world where differing opinions are tolerated, so computer-assisted methods of interpretation can open spaces of interpretation rather than trying to resolve things definitively. We are all sceptics to some degree, open to the idea that our most cherished theories could be proved wrong and always interpreting evidence and tradition. We are eager to encounter new evidence as the total space of understanding is enriched by the diversity of possibilities and interpretations, and, as Steven Ramsay has pointed out, the computer is an excellent tool for generating new evidence to consider. What better text to interpret with the help of hermeneutica than an artificial dialogue that models the questioning of certainties, methods, and results?

This chapter, our final interlude, is designed to show how you can do sustained text analysis across a single prepared text. Where does one begin when studying a text? The cost of entry can seem dauntingly high for a textual scholar contemplating all the tools, technical terms, and methods that one must master just to decide whether a computer can help. Playing with a text you know well is one way to start. For this reason, in this chapter we will give you a sense of what doing complex text analysis is like by telling the story of our interpretation of Hume's *Dialogues Concerning Natural Religion*. This artifice of a story of interpretation is designed to illustrate how you can use Voyant to study a single text that you already know but are re-searching.[4] On the way we will also talk about the dialogue of interpretation and about where text analysis can fit in a hermeneutical process.

Start by Bringing Questions to a Text or a Text to Questions

Our first step was to identify a text we knew well that we wanted to question. We then discussed questions we wanted to ask of Hume's *Dialogues*. (Starting with a text you know is a good way to test whether computer-assisted text analysis can provide further insight, as familiarity provides starting points for inquiry.)

Try Voyant on a text you know, one you have found or written, and see if interactive visualizations can show you something new. Test how it plays with the reading practices you have already developed. Alternatively, start with questions for which you then have to develop a text or collection of texts. We provided examples of these sorts of projects in the chapter 6, where we started with questions about Barack Obama's position on race and proceeded to find, analyze, and interpret his speeches on race.

You could begin with a single text or work or with a body of works—an artificial "corpus" or collection. Either way, as you find and prepare a text, you should develop initial questions or hypotheses that you want to explore using hermeneutical tools. Don't worry too much about your starting questions; you will find the questions change as you delve deeper into the text. You will discover anomalies in results offered by Voyant that spur new lines of enquiry. New questions will come faster than answers.

Adapt Questions to Hermeneutica

To do text analysis you need to formulate and formalize your questions, at least initially, into something that the searching, matching, counting, and visualizing capabilities of a text-analysis tool can help you with. You can't just ask what themes are important in a text, or what the text has to say about friendship; however, you can ask what clusters of words (which might indicate themes) have a high frequency (which might indicate importance), and you can ask to follow a cluster of friendship words through the text. This formalization is the hard work, but it is also where you practice thinking through analysis without even turning on the computer.

Even though you will have to formalize questions in order for the tool to be able to produce results, it is important to remember that the interpretive enterprise, as a whole, is not limited to computational results. You can use results produced by the tool to ask further questions or formulate arguments that are pursued by other means. Interpretive text analysis is a hybrid practice, one that is only assisted, or augmented, by the tool.

The Text You Use Matters

For our experiment we looked for an electronic edition of the *Dialogues* that we could mount in Voyant. We chose the Project Gutenberg version chiefly for pragmatic reasons: the text is freely and readily accessible.[5] Scholars should always carefully double-check text editions, even those sourced from well-established projects such as Project Gutenberg. They should be sceptical of the quality, and should check passages against other editions, especially for terms that matter to the analysis. Sometimes a digitized text is not the best version; sometimes a digital version contains typos or even missing chapters; often the text contains extra metadata. We periodically cross-referenced this digital version with a print edition.

Analysis Develops Many New Texts

A text-analysis research cycle generates many intermediate model texts. The cleaning and preparation phase—isolating the body of the text from the metadata, correcting flagrant typos, normalizing titles and other structural elements, creates a version. The second phase, breaking apart the text in various ways to create new texts, creates additional versions. Analysis, in the etymological sense of a breaking something into parts, by its very definition produces new fragmentary texts. These parts gets recombined in different ways into new hybrid texts or "results" that you can save and use for further reading and analysis. It is like a branching dialogue of potential texts.

In the course of our experiment, we found ourselves saving numerous intermediate results and having to make sure we noted how they were generated in case we wanted to recapitulate or explain how we produced them. The combinatorics of this get even more dizzying as branches are made and corrections or adjustments must be applied to multiple versions. It is critical to keep track of the many texts. We accomplished this through expressive but succinct file-naming strategies.

To support different types of questions, we created different input texts for different tools. We first converted the plain-text file into an XML representation in which important structural features were tagged—especially chapters, titles, speeches, and paragraphs. Producing XML representations may be excessive in a lot of instances where a text can be treated as a simple sequence of words, but it was necessary for our purposes in order to produce multiple views of the text. This allowed us to create separate documents from each of the chapters (also called books or parts) in Hume's *Dialogues*.[6] Adding tagging for the speeches uttered by each character allowed us to recombine all the speeches from each individual character into separate documents. Not only is such tagging useful for creating new texts as views of the source text; it also makes it easy to apply styling when viewing each representation. For instance, we have a view of the full text in which the words of the different speakers are colored to make it easy to see who says what.[7] We would like to say that we anticipated all these needs and created all these variants at the beginning, but the truth is that we had to go back and create new input texts as new questions arose. New texts are produced iteratively as needs arise; data are taken and remixed, not merely given.

Analysis Unfolds through the Iterative Development of Model Texts

Returning to the starting issue of scepticism, we then had to decide how Agile Hermeneutics could help us think through the scepticism in Hume's dialogues. Hume's dialogues, like other philosophical dialogues, are hard to interpret if what you want is to figure out is what the author thought, because nowhere does Hume write in the first person (though even if he had it may not help determine authorial intent, as we know well from literary criticism). The narrator who tells the story of the dialogue (in a letter to Hermippus) is Pamphilus, not Hume, a hint that the narrator should not be confused with the author. Understanding scepticism in the dialogue will depend on understanding its dramatic structure and asking how different characters might represent (or not) different positions the author considers relevant. How then can we read Hume's presentation of scepticism in this work that is not in his voice?

Analysis Is a Comparison with a Model: Looking at Characters

The easiest interpretation of a dialogue is to see if there is a principal character who may stand as a model for the author the way Socrates does so often in the Platonic dialogues. Assuming that quantity represents authority, we measured the number of words each character speaks to see if one character is speaking more often. Text tools give us a way to do this. We decomposed the full text into subtexts by character and compared those subtexts with other subtexts in different ways. You can use Voyant's Summary, or any tool that counts words, to ask which character speaks the most.

According to the lexical counting algorithms of Voyant, Philo has 23,085 words, Cleanthe 7,455, and Demea 3,998. Philo talks three times as much as the next most verbose other speaker, Cleanthes; that is a dramatic difference. The scale of Philo's speech acts would seem to confirm what most

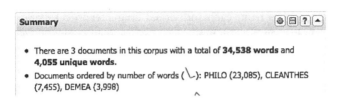

Summary   ⊕ ⊟ ? ▲

- There are 3 documents in this corpus with a total of **34,538 words** and
  4,055 unique words.
- Documents ordered by number of words (⌐): PHILO (23,085), CLEANTHES
  (7,455), DEMEA (3,998)

Figure 10.1
Voyant Summary. To get this summary we created a corpus with the extracted
texts for each speaker (except the narrator Pamphilus, see http://voyant-tools.
org/?corpus=hume.dialogues.by.speaker&stopList=stop.en.taporware.txt. This corpus then treats each speaker's text as a document in a larger corpus and counts the
words for the documents. Note that the text has the same words, but out of order.

readers instinctively end up believing: that Philo is set up to be the hero of
Hume's *Dialogues*. One could cautiously assume Philo represents the position Hume wants us to take most seriously as you cannot help but sympa-
thize with Philo through the dialogue.

Experiment through Code and Visualization

Once we realized the magnitude of the difference in how much the speakers
talk, we remembered that some chapters seem to be mostly Philo talking;
those chapters can hardly be called dialogical. Other chapters, however,
have more lively exchanges. To further examine the difference, we decided
to graph the speeches against chapters to see where there are long speeches
and where there is more exchange. For this visualization we wrote custom
code, though one could do it manually entering word counts into a spread-
sheet.[8] After a number of iterations we ended up with figure 10.2, which
clearly shows the large set-piece speeches near the end of the *Dialogues*, in
chapters 11 and 12 (labeled sections 12 and 13 in the figure), in comparison with the tighter exchanges earlier in the *Dialogues*. It almost graphs the
drama of the dialogue climaxing at the beginning of chapter 10, at least
insofar as exchange indicates drama. Philo then dominates the last two
chapters. He has one long speech in chapter 11; in the last chapter he has
four medium length speeches broken by short exchanges.[9]

Synthesize New Views for Comparison

Graphs are one of the engaging outcomes of interpretive tools. They can be
fascinating to explore and frustrating to translate into prose; it is no surprise

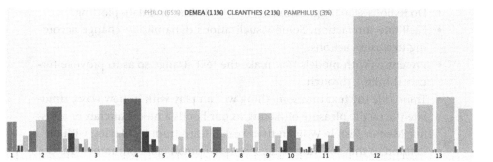

PHILO (65%) **DEMEA (11%) CLEANTHES (21%)** PAMPHILUS (3%)

Figure 10.2
Distribution of Speeches by Speaker. The parts are numbered starting with Pamphilus' prologue, and thus the numbers are off by +1.

that the overabundant digital visualizations on the Web are accompanied by little or no commentary. (See, for instance, the beautiful but under-interpreted visualizations of the *Lord of the Rings* at http://lotrproject.com/statistics/books/.) Good visualizations seem to articulate meaning, but that meaning is difficult to define, at least in words.[10] This shouldn't surprise us as visualizations transcode text into images—they create new visual texts or pictorial concordances by translating textual code into visual code.[11] One might wonder if they really need to be further interpreted, or if that is a discursive habit. Just as art is meant to be individually and idiosyncratically experienced, we might want to allow for aesthetic visualizations that produce irreproducible effects, especially when they are interactive in ways that would be difficult to re-enact.

Our visualizations are artificially generated models of Hume's original text; readers should be sceptical of what our visualizations show and what they hide. Like any interpretation, they produce meaning differently for different people. Therein lies the challenge of text analysis: it can be fascinating for those involved in the modeling but impenetrable to those who aren't accustomed to computer-based methods or aren't familiar with the nature of a particular model.

Model Visualizations for Serious Play

As facilitated by computers, interpretive tools and embeddable toys can do a number of useful and interesting things, such as the following:

- Do tedious searching, counting, manipulation, and data-plotting.
- Facilitate interaction. Some visualizations dynamically change according to a user's actions.
- Present us with models that make the text strange so as to provoke further thinking through.
- Transcode the text into something we can play with in new ways; simulate the tactile pleasure of having in our hands a model aircraft or a Visible Man or Visible Woman that we can learn from by playing with it.[12]
- Remind us that software doesn't replace human labor but rather is a tool that can extend our reach or augment our intellect.[13]

The visualizations we produced with Voyant, although interesting, didn't help to answer our question about Hume's scepticism as it is presented in the *Dialogues*—especially at the end, where Philo recants. After spending the whole dialogue as a model sceptic who breaks apart arguments for the existence of God, Philo changes tack in the final chapter and acknowledges the obviousness of God's existence: "Notwithstanding the freedom of my conversation, and my love of singular arguments, no one has a deeper sense of religion impressed on his mind, or pays more profound adoration to the Divine Being, as he discovers himself to reason, in the inexplicable contrivance and artifice of nature."[14] And Pamphilus—the fictional author-narrator telling us of the dialogue, and a candidate for Hume's final judgment—concludes the dialogue by telling us that he prefers Cleanthes' "accurate philosophic turn" to Philo's "careless scepticism."[15] If the narrator for whom this conversation has been staged, and who reports it to his friend in a letter, closes the work with such a judgment, we need to consider whether it hints at how we should interpret the work. Perhaps Hume doesn't think Philo's position is the whole story. Perhaps Hume is playing with his reader.

Analytics Show There Is Something; Interpretation Judges Meaning

Philo's sceptical reversal illustrates one of the dangers of text analysis and visualization: The tools can show you *where* characters speak and *how much* they speak, but they don't tell you what the speaking *means*. Only a reader of the text would know that there is a surprising reversal in part 12 that seems to undo all of Philo's persistent questioning. The graph reproduced here as figure 10.2 shows only *that* Philo gives several long set-piece speeches at the end, not how or why he changes his mind.

We may get human-quality interpretation from computers someday, but at the moment computers are not very good at finding or defining meaning. It is questionable if they will ever match our human ability to sniff out irony or other forms of layering meaning. True artificial intelligence has seemed just beyond our grasp since early successes of the 1960s. That is why returning to the text to confirm interpretation is critical,[16] and why Voyant puts a reading panel in the center of its main reading skin, an environmental mode, to make it possible to get at the original text. We believe that text analysis is a form of re-reading or reading through; the original text should be revisited alongside new forms of data analysis and visualization.

Literary Analysis Returns to the Text

Philo's reversal has puzzled interpreters of Hume for some time; many are tempted to dismiss it as a ploy by Hume to mask his radical scepticism.[17] Is it just Hume trying to play it safe by tacking back to religion at the end of his dialogue in a way that makes doubly sure that he can respond to accusers that his most talkative character is not an atheist? For that matter, is Philo actually recanting, or is there a subtler interpretation of his evolving position? In short, the reversal raises questions not only about Hume's position on the existence of God but also about Hume's variant of scepticism as a philosophical practice.

If Philo seems to be constructed by Hume as an example of how a sceptic should argue, what does it mean when the sceptic flip-flops at the end and is judged second to the theist? Is that a sign that Hume actually found scepticism wanting? Does it signify that Hume advocates switching positions to suit the audience? Could Hume be showing a deeper scepticism of scepticism? We need to look more closely at how scepticism is discussed in the dialogue, and text analysis can help us to do so.

Following a Theme

Software cannot summarize a theme the way a human would. However, it can identify the words that would mark the theme and then track their interactions through the text. This is not new functionality; one does roughly the same thing when using an index to find the passages on a certain subject. The software, however, quickly provides a thorough and reliable index and then provides the user with interfaces for exploring those occurrences as a trace of a theme.

Synthesizing New Readings from a Text

In the case of Hume's *Dialogues*, we first identified the words that we wanted to follow in order to study scepticism. To do this, we searched the Words in Entire Corpus list of Voyant for the forms of the word, using the pattern "s[ck]eptic" (which finds all the variant spellings with either a "c" or a "k").[18]

As was noted in chapter 1, using the Key Word in Context panel made it clear that in our edition "skeptic" is used to represent the school of philosophy, as in "the dispute between the Skeptics and Dogmatists is entirely verbal," and that "sceptic" is used to represent individuals and their beliefs. Selecting all the sceptical words, we then got a distribution graph of where the thematic words appeared across the text. From the Word Trend graph it was clear that scepticism as a philosophical issue is dominant, at least lexically, at the beginning of the text up to chapter (or part) 3 and then tapers off, being dealt with less in any of the other parts. We therefore expected the issue to be explicitly raised in the first chapters and then returned to in the course of the dialogue in ways that might modulate our understanding.

When we looked at the distribution of the words across the three speakers in the dialogue (ignoring Pamphilus, for the moment, because he is the narrator and not a speaker), we saw something interesting: Cleanthes, not Philo, uses these words the most relative to how much he talks. Even if Philo is the sceptic, it is Cleanthes who is fascinated by scepticism.

Cleanthes, despite talking about scepticism the most, talks about it only in the first half of the dialogue. After the initial chapters, he abandons the

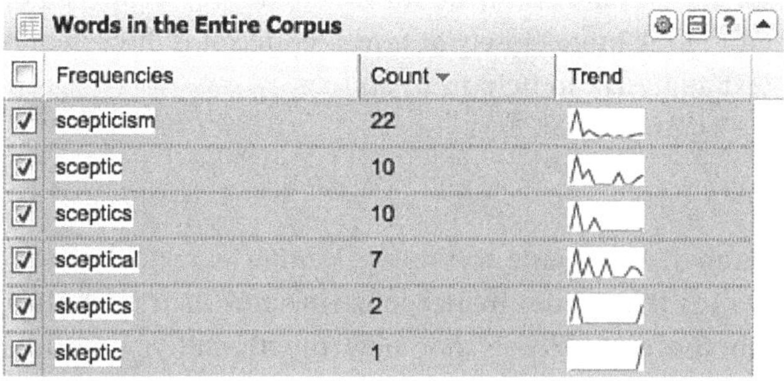
Words in the Entire Corpus

Frequencies	Count	Trend
scepticism	22	
sceptic	10	
sceptics	10	
sceptical	7	
skeptics	2	
skeptic	1	

Figure 10.3
Sceptic words in the Words in the Entire Corpus. To get this view, go to the URL http://voyant-tools.org/tool/CorpusTypeFrequenciesGrid/?corpus=hume.dialogues.by.book&stopList=stop.en.taporware.txt&query=s[ck]eptic.

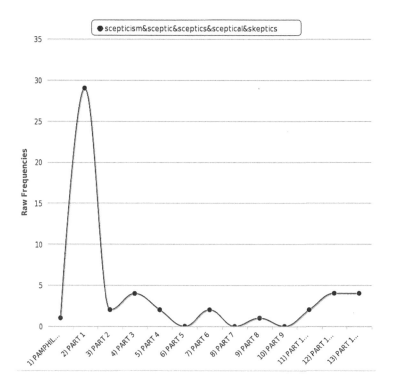

Figure 10.4
Word Trend of sceptical words across parts of the *Dialogues*.

subject and lets Philo speak uncontested. His last sustained input on scepticism is in chapter 4. In short, Cleanthes raises the issue of scepticism in the first half; Philo plays with it in the second half; Cleanthes continually mentions scepticism in the early parts of the *Dialogues* as way of belittling what Philo has to say; Philo models it in how he argues. These visualizations suggested the need to investigate how scepticism is raised in the first chapters of the *Dialogues*, and how Cleanthes explicitly leaves the issue in chapter 4. Finally, we decided to see how Philo models scepticism in the rest of the *Dialogues*.

On Beginnings and Ends: Visualize the Flow of Words across a Text

Scepticism, in connection with natural religion, is one of the framing issues in Hume's *Dialogues*. Using Voyant as a concording tool, we surveyed the way scepticism is introduced and read in extensive passages. We used the

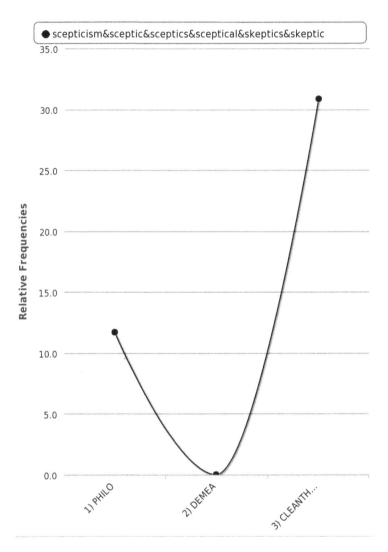

Figure 10.5
Word Trend of sceptical words across speakers in the *Dialogues*.

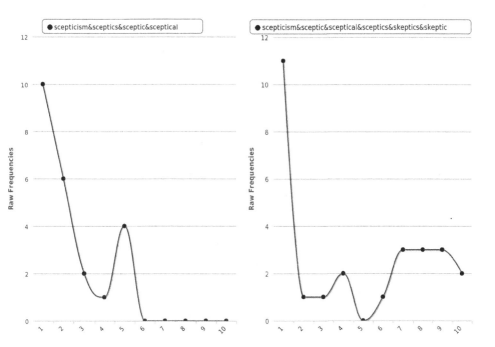

Figure 10.6
Word Trend of sceptical words of Cleanthes (left) and Philo (right). These distribution graphs are of the skeptical words across the text of just what Cleanthes said or Philo said, so they do not represent the distribution across the book. This is a limitation of Voyant. To graph a speaker's use of a word, we have to extract their words as a separate text.

Key Words in Context panel to work through the concordance entries as "hits." By default, Voyant's preview includes five words on each side of the key word, but it can be expanded to see more context. We discovered that the dialogue begins with Demea congratulating Cleanthes on the education of Pamphilus. He quotes a maxim of the ancients: that students "ought first to learn Logics, then Ethics, next Physics, last of all, of the Nature of the Gods."[19] This unusual order of learning (unusual, at least, for a religious man such as Demea) leads Philo to congratulate him on his principles. The demotion of religious learning is a veiled promotion of scepticism, a move that raises Cleanthes' suspicions. Pamphilus describes Cleanthes' reaction this way:

But in Cleanthes's features I could distinguish an air of finesse; as if he perceived some raillery or artificial malice in the reasonings of Philo.

You propose then, Philo, said Cleanthes, to erect religious faith on philosophical scepticism; ... whether your scepticism be as absolute and sincere as you pretend, we shall learn bye and bye, when the company breaks up: We shall then see, whether you go out at the door or the window; and whether you really doubt, if your body has gravity, or can be injured by its fall.[20]

Scepticism is linked with the titular issue of the dialogue, natural religion, and with the opening issue, education. Cleanthes also raises questions about the everyday practice of scepticism and common sense. He challenges Philo on the consistency of his scepticism and asks what he will do at the end of the dialogue. A few lines later, Cleanthes seems to anticipate Philo's recantation, arguing that "it is impossible" for Philo "to persevere in this total scepticism, or make it appear in his conduct for a few hours."[21] Either Philo has to be consistently sceptical, questioning common sense exits like doors, or he has to be inconsistent and appear to only play scepticism as artifice during conversation. He is being put on notice that how he ends the dialogue matters. This foreshadowing sheds new light on Philo's final position on scepticism.

We then decided to explore the collocates using the Collocate Clusters tool. The words that collocate with (that is, occur within close proximity to) "scepticism" in Cleanthes' and Philo's dialogue illustrate some of the tension between Philo and Cleanthes.[22] The Collocate Cluster shown in figure 10.7 also contains some unexpected terms Cleanthes uses in the

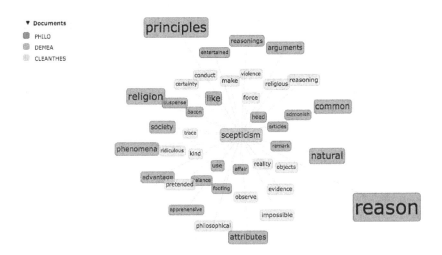

Figure 10.7
Collocate Cluster for "scepticism."

context of "scepticism," among them "violence," "conduct," "ridiculous," and "pretended." For Cleanthes scepticism is a "violence" that people impose on their "conduct." It is "ridiculous" to reject Newton's explications, and in fact sceptics end up following common sense despite their "pretended" scepticism. Exploring collocates reinforced and clarifies for us the disdain that Cleanthes has for Philo's scepticism as a way of life. He focuses in specifically on sceptical conduct, not on the rationality of scepticism. He doesn't attack the rationality of scepticism because he sees it as an excess or pretended rationality; he deals with it by repeatedly mocking it as a form of raillery or jest that is so impractical that it can have no effect.

Cleanthes' mockery of Philo's scepticism peaks at the end of chapter 4 when Cleanthes contrasts the sceptic to the "ignorant savage"; scepticism is, for Cleanthes, a form of ignorance. He introduces ethical terms when he tells Philo "your sifting, inquisitive disposition, my ingenious friend ... suppresses your natural good sense."[23] Cleanthes patronizingly suggests that Philo's scepticism is an error of excess "not from barrenness of thought and invention, but from too luxuriant a fertility."[24] It may not stem from ignorance, but nonetheless it leads into a form of ignorance by excess. Philo, Pamphilus tells us, "was a little embarrassed and confounded: But while he hesitated in delivering an answer, luckily for him, Demea broke in upon the discourse, and saved his countenance."[25] That Hume has Pamphilus interject here struck us as important, as it is one of the few times he interprets the dialogue for the reader. Whereas the interlocutor's words dominate the *Discourse*, here Hume presumably wants to underline the ethical challenge to scepticism that temporarily silences Philo. How then does one answer such a personal attack from one's host? How does one answer Cleanthes in front of his ward and student without being rude? Cleanthes doesn't dispute sceptical reasoning (Philo could sceptically answer any rational questions about scepticism); rather, he characterizes scepticism as a futile excess of imaginative thinking. He is calling into question Philo's good sense and behavior. A response or a rationalization, if even possible, would only reinforce Cleanthes' point and demonstrate Philo's further lack of good social sense. Here is the first hint of how Hume has Philo deal with Cleanthes. Hume deliberately changes the subject, though Philo will return to it later. Philo shows social intelligence by not taking the bait.

This brings us back to the practice of text analysis. There is real drama in this dialogue, and text analysis helped us find it. It would be easy to say that any close reader would have noticed this, and that may be true, but in our case it was through text analysis that we found the turning point where Hume uses Philo's silence to make a point. Further, this dramatic dimension of scepticism as sensible practice, rather than philosophical practice, has not been dealt with adequately by philosophical interpreters, because it really isn't about philosophical arguments or theories; it is about how you are a practicing and ethical intellectual in the world—something we all deal with, and something we are going to look at next.[26] Following the logic of the arguments, as philosophers tend to do, one misses the social moves that become evident when the text can be concorded and reorganized according to different principles.

Skeptical Practice as a Response

Demea interrupts at the point of insult or ethical challenge and changes the subject. It is possible that even Demea feels that Cleanthes has gone too far and has exhibited unbecoming conversational behavior. The interruption leads to a series of chapters dealing with proofs of God's existence—proofs that Philo demolishes in a virtuoso display of philosophical argumentation. Then, in chapter 11, Philo raises the problem that misery and evil presents for those who want to argue for God's existence from the design of the world.

As has already been mentioned, this doesn't mean that Hume drops the issue. Hume's answer to Cleanthes' challenge lies not in what Philo says, because one can't really refute such a rude challenge, but in what he does in the evolution of the drama of the dialogue. Philo's actions through the rest of the dialogue provide an indirect answer to the claim that he is excessive in his scepticism. Put simply, Philo is portrayed as a perfectly sociable character. When madness through excess of scepticism can be perfectly rational, no argument can decide the question. Instead it is the ongoing reasonableness of character that does so.

The reversal in chapter 12 provides an example of how a sceptic comes back to earth. Although Cleanthes has suggested that sceptics cannot gracefully return to the natural habits of using doors, chapter 12 shows us a sceptic who does just that: Philo returns to the natural pieties he was raised on. The reversal has, in this interpretation, a positive role in the definition of the character of the reasonable sceptic. It is not something to be explained away. It is the necessary return of sceptical flight, because true scepticism should be sceptical of scepticism itself. A sceptic who is truly consistent will be cognizant of the limitations of scepticism itself and will not take it too far, especially in the company of students. Good manners, reconciliation, and piety are what a self-respecting citizen returns to ultimately, especially when a guest.[27]

The reversal, though it may be philosophically contradictory, is dramatically realistic. How often do we back down on issues in conversation in order to preserve the peace with friends? How much more likely is it that Philo, having alienated Demea, would retreat at the close of a conversation to a position that is close to that of his friend, especially since this conversation takes place before the friend's ward and in the friend's house? In conversations it is common to challenge someone to get the conversation going and then to try to find a common ground at the end. This doesn't negate the challenge; it mitigates it. The challenge still stands, because Pamphilus recorded the conversation. It stands to be reopened by readers who have to make up their own mind. Backing down in the way Philo does is far more likely to be the way a socially adept sceptic would finish a conversation with people he wished to keep as friends than the ways interpreters might wish for in the name of consistency. Nor does one have to interpret everything said in the reversal as ironic (an irony that Philo's good friend Cleanthes would have noticed anyway, as Rich Foley points out).

Reversals are a dramatic feature of a number of other dialogues that can be traced back to Plato's *Phaedrus*. In the *Phaedrus*, Socrates demonstrates to the character Phaedrus how he is a better rhetor than Lysias by first arguing one side of the question of who is the better friend and lover and then arguing the other. Socrates then makes up for this shameful showing off by engaging Phaedrus in dialogue—an even better way to write on another's soul. The dialogue is uniquely suited to presenting different sides to a question, especially if the goal is to encourage readers to think for themselves instead of telling them which is the preferred position. Reversals are one way to ensure that the reader doesn't leave the reading comfortably sure of what the author believes. They are a way to provoke the reader to decide what he or she thinks. The sceptic Philo shows that he can play both sides, and the author Hume makes it hard for the reader to take either side without thinking through the issue of scepticism as countless commentators have.

Scepticism at the End: Analytics Can Help to Find Patterns or Can Suggest What to Find

This brings us to the most important point to be made about how Hume portrays scepticism. As was noted above, the dialogue opens on the question of education and connects that with natural religion and scepticism. The dialogue also ends on the question of education and scepticism. We saw this when we used Voyant's visualization of the results of correspondence

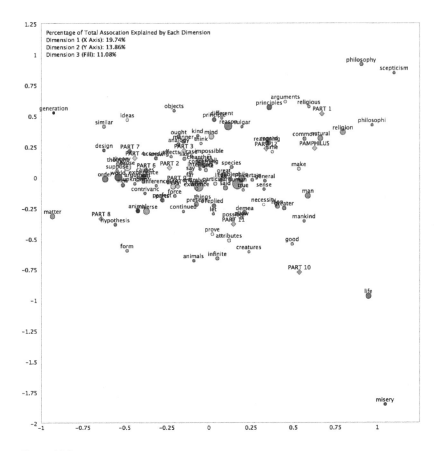

Figure 10.8
Scatter plot of correspondence analysis of Dialogues.

analysis to show how words and chapters correspond. In the upper right quadrant of figure 10.8, one sees that the opening letter from Pamphilus, part 1, and the final part 12 cluster with words such as "scepticism," "religion," and "philosophy."

Such text-mining visualizations are the opposite of the usual searching and concording techniques. They are exploratory. They illustrate the whole text in new ways that encourage you form hypotheses rather than answer them. Visualizations enable scholars to browse the big picture. In this case the visualization suggests that the dialogue is framed by chapters 0 and 1 at the beginning and by chapter 12 at the end, all of which have similar vocabulary. The visualization suggests that scepticism is raised at the

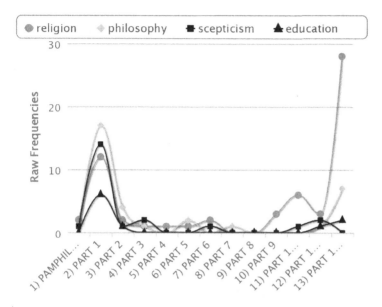

Figure 10.9
Word Trends of "religion," "philosophy," "scepticism," and "education."

beginning and then returned to at the end along with related philosophical issues. We can see the framing issues in the Words Trends graph reproduced here as figure 10.9. The hypothesis of framing was confirmed when we looked at Philo's closing words, which take us back to the beginning of the *Dialogues* and to the issue of the education of Pamphilus:

> To be a philosophical Sceptic is, in a man of letters, the first and most essential step towards being a sound, believing Christian; a proposition which I would willingly recommend to the attention of PAMPHILUS: And I hope CLEANTHES will forgive me for interposing so far in the education and instruction of his pupil.[28]

We saw parallels between how Hume designs the dialogue to show scepticism at work and how Philo practices imaginative scepticism in his arguments. Hume presents us a Philo who has sparked and then managed the discussion that Pamphilus admits made a great impression on him.[29] Philo's imaginative scepticism is the dramatic engine of the dialogue. It provided Pamphilus with an actual example of the value of a sceptical education. By extension, it provided us with an example of scepticism in practice that is dramatically effective. Philo plays out what he advocates; he acts on his belief in the educational value of scepticism, and Hume shows the sceptic having an effect when he interposes in education. Philo (and on another level, Hume) handles the insulting challenge to scepticism not with arguments, but by showing us how educationally effective scepticism can operate in dialogue. Could you imagine a lively dialogue if Philo had not been inventive in his arguments? The dialogue itself is the answer to Cleanthes' challenge.

Text Analysis Animates Questions

Cleanthes is also right: Philo is imaginative, and does indulge in raillery, at least toward Demea. The difference between the picture painted by Hume and Cleanthes concerns the worth of this imagination. For Cleanthes the arguments of Philo are an excess of imagination, no matter how rational. For the reader the scepticism of Philo is what animates the dialogue and provokes thought. Without Philo's imaginative arguments there would be no dialogue worth reading in the first place. Pamphilus hints at this in his letter introducing the dialogue when he mentions how excited Hermippus, the person to whom he is sending the dialogue, was on hearing about the reasoning.[30] For Pamphilus the conversation he had is worth writing down as a dialogue and sending to Hermippus precisely because of the "remarkable contrast in their characters" and the "whole chain and connexion of their arguments."[31] Pamphilus doesn't tell us what to think; he shows us the dialogue.

The dialogue is an artifice that models how different educated people might talk about natural religion. Hume's work is not merely philosophy; it is a work of ethics that uses the drama of dialogue to model behavior. It is an invention that Cleanthes might find excessive, but it is nonetheless educational in that it models pleasurable intellectual society. In his opening letter, in which he talks about what dialogues as a rhetorical form are good for, Pamphilus comments: "If the subject be curious and interesting, the book [dialogue] carries us, in a manner, into company, and unites the two greatest and purest pleasures of human life, study and society."[32]

The ultimate irony is that the central arguments of the *Dialogues* are about arguments from design or artifice. On the one hand, Cleanthes sees pretense and raillery in Philo's imaginative scepticism; on the other, he sees the design of God in the imaginative artifice of nature. Though he insults one form of creativity, he sees another as proof of the divine. Could Hume be presenting Philo's scepticism—and, by extension his dialogue writing— as creativity analogous on a human social scale to the divine artifice we think we see in nature?

Skeptical Text Analysis

The computer-assisted practices described above have a number of virtues for those who want to use them to research their intuitions or the claims of others. They provide a different way of reading the text that is therefore not liable to the same types of errors as close reading tactics. That is not to say that there are not all sorts of ways text analysis can distort reading; it is just to say that the distortions are not those of the usual ways of imaginative reading and therefore serve as a useful alternative. What follows is an attempt to capture some of the virtues of skeptical text analysis.

Digital text analysis encourages a new form of dialogue. Digitally enabled hermeneutical practices involve formalizing claims, or parts of claims, so they can be shared and verified. What were we doing, then, when we tried text analysis? Like Philo's scepticism, text analysis is not an answer or a theory. It struck us at a certain point that text analysis was a method (or performance) of questioning, a thinking through similar to Philo's scepticism. We experienced new readings through re-examination. Rosanne Potter, in her survey of the statistical analysis of literature (1991), argues that "the vast mass of literary criticism rarely considers repeating or rechecking earlier 'discoveries' (usually simple assertions)," that replication is essential to the scientific process, and that scientific discipline will bring "a higher truth value to the practice of literary criticism." We do not believe that text analysis can provide the certainty of scientific process, but we do believe that Potter is right about revisiting claims made about texts, and especially about re-viewing them through different instruments such as those visualizations provide. To support this value, we developed Voyant export features, some of which, like exported URLs, take the reader directly to certain states of the tool that support certain arguments.

Interpretive tools make it practicable to re-apply the essential tenet of the scientific method. Text-analysis readings, when documented, can be re-run by others. An interpretation that is presented through hermeneutica, so that it can be tried again, checked, and played with, is going to be more rhetorically convincing whether or not one believes in the certainty of science. It is convincing because readers can draw their own conclusions by playing with the evidence. It may be difficult to formalize interpretations so that they can be modeled with computers, but, insofar as one can try to formalize some claims for replay, doing so give readers a new view on your interpretation.

Digital analytics facilitate interpretive negotiation in new ways. Text analysis can enlarge a dialogue by providing formalizations for negotiation. If you check my interpretation and disagree with my claims, you can criticize the analysis, the choice of texts, the techniques applied, and the interpretations of results—something you can't do if my interpretation is based on anecdotal quotes or on implied authority. The interpretive humanities are motivated not by a desire to prove things and move on but by a desire to renew understandings through conversations with the text and with others about the text. Text analysis as an interpretive practice is about an ongoing conversation about the text, but with the artifice of computing.

Computer-assisted text analysis is an imaginative practice that makes use of information technology. You could, like Cleanthes, accuse us of being too imaginative in our distortion of the text (and, for that matter, our distortion of interpretation). To many people, text analysis seems an unnatural practice that is not warranted by texts that are written to be read, not processed (though of course the processing can lead to new texts to be read). Likewise, visualizations can be imaginative but unintuitive and unfamiliar in comparison with reading texts. Critics of analytics call for a definitive proof of the value of hermeneutica in the form of an interesting and original contributions to scholarship made possible by computers. Needless to say, nothing satisfies such critics. Examples don't satisfy, just as Philo can't answer the challenge of excessive imagination, because a conclusion that can be reached only through computer-assisted interpretation will be too artificial to be interesting to a computer sceptic and because if such an interpretation it is believable anyway then the role of computing can be dismissed. That leaves only spectacle, but humanists are generally suspicious of the spectacle of visualization and poorly trained to deal with it.

Conclusion

In this chapter we have tried to show that interpretations do not stand alone such that they could be unambiguous champions for one method or another. Interpretations are influential to the extent that they are inscribed into dialogues valued in the humanities. We have to pay attention to how analytics and visualizations become part of the practices of interpretation and discourse about texts not only in the academic literature but also in data-driven journalism. That visualization and analysis are now part of computer-mediated discourse is no longer in doubt. Perhaps we should pay attention to them now.

In *Reading Machines* (2011b), Stephen Ramsay writes about how text analysis can deform a text, presenting different readings that provoke thought. We have made similar to points about text-analysis tools presenting new views that support reading (Rockwell 2003a; Sinclair 2003). Hermeneutica synthesize artificial views onto the text that encourage a reader to read it differently. The computer is a modeling tool for developing these different views, many of which are playful and a few of which are artful. The practice of text analysis is thus one of re-reading a text in different ways with the assistance of computers that make it practicable to ask formalized questions and to get back artificial views. This process can be a dialogue of sorts, enhanced by the hermeneutical tools we build. Like the artifice of Philo's imaginative arguments, text analysis can enliven the dialogue one has with a text, which is at the heart of the humanities.

Perhaps we do text analysis just because these toys are available to us, much as Philo teased Cleanthes about God because he could do it. Ultimately, using computers to aid in analysis is in part an ethical decision in the sense that it is a decision on how to act as a scholar. On that, like Philo, we remain silent for the moment.

11 Agile Hermeneutics and the Conversation of the Humanities

Richard Sumner:

The purpose of this machine, of course, is to free the worker …

Bunny Watson:

You can say that again …

Sumner:

… to free the worker from the routine and repetitive tasks and liberate his time for more important work. For example, you see all those books there … and the ones up there? Well, every fact in them has been fed into Emmy. What do you have there?

Operator:

This is *Hamlet*.

Boss:

That's *Hamlet*?

Operator:

Yes, the entire text.

Sumner:

In code, of course. … Now, these little cards create electronic impulses which are accepted and retained by the machine so that in the future, if anyone calls up and wants a quotation from *Hamlet*, the research worker types it into the machine here, Emmy goes to work, and the answer comes out here.[1]

In 1957, the same year in which Paul Tasman published "Literary Data Processing," the movie *Desk Set*, with Katherine Hepburn as Bunny Watson and Spencer Tracy as Richard Sumner, made comedy of the research potential of computers. The movie, based on William Marchant's play *The Desk Set*, has Sumner introducing computers into a broadcasting company to automate payroll and to speed up question answering in the research department run by Bunny Watson. In the scene transcribed above, Sumner shows the boss and visitors what the computer (nicknamed Emmy, short for EMERAC) can do; Watson comments ironically. Watson is rightly concerned about the computer replacing her staff in the research department, though Emmy turns out to have been designed not to replace her researchers but to assist them.

Desk Set, the last of a series of romantic comedies that featured Hepburn and Tracy, dealt with a very real concern: that computers were going to put people, especially, women out of work. The line between freeing people for more important work and freeing women of a job was being negotiated in the workplace, in the news, and in movies such as *Desk Set*.

The present book has been about a similar negotiation, currently taking place in the humanities, about how we are to weave computing into our practices—especially the interpretation of texts, one of the central activities of the humanities. While recognizing that computing changes how we enter into dialogue with others, we have taken the position that it can fit into our practices; it can assist without replacing interpretation. We propose hermeneutica as a type of computing tool that can be flexibly integrated into existing research methods while offering new interpretations in the sense of new interventions. This concluding chapter is about how hermeneutica can be woven into our traditions of practice and how they can modulate the conversation of the humanities. To understand how hermeneutica could be woven into our traditions of practice, we need a working model for the humanities. In proposing such a model, we start from the view that the humanities can be characterized as a dialogue across time, a conversation that goes on both with others and with ourselves.[2]

Hermeneutica and Dialogue

How do hermeneutica fit in the conversation of the humanities? One place to look for answers is in the works of Plato, a masterly writer of dialogue. In the dialogue *Phaedrus*, Socrates discusses innovative information technology: writing. He tells the story of a conversation in which the Promethean Theuth presents writing as a tool for wisdom only to have his invention critiqued by the philosopher-judge Thamus:

This, said Theuth, will make the Egyptians wiser and give them better memories; it is a specific both for the memory and for the wit. Thamus replied: O most ingenious Theuth, the parent or inventor of an art is not always the best judge of the utility or inutility of his own inventions to the users of them. And in this instance, you who are the father of letters, from a paternal love of your own children have been led to attribute to them a quality which they cannot have; for this discovery of yours will create forgetfulness in the learners' souls, because they will not use their memories; they will trust to the external written characters and not remember of themselves[3]

In this story of a dialogue in a dialogue, Theuth presents writing as an invention that will help our memory and thus make us wiser. In response, Thamus reflects on the technology and its justification (though it is not clear that he tried it, which might explain why no one, even Plato, listened to him). Thamus then makes an interesting meta-theoretical move. Theorizing about the relationship between developers and their developments, he compares it to parenthood. He opines that inventors are not the best judges of their inventions, because, like parents, they are biased. However, both Socrates (in the dialogue) and Plato (in writing it) understand that proclaiming a judgment about a technology such as writing probably isn't sufficient to change someone's mind. If you want to change someone's mind, you must interact with him:

Writing, Phaedrus, has this strange quality, and is very like painting; for the creatures of painting stand like living beings, but if one asks them a question, they preserve a solemn silence. And so it is with written words; you might think they spoke as if they had intelligence, but if you question them, wishing to know about their sayings, they always say only one and the same thing. And every word, when once it is written, is bandied about, alike among those who understand and those who have no interest in it, and it knows not to whom to speak or not to speak; when ill-treated or unjustly reviled it always needs its father to help it; for it has no power to protect or help itself.[4]

In earlier chapters of this book, we discussed how the rhetorical potential of hermeneutica lies in their interactivity. It would be easy to claim that hermeneutica make possible a real dialogue with a text—something that Socrates felt was missing by definition. We could argue that analytical toys bring the dead corpus to life, as Dr. Frankenstein brought dead flesh to life, so that it could become a companion in interaction. There is a way in which we talk about the intense reading of an author as a dialogue by analogy, but if it is a conversation then it is a conversation, within the reader, with an imagined author.

Though it is true that text-analysis tools can help you ask questions of a text, and that they can provide responses of a sort, this asking of questions is merely dialogue by analogy, and the responses are not of the same nature as one gets in dialogue with other humans. The responses are a rearrangement of the text, or a hybrid representation. In using text-analysis tools you are no more entering into a dialogue with the inanimate text than you are by just having the book before you. Both the book and the tool, as we have seen, are technologies that you can use to animate an inner dialogue such as the one Smith added to his article "Computer Criticism."

There are, however, two ways in which hermeneutica can assist the dialogue of research. In Plato's *Phaedrus*, Socrates illustrates his point about writing by engaging Phaedrus in a discussion that is more effective than telling stories about the judgment of writing. Likewise, Plato's *Phaedrus* illustrates the effectiveness of dialogue by showing how Socrates uses it to greater effect than the written speeches Phaedrus was initially fascinated by. But Socrates' story is not a dialogue; rather, it is a *story of* a dialogue. Plato's written dialogue is, likewise, a story of different practices (writing and conversation) and their effectiveness. Both are ways of showing conversations. Obviously Socrates and Plato feel that there is a role for stories and writings, and that role is to represent discussion.

Stories and writings may not be dialogue, but they can be deployed within dialogue, along with a rich array of other moves that provide fodder for conversation. Hermeneutica are woven into dialogue as demonstrative tools for showing things we want to talk about rather than keeping the computing in the basement. Thamus' worry that these things will be "bandied about, alike among those who understand and those who have no interest" still applies. Hermeneutica, like other artifacts of interpretation, can be woven into research conversation (i.e. scholarship), becoming the very subject of discussion, not just tools for enhancing dialogue.

Thamus makes the interesting move of stepping back and discussing how one should judge technology when it is brought before one. Text analysis, text mining, and visualizations are not found the dialogue, but they are what we should talk about now that they are before us. At a time when surveillance being done by the National Security Agency and other governmental and corporate analytic projects are being discussed in public, the humanities should be contribute to the ongoing dialogue. We should make the meta-theoretic move that Thamus made and assert the importance of judging the value of information technologies, whether or not anyone will listen to us. In the humanities we have a tradition of discussing interpretation and misinterpretation, of asking how technologies can be used appropriately or misused, especially technologies of the word. Now is the time for us in the Digital Humanities (and beyond) to be engaged in the critical use and interpretation of these analytical tools. More than anyone, we know how they fail and need to remind people of their particular limits, especially when used outside of active hermeneutical traditions that ask about how they work. In short, like Thamus, those working in the Digital Humanities are positioned to make the move to creative and critical engagement with analytical and visual text tools.

Hermeneutica in the Research Cycle

This brings us to pragmatic question of how Voyant and other text-analysis tools fit into the traditions of research practices of the humanities if they cannot really be said to animate a dialogue. How can they be used to represent our conceptual models for research, and how can we stand back and interpret the tools? This brings us back to the issue of method. How could hermeneutica fit into the methods of humanists, and how could we talk about them? How would Descartes have used Voyant if he had been persuaded to try? How would he have engaged Voyant to understand the challenges of large-scale interpretation? The problem with answering questions about method is that we humanists don't have formal methods that describe what we do or what we should do; what we have are the stories told by the likes of Plato and Descartes. In fact, we are suspicious of method as method, and we worry that methods carry intellectual baggage of which we should be critical. Much as we feel a need to be sceptical even of skepticism, we might like to find some way to deconstruct all methods—and even un-methods such as deconstruction. Alas, this distaste for method also means that, instead of formal methods openly described, we humanists have practices (rarely discussed) that are closer to the precepts for thinking in the face of uncertainty that Descartes set out in his discourse.

Humanists' aversion to method has been discussed before. John Unsworth (2005) commented on the lack of formal methods and how that lack makes it hard for DH to imagine new methods or new tools for old methods. He noted that research in the humanities is idealized as a solitary and private practice, as Descartes imagined it. The practices that actually exist can be described, but because they aren't formalized it is difficult to draw conclusions about their epistemological commitments or about the place of tools in them.

For our purposes, a model of the life cycle of a research project is sufficient to identify where researchers could and are using tools. The model we propose is loosely based on our experience and on research about research activities in the humanities. In particular, we have drawn on a report titled "Scholarly Work in the Humanities and the Evolving Information Environment" (Brockman et al. 2001) and on John Bradley's work on *Pliny*. Our model for digital scholarship is primarily meant to show the possible roles of various tools. Taking the *project* as the emblem for what we do, we simplify the process into four phases.

Wide Browsing

The first phase, *Wide Browsing*, is the wandering, general reading, and browsing that researchers do outside of particular projects. This includes browsing shelves in bookstores and reading blogs and journals in one's field. It is reading that is not purposeful in the sense that it is not aimed at a particular outcome. Generally researchers don't take extensive notes or record such reading, though they might set interesting works aside. This is the reading we do for "fun" and breadth. This is the space for serious play. It is also often woven into teaching, conferences, and other social activities and therefore prone to the errors of influence Descartes fled the city to avoid. Many kinds of tools exist to support such serendipitous browsing, including the *New York Review of Books*, Digg, and Google. For that matter, bookstores and libraries could be considered technologies that support browsing.

Gathering and Note Taking

The second phase, *Gathering and Note Taking*, starts when a researcher conceives of a project and begins to gather materials for it. Projects may be provoked by some external invitation to give a talk or by an insight gleaned in reading. Here wide reading for pleasure shifts to more purposeful activity that includes thinking about an end, both in the sense of an end to the project and in the sense of a publication or some other outcome. With a project in mind and a frame in hand, we begin to collect materials and document those materials for later reference. There are many kinds of note-taking tools and reference management tools, among them index cards and bibliographic management tools such as Zotero. John Bradley's Pliny is an important attempt to prototype how note-taking tools can be enhanced with analytics.

Writing and Thinking

The third phase, *Writing and Thinking,* is particular to fields in the humanities in which writing is a way of externalizing thought rather than simply reporting on a project. Writing and thinking through (meta thinking about) writing happen in a project when the researcher shifts to activities aimed at inscribing a sharable or publishable outcome. It could be the writing of a paper proposal for review and then a conference paper. It could be the writing of a paper for publication or the preparation of a PowerPoint deck. Once there is an anticipated outcome, and often a deadline, the activities of the research change to support a specific writing project. Often gathering and note taking stop in a late-night rush to complete a paper; the paper itself becomes the holder of new ideas. Often the specificity of the writing narrows what is gathered and noted. Once you are writing, you only need to read stuff that supports your paper. Most important, for humanists writing is a thinking-through. Obviously thinking happens throughout the cycle, but in the humanities it is when you are writing about something for others that you project your thoughts outside yourself so as to reflect on what you think you want to say. You enter into a dialogue with yourself before an imaginary audience of peers, and you decide what you think should say. This is when you are forced to think through and analyze all the gathered evidence, judging your children (to echo the *Pheadrus*). In other disciplines the writing is more reporting, but in the humanities the writing is a creative reflection and transformation of research. And again, there are tools that support this, including the note-taking tools that represent information during the writing and the word processors with which we write.

Sharing and Publishing

Finally, there is a phase of closing down the project. A projects is, by definition, an activity that has an end. *Sharing and Publishing* includes all the work we as scholars have to do once the writing is more or less finished and we concentrate on sharing the ideas in various ways, including publishing it. This is when we try to contribute our intervention to the larger conversation in some concrete way, through a journal or online. To some extent sharing happens at all phases; humanists may read and write alone, but they informally share ideas broadly by means of email, at symposia, and at conferences. Publication is a more formal sharing in which the original research is submitted to some sort of scrutiny (including peer review), we end up editing it as we get comments, checking page proofs, or we have to rewrite it if it is rejected. This last phase is often the most time consuming and often not considered research at all but rather a necessary part of the drudgery of publishing in order to have your thoughts entered into a more permanent record so that others might engage them years later. All sorts of publishing tools exist to support this last phase, including online journal frameworks such as Open Journal Systems and generic tools for publishing on the Web.

Needless to say, real research is not so paced or linear. We call this a research cycle because during or after each project is completed another research project might emerge and it is from reading how others respond to our projects that new cycles start. After publication, a researcher may turn again to broad reading, or another researcher may be inspired to respond to the publication with his or her own project, creating a cycle of conversation that characterizes our research culture.

Analytics

The hermeneutic model presented above is just that—a model or a simulacrum that we want to manipulate to see where tools can fit. Of course real research is much messier, but this model is meant to be something like the "scientific method" in that it is an ideal progress that compromises detail for clarity. Where do hermeneutica fit?

Analytical tools are traditionally described as a fitting in the second and third phases. Analytical tools allow you to gather a large corpus so as to be able to search it when writing. We can think of it as gathering on a large scale for searching. Analytical tools are presented as tools that can speed up the asking of questions such as "Where does Plato write about writing?" After investing time in developing a computer-searchable corpus, you get in return something that helps your memory even better than just writing. Writing meant that you didn't have to memorize; text-analysis tools mean that you can handle much larger corpora and can find things even faster than by re-reading. At some point the speed of searching and the ability to create concordances allow you to explore the language of an author or a time. (This was Father Busa's point about concordances: They can be used for philological thinking that tries to enter sympathetically into dialogue with a different time that uses language differently.)

But analytics can fit into humanities scholarship in other ways. As we saw in earlier chapters, Etienne Brunet and John B. Smith have other ideas about how analytical tools can be used. Smith specifically designed ARRAS so that it could be used alongside writing as a tool for thinking through structures in a text. He also experimented with visualizations that allowed him to explore the text in radically different ways that again, encourage asking different questions of a text and thinking differently about it. He then shared static graphs in publications as a way of letting readers explore.

Voyant takes a further step in that it is designed to directly integrate into the Sharing and Publishing phase. Assuming that more and more publications will be shared online we provide a way for results to be carried through from the Writing and Thinking phase to the Sharing phase. Results can be shared as interactive panels or as hermeneutical toys embedded in online interventions. The hermeneutica cease to be just tools to assist in representing for thinking and become an interpretation that can be shared so that others can recapitulate your analysis. Such hermeneutica leave the solitary study and become something that aids interpretation and that can be shared for interpretation itself. When shared, the hermeneutica themselves become objects for study, as opposed to transparent tools that are difficult to interpret or the hidden ad hoc code we don't share for interpretation. We work with technologies as a way of also thinking about them; we then make hermeneutica available for others when they are Wide Browsing. Hermeneutica are designed to travel in different ways through the entire research cycle; they are analytical tools that can be encountered at every stage of what we do as humanists in a digital age. This book is the story of that travel.

There is another way in which tools can fit into this research cycle if one doesn't think of it in Cartesian terms as a solitary practice. In chapter 1 we described the practice that we call Agile Hermeneutics—a practice of team interpretation in which we both interpret and make the tools we need to interpret. This practice makes a virtue of the use of hermeneutica both as tools that represent *for* thinking and as tools *about* which we think. This practice is what this jointly authored book tries to illustrate, though not as a dialogue.

Unlike Descartes, and unlike all those humanists who want to escape the other, we believe that research can start with others. Agile Hermeneutics starts with the assumption that you will work with others rather than alone. AH is not about freeing yourself of the errors of others, but about practicing research with others while thinking about how to do it. AH doesn't limit its engagement to reporting back after thinking as if research were about black boxes (solitary researchers) thinking alone and then messaging through publications as if scholarship was like the model of communication that Claude Shannon made popular. Rather, if you start in dialogue, the research phases discussed above become negotiated and talked through. If you work in teams, you can have one person interpreting a text while the other looks over his shoulder and asks about the interpretation itself and the tools of interpretation. As in Socrates' story of invention, we play Thamus and Theuth, inventing and judging, but we alternate roles. We would like to say this is a new way of doing research, but of course it is not new at all, it is just overlooked. The history of thought is full of stories like those of Plato that describe research in communion with others. One wonders why it seems so novel to the humanities that groups of people can think together in informal conversations, symposia, or structured groups. We suspect that we have inherited a Renaissance idea of genius according to which one person has to be credited with all the work, and that this has been encoded into our professional structures for recognizing the origins of ideas and allotting credit, but that is another story. What matters here is curing method (generally) of its solipsism.

The Rhetoric of Analytical Failure

For a long time computing humanists complained that computer-assisted criticism couldn't escape from the ghetto of specialist periodicals to the mainstream of literary dialogue.[5] In view of the attention the Digital Humanities have received from the likes of Stanley Fish in the last five years, that is clearly no longer true. This attention should be welcome after the long years of having no discernible impact on literary and textual studies, especially since digital humanists have, on a few occasions, promised funders that digital tools or methods would be transformative if funded. Attention doesn't mean that analytics are now woven into the conversation as we wish they were. There is, in fact, a minor industry in the Digital Humanities of bemoaning our lack of influence and speculating about what we should be doing. That began in 1966 with the very first issue of *Computers in the Humanities*, in which Louis Milic, in a paper titled "The Next Step," wrote:

We are still not thinking of the computer as anything but a myriad of clerks or assistants in one convenient console. ... We do not yet understand the true nature of the computer. And we have not yet begun to think in ways appropriate to the nature of this machine.[6]

In 2003, John Unsworth rightly noted in a paper titled "Tool-Time, or 'Haven't We Been Here Already?'" that we keep circling around tool development and disciplinary impact to the point that "this sense of *déjà vu* is particularly keen when it comes to tool-building for humanities computing." Unsworth then proposed yet another diagnosis and another solution—a solution that led to the MONK Project.[7] Willard McCarty, in a series of lectures given at the University of Alberta in 2010, used this failure as a starting point for thinking about the "wider historical context in which computing has developed, multiplied, spread and interpenetrated our imaginations."[8] McCarty's project asks larger questions about our hopes and anxieties with regard to computing, including what we might expect it to do for literary studies and how we should always be sceptical of computing.

Fortunately for computer-assisted text analysis, things are changing and failure is not about being ignored by mainstream scholarship. As we move away from scientific models for the discipline where analytics are meant to prove things, DH has begun to accept productive failure as a part of the learning curve. Both Unsworth and McCarty have noted the value of failure in the Digital Humanities (though not in the context of tools). Unsworth (1997) calls for digital humanists at this critical stage in the rapid evolution of electronic textuality to document their failures, along with their successes, for posterity. We can learn much from failure, though we may want to learn from the failure of others but not to admit our own.

For the same reasons of productive failure, it is important to document experiments with tools. McCarty, in *Humanities Computing* (2005), theorizes that failure is how we learn from computing. If what we do is model phenomena formally with computing, we do that to discover the limitations of our formalizations, and thereby learn about the anomalous, the ineffable, and the details that always escape formalization. Just as interpretation never ends satisfied that nothing more can be said about a text, so digital experimentation and modeling should never be satisfied that they have succeeded in completely mapping something. Failure is often the way forward, and digital representations will never exhaust the originals, though they can be confused for the originals.

Thomas Corns recognized the more playful and poetic uses of analytics, suggesting that "opening a text by way of text processing may be singularly timely, replacing the reproachful 'So what?' rejoinder to quantitative approaches with the more stimulating 'What if … ?'"[9] Playful text-analysis experiments that don't claim to prove things through pseudo-scientific quantification are less likely to fail by their own standards, though they may fail by the standards of toys.

Perhaps the rhetoric of failure and success is the source of the melancholy and deeply humane features of the Digital Humanities. After all, complaining that all that came before misunderstands the phenomena is as old as grant writing and may be as old as the humanities. How many grant proposals tell a story that starts with a problem which funding can cure? How many philosophers start afresh, discarding all previous work, as Descartes did, in order to not introduce error? How many people, when judging a technology as Thamus did, end up saying something patronizing to the effect of "You may be fond of your invention, but you can't judge it, and I can; and I find it wanting"?

The temptation to see only limits in technology is the other side of an orientation toward what technology will become. It is in the nature of the present-day culture of technology to be perpetually focused on the potential of the next future technology rather than satisfied with what we have. A certain dissatisfaction with the tools available is understandable, because they suggest what could be. Every time we teach Voyant, we are asked for more features, not because Voyant has few features, but because participants can imagine what they could do in original ways. It would be impossible for any one project or hermeneutica to satisfy everyone. A scholar using hermeneutica starts building his or her own rather than complaining that the work of others is limiting, and that building-on is a way forward for DH. It is therefore not surprising that many digital humanists advocate learning to program so that algorithmic interpreters can always go beyond the inevitable limitations of what already exists. The time has come to turn from complaining to understanding the history of building as part of the history of computer-assisted interpretation.

We should also be sceptical of some forms of discourses of failure, especially those that promise solutions that are not in our traditions of ongoing dialogue, such as big tool projects that promise to end all projects, so that humanists need not bother themselves with engineering. Whenever we hear someone calling on humanists to stop "re-inventing wheels" and get behind a project that purportedly will end all fiddling by humanists with developing tools, we worry that this is really a call to shut down a form of re-interpretation in the humanities or to exclude humanists from engaging in the tools that bear method. Would we ask people to stop re-interpreting Plato because it has been done before? No, the whole point of the humanities is encouraging people to think and interpret for themselves as an ongoing discipline of keeping ideas animated. It is not about settling questions; it is about unsettling people in order to re-engage them in conversation. If we want to understand the potential effects of big data and analytics, we should experiment publicly and encourage others to do so. This is far too important to leave to software engineers; these are the very tools of interpretation.

Returning to the question of failure, we should add that there has been a change, noted in previous chapters, in the impact of DH in general and in that of text analysis in particular. The attention that the DH is getting at meetings of the Modern Language Association, the attention that large-scale literary-historical work by Moretti and Jockers is getting, and the criticism from Fish have exposed more and more people to digital methods and results. Analytics are everywhere in the news. The *New York Times* and the *Guardian* now routinely weave analytics and toys for interpreting texts into their news on the Web. The *Guardian* has made this an explicit feature of its approach to the news by hosting a Datablog and a Data Store; the latter allows readers to play with data or to download data to try in their own tools.[10] Voyant gets more than 40,000 visits a month and hundreds of thousands of invocations of the underlying tools. The Text Encoding Initiative, Zotero, and Omeka are used even more widely.

The question is no longer "Why is no one paying attention?" Now the question is "How can the audience interested in agile co-development be responsibly engaged?" Now that text analysis is no longer a backwater, we have to ask how we in the humanities should engage an audience beyond those who show up at our conferences. What sort of a conversation should we have about these tools of knowledge and surveillance? Open and documented research tools such as Voyant are one type of response that puts the tools of interpretation into your hands to interpret. Another response may be the development of traditions and schools that maintain traditions of interpretation.

We think the perception of impact has been biased toward theory in the humanities. As we pointed out in chapter 9 about Stanley Fish's fishing for theory, it is wrong to measure impact in terms of theory books. The impact of the Digital Humanities should be digital. When we look at the proliferation of analytics in the popular media and in work being done in the humanities, we see signs that they have become part of the public and literary conversation.

Addendum

But we get too enthusiastic and too fond of our developments. By way of a sobering afterthought, we leave you with the difficult challenge before the humanities: the challenge of busy-ness. Heidegger aptly captured the postwar transformation of the academy from an institution in support of scholarship to one manufacturing research. In "The Age of the World Picture" he characterized the life of the busy researcher:

The decisive unfolding of the character of modern science as constant activity produces, therefore, a human being of another stamp. The scholar disappears and is replaced by the researcher engaged in research programs. These, and not the cultivation of scholarship, are what places his work at the cutting edge. The researcher no longer needs a library at home. He is, moreover, constantly on the move. He negotiates at conferences and collects information at congresses.

From an inner compulsion, the researcher presses forward into the sphere occupied by the figure of, in the essential sense, the technologist. Only in this way can he remain capable of being effective, and only then, in the eyes of his age, is he real. Alongside him, an increasingly thinner and emptier romanticism of scholarship and the university will still be able to survive for some time at certain places.[11]

Heidegger could have been talking about the busy digital humanist. At the risk of clairvoyance, the challenge to the Digital Humanities will not be to find a place for hermeneutica or other forms of building; it will be to deal with the illusion of busy success as we get funded, noticed, copied, and critiqued. And it will get even worse when the party is over and the Digital Humanities are the old new thing. Then, tempted to join or remain in the frenzy, demarcate boundaries of belonging, and commit the same sins of pride we disliked in the traditions we came from, we will just get busier. We worry about being let in and letting others in; that is another form of busy-ness, as are many other anxieties. Let us try to remain agile in our interpretation, open in our discipline, and attentive to what matters. Let us make miniature trains for the mind that go somewhere interesting and then document their limitations.

Notes

Chapter 1

1. Descartes. *Discourse on Method* (2006), part 2, p. 12.

2. See Deegan and McCarty 2012.

3. The online version is available at http://hermeneuti.ca.

4. "Now Analyze That!" is included in print in this book as chapter 6. An interactive online version is available at http://hermeneuti.ca/now-analyze-that.

5. We use the word "skeptic" to represent the school of philosophy, as in "the dispute between the Skeptics and Dogmatists is entirely verbal." We use the word "sceptic" to represent individuals and their beliefs.

6. On Descartes' method of analytical reflection, see Miles 2008.

7. See http://hermeneutic.ca for links to the texts we used, the tools, and our notes.

8. The full title of the *Discourse* is *A Discourse on the Method of Correctly Conducting One's Reason and Seeking Truth in the Sciences*. As was mentioned above, Descartes' "method" is different from, though closely related to, his story of how he went about correcting his thinking until it led to the method. It is only in the three appendixes to the *Discourse* that you get results from Descartes' method. They are the case studies showing how his method could be employed scientifically.

9. Collaborative research is a new phenomenon in the humanities that is often dealt with by assigning percentages to the final outcomes as if writing a paper collaboratively were simply a division of labor ("I wrote that part worth 30 percent, and she wrote the remaining 70 percent"). For more on this, see The Evaluation of Digital Work, a wiki maintained by the Modern Language Association (http://wiki.mla.org/index.php/Evaluation_Wiki).

10. McCarty 2005, p. 81.

11. There is something comedic about the strange pairs of computer science student programmers and senior scholars that do many humanities computing projects. Humanities computing attempts to bridge the mismatch of backgrounds, age, and interests.

12. For an introduction to Extreme Programming, see Beck 2000 or Auer and Miller 2002.

13. Shore and Warden 2007, pp. 76–77.

14. For information about PRORA, see Glickman and Staalman 1966. For information about TACT (Text Analysis Computing Tools), see http://projects.chass. utoronto.ca/tact/. For information about TAPoR, see http://tapor.ca.

15. McCarty 2007, p. 1.

16. Development as a form of research is common in the design field (Galey and Ruecker 2009).

17. Voyant Tools is available at http://voyant-tools.org. It was previously found under the name Voyeur. Many of our experiments were conducted with the earlier version.

18. For Voyant documentation see, http://docs.voyant-tools.org.

19. See http://docs.voyant-tools.org/resources/run-your-own/voyant-server/.

20. For a more in-depth examination of dialogue, see Rockwell 2003b.

21. Xenophon 1968, 4.5.12.

22. For more on this, see http://wo.ala.org/gbs/ or http://www.googlebooksettlement. com/.

23. One computing humanist who anticipated this issue of scale was Greg Crane. See Crane 2006.

24. According to Lyman and Varian (2003), about 5 exabytes of new print, film, magnetic, and optical information were produced in 2002, a number that increases by 30 percent or more a year. Of this only a small amount—a mere 1,634 petabytes— is print, but consider that 2 petabytes is sufficient to represent all the academic research libraries in the United States. Most of this print information is office documents: in 2003, North Americans were consuming 11,916 sheets of paper per person, and Lyman and Varian estimated that half of that was used in printers and copiers for office documents. (A petabyte is 10^{12} bytes.)

26. Lyman and Varian 2003.

27. See http://www.emc.com/leadership/digital-universe/iview/big-data-2020.htm.

28. See http://cautbulletin.ca/default.asp?SectionID=0&SectionName=&VolID=34&
VolumeName=No%205&VolumeStartDate=May%2018,%202007&EditionID=
7&EditionName=Vol%2054&EditionStartDate=January%2009,%202007&
ArticleID=0.

29. Quoted, with permission, from a course blog maintained by Garry Wong at the
University of Alberta in 2009.

30. McCarty 2005, 81.

31. On connoisseurship one might compare two articles from *Artibus et Historiae*. In
"Connoisseurship: The Penalty of Ahistoricism" (1988), Gary Schwartz argues that
connoisseurship is ahistorical as it is based on characteristics of the object itself and
therefore can't tell us much about the history of production of a work. In "Connoisseurship as Practice" (1988), David Ebitz argues for connoisseurship as the tacit craft
knowledge of the physical artifact that resists linguistic expression. In either case the
connoisseur's knowledge is the human equivalent to a black box—it is opaque to
the receiver.

32. In humanities computing, as John Unsworth points out (2003), we keep on proposing new tool projects that will eventually make it easy enough for humanists to
use analytics (and thereby transform interpretation). We are of the view the problem
is deeper and involves a change in interpretive culture that has to start with rhetorically effective examples using analytics. People will not use the tools if they can't
imagine what they would say with them.

33. We have argued for some time that text-analysis tools should be designed to
assist reading. In "Computer-Assisted Reading: Reconceiving Text Analysis" (2003),
Stéfan Sinclair argued that "by thinking more about process than outcomes, about
multiplying meanings (not data) rather than converging on answers, we can consider how to make the computer an extension of reading and interpretive practices
in which humanists are *already* engaged."

34. As the readership of *Computers and the Humanities* and *Literary and Linguistic
Computing* attests, there is an audience interested in technique. Perhaps text analysis
is destined to be a specialized domain really of interest only to those interested in
textual computing. Perhaps we should give up pretensions of addressing the needs
of all the unwashed out there and do pure research. Nonetheless, the challenge
should be to make these tools more widely accessible.

35. To a certain extent this is a limitation of the economics of the scholarly journal
article and monograph, which rarely include the long appendixes needed to fully
explain a method and document the data. The costs of printing and the awkward-
ness of such appendixes discourage printing everything needed for a reader to recapitulate an experiment. In the hypertext environment of the Web, these appendixes
can be included at no extra cost.

36. See Moretti 2013a, 154.

37. See http://monk.library.illinois.edu/ and Clement 2008.

38. See Shaftesbury 1963, p. 132. The original passage reads: "For here (in dialogue) the author is annihilated, and the reader, being no way applied to, stands for nobody. The self-interesting parties both vanish at once."

39. See Harpham 2006.

40. See Hayles 1990.

41. Instructions on how to contribute are available at http://hermeneuti.ca/contribute.

42. See http://docs.voyant-tools.org.

43. On TAPoR, see http://tapor.ca.

Chapter 2

1. Powers 1996, p. 326.

2. For an accessible introduction to Artificial Intelligence, see chapter 5 of Floridi 1999. Alternatively, see Oppy and Dowe 2011.

3. Kenny 1992, p. 1.

4. One could argue that computers such as the ENIAC were used first to solve numeric problems, and that only later were textual applications developed. Thus the computer may be said to have been developed for quantitative purposes. This, however, ignores the Colossus and other early computers developed for cryptanalysis of strings. See http://en.wikipedia.org/wiki/Colossus_computer.

5. A string can also be a ring of characters that has no beginning or end, but that is a less common form of string.

6. See http://en.wikipedia.org/wiki/UTF-8.

7. It actually gets even more complicated. You can define a character as what we humans consider a return, but it is up to the programmers to make sure the computer actually outputs to the screen, or to a printer, something like a carriage return that would create a new paragraph. A character set is aspirational, connecting a binary code to a human definition of the glyph that you hope programmers will make appear as intended.

8. If your characters are meant as instructions for a typewriter-like printer, you need two characters to create a new paragraph. (This is the standard in Windows, though Mac and Linux both use single characters to indicate new lines.) First you need the "line feed" to roll the paper up a line; then you need the "return" that moves the

print head to the beginning of the blank line. Take a look at the control characters in ASCII at http://en.wikipedia.org/wiki/ASCII#ASCII_control_characters.

9. Obviously you failed; otherwise you wouldn't be reading this note. Now think about how much you know tacitly about using endnotes and other textual features that make these paper machines we call books work so smoothly. What would it take to build an AI that would know all that?

10. See http://www.tei-c.org.

11. Encoding text is a complex art. We recommend that people new to it take a course or start with some tutorials such as those gathered by the TEI at http://www.tei-c.org/Support/Learn/tutorials.xml.

12. See http://hermeneuti.ca/finding-preparing-text.

13. Microsoft and some other companies have developed ways of adding formatting information of all sorts to plain old strings. When Word saves a file to a hard drive, it saves not only a sequence of characters but also formatting information about those characters. You can search by formatting in Word. I could, for example, search for the characters in the Zapf Dingbats font that I used above to illustrate how computers can't read. For text analysis, however, you typically don't want that information mixed in with the words being analyzed.

14. Escape characters are fundamental to how we can layer more and more information using simple character sets. You might ask what we do if we actually want a < in the text. In XML we use another escape character, &, with quotation marks around it, to indicate special entities such as characters otherwise used as escapes: < is then encoded as "<" (lt standing for "less than").

15. For a good humanist introduction to regular expressions, see Stephen Ramsay's "Using Regular Expressions" (available at http://solaris-8.tripod.com/regexp.pdf).

16. Adapted from the synonyms provided by http://thesaurus.com.

17. John Kirk and some other linguists talk about the different types of words from the phonemic to the orthographic to the statistical. What counts as a word when you talk may not count as a word when you write. On how this affects the way we count with computers, see Kirk 2009.

18. For an accessible discussion of different senses of "word," see What Is a Word? (a working paper from the University of Sussex). Susan Hockey (2000, p. 52) also discusses this.

19. The notion of a word unit doesn't map well onto all languages. Tokenization is especially challenging in languages that have no word boundaries, such as Mandarin.

20. Voyant and some other tools will give you a measurement of vocabulary density by dividing the number of types by the number of tokens and multiplying that by 1,000. The higher the density, the more unique words there are (or the fewer words are used repeatedly). Type-token frequency is one of a number of measures of lexical richness or vocabulary richness that can have interesting applications. Ian Lancashire describes in *Forgetful Muses* (2010) how he and Graeme Hirst used various measures of lexical size and richness to study Alzheimer's-related dementia in the writing of Agatha Christie.

21. For a critique of the value of word clouds, see Harris 2011; for a fuller discussion of word clouds, see Friedman 2007.

22. A computer, of course, doesn't know the difference between a text and a collection of texts. However, it does know the difference between one text file and many text files concatenated. If you concatenate all of the individual plays of Shakespeare into one text file, a computer will treat it as one long string unless you have markup that can be interpreted by the computer to indicate the individual texts in the corpus.

23. For more on assisted reading, see Sinclair 2003.

24. See Orlandi 1997 (in Italian) or Orlandi 2002 (in English). Orlandi is one of the theoretical pioneers of humanities computing, but because he writes mostly in Italian he gets overlooked in English-speaking circles.

25. Though it is true the user can do that analytic and explorative work with text-analysis tools on texts with little or no previous formalization, the user is then dependent on the formalizations encoded into the system by the developers.

Chapter 3

1. See http://www.nytimes.com/ref/washington/20070123_STATEOFUNION.html.

2. For an article from *Wired* on what was called then the Search Inside the Book project, see Wolf 2003. That was one of the first big book-digitization projects, though it was not designed to provide full-text access so much as to help people find books they would want to buy.

3. For the Amazon Product Overview page for Douglas Hofstadter's book *Gödel, Escher, Bach*, see http://www.amazon.com/Godel-Escher-Bach-Eternal-Golden/dp/0465026567/. For the Concordance and Text Stats, see http://www.amazon.com/G%C3%B6del-Escher-Bach-Eternal-Golden/dp/sitb-next/0465026567/ref=sbx_con#concordance.

4. Howard-Hill 1979, p. 4.

5. For more on the concordance, see McCarty 1993.

6. Rouse and Rouse 1982, p. 212.

7. Ann Blair (2010, p. 59) talks about this type of reading as actually preceding what we now consider the normal "linear" way of reading novels: "Consultation reading existed amongst the learned in earlier centuries, and in an unbroken line of transmission at least as far back as the thirteenth century, so that the most distinctively new kind of reading in the eighteenth century was not consultation reading but rather engrossment in the novels that were a new and successful genre."

8. Exactly how Google generates its result pages when you search is a guarded secret, but an important ingredient is the PageRank algorithm that weights links into a page. (See http://en.wikipedia.org/wiki/PageRank.) Recently Google introduced Panda, a ranking algorithm that was trained by humans to better discriminate quality information. What is not hidden is the way Google synthesizes a concordance-like page of results for you.

9. McCarty 1993, p. 49.

10. For a discussion of the hermeneutical assumptions of stitched texts, see Rockwell 2001.

11. Burton 1982, p. 24.

12. See "Paul Tasman, Executive, 74" (obituary), *New York Times*, March 7, 1988. For a review of the *Index Thomisticus*, see Burton 1984. For Busa's story of the development of the *Index Thomisticus*, see Busa 1980. Here is how Busa describes his first encounter with Watson: "I knew, the day I was to meet Thomas J. Watson, Sr., that he had on his desk a report which said that IBM machines could never do what I wanted. I had seen in the waiting room a small poster imprinted with the words: 'The difficult we do right away; the impossible takes a little longer.' (IBM always loved slogans.) I took it with me into Mr. Watson's office. Sitting in front of him and sensing the tremendous power of his mind, I was inspired to say: "It is not right to say 'no' before you have tried." (p. 84) For more on the extraordinary process behind the *Index Thomisticus*, see Burton 1981a.

13. This project spanned the major shifts of the twentieth century in humanities research technology, having started with early punch-card technology aimed at print as the outcome, then evolving to publishing a CD-ROM for use on the computer, and finally ending up free on the Web. See the English version of the Web edition by Eduardo Bernot and Enrique Alarcón at http://www.corpusthomisticum.org/it/index.age.

14. Parrish 1959, p. vii. Parrish goes on to describe how the Arnold concordance was produced with the help of a computer: "This concordance was produced by an electronic computer, the IBM 704 Data Processing Machine. The lines of Arnold's verse, without punctuation, were punched on IBM cards, one line per card (this took one key-punch operator 69 hours)."

15. For more on punch cards, see Lubar 1992.

16. Howard-Hill (1979, p. 51) points out the connection between the development of the concordance and the KWIC: "The irony is that a general concordance programme (KWIC software) which was rewritten to facilitate special technical indexing is now widely used again, after special modification, for general concording of literary texts." Concording influenced the KWIC for technical indexing, which provided software tools that could be used by humanist concordancers experimenting with computing.

17. McCarty 1993, p. 57.

18. Fischer 1971, p. 122.

19. For more on the history of concording software, see Burton 1981c, Lancashire 1986, or Susan Hockey's chapter ("The History of Humanities Computing") in Schreibman et al. 2004.

20. In a lecture titled "Computer Applications in the Arts and Sciences" R. F. Churchhouse (1972) describes how, before leaving Chilton, he hired Hockey to work on literary research. "For the Arts people present," he writes, "I point out that Mrs. Hockey had no scientific training beyond O-level thus providing a counterexample to the idea that computers are only for scientists."

21. Howard-Hill 1979, p. 77.

22. Smith 1985, p. 1-1

23. Smith 1984, p. 20.

24. Ibid., p. 29.

25. Ibid., p. 20.

26. Ibid., p. 31.

27. Rheingold 1985.

28. Smith 1984, p. 21.

29. Brunet 1989.

30. Tompa 1996.

31. Before then, the ACH and the ALLC had held separate conferences. This joint conference survives today, now called DH.

32. CATMA (Computer Aided Text Markup and Analysis) is an attempt to create a modern equivalent to TACT. See http://www.catma.de/.

33. For more on this project, see Rockwell et al. "The Visual Concordance: The Design of Eye-ConTact" and "Eye-ConTact: Towards a New Design for Research Text Tools" at http://www.chass.utoronto.ca/epc/chwp/rockwell.

34. More recently T2K (Text to Knowledge) and SEASR provide a similar visual programming environment of what SEASR calls "itineraries." See http://alg.ncsa.uiuc.edu/do/tools/t2k and http://seasr.org.

35. Rockwell et al. 2010.

36. On the effectiveness of TACTweb, see Rockwell, Passmore, and Bradley 1997. The TAPoR Portal Recipes (which can be found at http://tada.mcmaster.ca/Main/TaporRecipes) were initially developed and reported on by Shawn Day, who was working with us. With support from SSHRC these are being generalized and extended to cover more tasks and to help with other tools at the Methods Commons (http://methodi.ca).

Chapter 4

1. Humanist Discussion Group, volume 15, no. 1 (www.digitalhumanities.org/humanist/Archives/Virginia/v15/0000.html).

2. This was more the case before the rise of an active community on Twitter.

3. Canadian Academies 2006, p. 10.

4. Pannapacker 2009.

5. Unsworth 2010.

6. Fish 2011, 2012a, 2012b.

7. This is the opening line of the "Welcome to Humanist" message of May 14, 1987. See http://www.digitalhumanities.org/humanist/Archives/Virginia/v01/8705.1324.txt.

8. Some of the limitations include the fact that it is often dominated by announcements and discussions initiated by its moderator, Willard McCarty. Another issue is the structure of the list messages. The common components can throw off text-analysis tools, as they appear with every message. There were also changes in the structure of the messages over time.

9. For more on the data preparation phase, see http://tada.mcmaster.ca/view/Main/HumanistArchives.

10. For glimpses of this debate, see Ramsay 2011a and Liu 2012.

11. For more on network analysis, see chapter 8 below.

12. Caution should be taken with such work. Stanford NER doesn't recognize all entities or all instances of those entities recognized. It has difficulty disambiguating who "he" or "she" refers to, it tends to look for capitalized names, it treats variant names of the same person as different people, and it can mis-categorize entities.

Chapter 5

1. In an online review titled "Talk Radio" (http://www.reverseshot.com/article/pontypool), Adam Nayman referred to *Pontypool* as a "semiotic zombie movie."

2. Willard McCarty, Humanist 21, no. 379.

3. Parunak 1981, p. 24.

4. Smith 1978, p. 343.

5. Smith 1973, p. 220.

6. Ibid., p. 223.

7. Ibid.

8. One might wonder whether, if he were working today, he would be likely to make his list available somewhere on the Web. See Smith 1973, p. 224.

9. Smith 1973, pp. 223–224.

10. If one wanted to recapitulate his precise imagery plot, one would need access to this axiomatic list, but it isn't provided and we don't have much to go on other than the number of words.

11. Smith 1973, p. 224.

12. Five hundred words is a commonly used chunk size corresponding roughly to the number of words on a page of the standard edition.

13. Smith 1973, p. 224.

14. If you find yourself exploring the graph and checking your interpretation of it against Smith's, you have already been sucked into the methodological assumptions giving them tacit assent.

15. Joyce 1968, p. 212.

16. Ibid.

17. Ibid., p. 213.

18. Ibid., p. 213.

19. In "The Visual Concordance: The Design of Eye-ConTact" (1998), Rockwell argues that visualizations function like concordances that bring into a new synthesis a collection of passages broken out from the original.

20. The FRANTEXT database of the *Trésor de la langue française* is available in North America through ARTFL, http://artfl-project.uchicago.edu. Brunet discusses the advantage of using the Stella software that could be accessed over a terminal to analyze FRANTEXT. This article documents an important early example of a networked large-scale text database accessible through a suite of interactive text-analysis tools. There was probably nothing like it in the world at the time.

21. "The testimony of statistics isn't solid except in large numbers. Its value is collective, like that of aggregated visualizations (portraits-robots), and not individual, like that of the finger-print." (Brunet 1989, p. 121)

22. Our translation of Brunet (1989, p. 122).

23. Toby-Dog and Kiki-the-Sweet are the interlocutors in Colette's *Dialogue of the Animals: The Cat and the Dog.*

24. The workbook is available at http://tactweb.cch.kcl.ac.uk.

25. For more on TACTWeb and the workbook, see Rockwell, Passmore, and Bradley 1997.

26. Smith 1978, p. 351.

27. One can also see the NEH-SSHRC-JISC Digging into Data Challenge of 2009 as a form of validation of Brunet's point about scale.

28. For more on these experiments, and for some of the raw materials, see http://tada.mcmaster.ca/Main/ExperimentsInTextAnalysis.

29. Willard McCarty, Humanist, volume 21, no. 379.

Chapter 6

1. From Jeremiah Wright's speech to the NAACP. An online version of this speech with interactive analytical panels is available at http://hermeneuti.ca/now-analyze-that.

2. See "Jeremiah Wright controversy" at http://en.wikipedia.org/wiki/Jeremiah_Wright_controversy.

3. See Campbell Robertson, "A Pulpit-and-Pews Gulf on ˙Obama's Ex-Pastor," *New York Times*, May 2, 2008 (http://www.nytimes.com/2008/05/02/us/politics/02carolina.html).

4. Obama 2008.

5. Wright 2008a.

6. We looked at Wright's speech to the National Press Club on April 28, 2008 (Wright 2008b). Despite our interest in dialogue, we chose not to use that speech because a large portion of it took the form of questions and answers and therefore would not necessarily reflect how Wright wanted to shape the issues.

7. We have not proofed either against the video records, letting the record stand. There are "typos" in both that suggest either problems in transcription or oral infelicities.

8. When comparing texts using the computer, it makes sense to compare their relative use of vocabulary—to see what words are used more often in one text compared with another.

9. For a specialized view in Voyant that that focuses on these terms, see http://bit.ly/1DCJ8Fy.

10. For a list of useful resources for analyzing these texts, see http://hermeneuti.ca/now-analyze-that.

Chapter 7

1. A version of this chapter was presented at Kansas THATCamp 2012 at the University of Kansas.

2. Glenn Greenwald, who at the time was working for the British newspaper the *Guardian*, has published a book about Snowden and his dramatic revelations, *No Place to Hide* (2014). For a good historical summary, see the "background" chapter of the 2014 Human Rights Watch report titled With Liberty to Monitor All..

3. Matthews (2013) estimates that in 2013 about $4.3 billion was spent on conducting cyber operations out of a total "black budget" of $52.6 billion.

4. Rosen 2005, p. 8.

5. Barbaro and Zeller (2006) describe how they were able to identify people with enough data.

6. Big Data: Seizing Opportunities, Preserving Values, a report prepared for President Obama by John Podesta (Executive Office of the President 2014), contains an accessible summary of the ethical and privacy concerns associated with big data. Mayer-Schönberger and Cukier 2013 contains an accessible chapter on "Risks" and useful suggestions for "Control."

7. We encourage readers to consult the *Guardian*'s page on "The NSA Files" at http://www.theguardian.com/world/the-nsa-files, EPIC at http://epic.org, and EFF at https://www.eff.org/.

8. See Laney 2001 and Eaton et al. 2012.

9. Data-processing technologies predate the computer. Herman Hollerith processed the 1890 census with punch cards and electro-mechanical tabulation machines. See Lubar 1992.

10. To be fair, Moretti (2013a) isn't so much dismissing interpretation as claiming that it is time to do some explaining. "In this situation," he writes on page 155, "'defending' interpretation from explanation misses the point: where the real challenge lies, and the hope for genuine breakthroughs, is in the realm of causality and large-scale explanations."

11. Feinstein 2013.

12. Greenwald 2013.

13. Jockers 2013, p. 35.

14. Moretti 2013b, p. 218.

15. The distinction between information or data "in motion" and "at rest" seems to be common in discussions of SIGINT (signals intelligence). See, for example, Bamford 2009, p. 213.

16. Gellman and Lindeman 2013.

17. Duhigg 2012.

18. Ibid.

19. Anderssen 2014.

20. You can imagine the intelligence uses: Where are you living? Where are you traveling? Do you buy unusual items, such as large amounts of fertilizer? Do you pursue unusual activities, such as taking flying lessons? We will return to information at rest later when talking about Digital Humanities applications.

21. Intel's co-founder Gordon Moore observed that the number of transistors on computer chips was doubling every two years (and, by extension, computer performance was doubling at about the same rate). See Turner et al. 2014 for some more specifics about the rate of production of digital data.

22. From the product page on NarusInsight at http://www.narus.com/index.php/products/narusinsight.

23. See Dewey 2014a,b.

24. Gartner, Inc. developed and branded the Hype Cycle as a representation and method for understanding technology adoption. See http://www.gartner.com/technology/research/methodologies/hype-cycle.jsp.

25. Manyika et al. 2011 is an example of a report that discusses the uses and opportunities for big data in commerce and government.

26. We will return to modeling in chapter 9.

27. See the video "Web 2.0 Expo NY: Clay Shirky (shirky.com) It's Not Information Overload. It's Filter Failure" at http://www.youtube.com/watch?v=LabqeJEOQyI.

28. For the current state of FRANTEXT, see http://www.frantext.fr/ or https://artfl-project.uchicago.edu.

29. For more, on TLG, see http://www.tlg.uci.edu and http://www.tlg.uci.edu/about/history.php. Also see Pantelia 2000.

30. Two other useful surveys of applications of text mining in the humanities are Moretti 2007 and Jockers 2013.

31. An archived page about this project can be found at http://cs-www.cs.yale.edu/homes/freeman/lifestreams.html.

32. On the MyLifeBits project, see http://research.microsoft.com/en-us/projects/mylifebits/. On the SenseCam project, see http://research.microsoft.com/en-us/um/cambridge/projects/sensecam/. On the Vicon Revue, see http://viconrevue.com/product.html.

33. See http://blog.stephenwolfram.com/2012/03/the-personal-analytics-of-my-life/.

34. On fitbit see http://www.fitbit.com/; on nike+ see http://nikeplus.nike.com/plus/.

35. For more on the results of the workshop, see http://ra.tapor.ualberta.ca/mindthegap/Home.html.

36. For examples of the sorts of assertions the Conjecturator generates, though on a different dataset, see https://twitter.com/conjecturator.

Chapter 8

1. Aarseth 2001.

2. Aarseth 2002.

3. Frasca 2003.

4. See http://gamestudies.org/1103/archive.

5. "Réseau" is French for "network." RezoViz is available at http://voyant-tools.org/tool/RezoViz.

6. A Named Entity Recognizer such as the Stanford NER uses various techniques to identify named people, places, and organizations. The Stanford NER (available at http://nlp.stanford.edu/software/CRF-NER.shtml) still produces some errors.

7. To get this list we created a table of variant names from the corpus, excluding bibliographies. For example, we assigned "Murray" and "Janet H. Murray" to "Janet Murray." We then ran the process again to get the frequencies and generate data for RezoViz to visualize.

8. The article that gets the most hits for "huizinga" is Rodriguez 2006, which begins "The modern study of play can be traced back to the publication of Dutch historian Johan Huizinga's groundbreaking study *Homo Ludens* ... ."

9. Three articles have more than five instances of "caillois" each: Eskelinen 2001, Rodriguez 2006, and Rockwell and Kee 2011.

10. Strangely unimportant to Game Studies is Bernard Suits, a philosopher of sport who wrote *The Grasshopper* (1978), a charming dialogue that tries to define what a game is. Games don't play with sports.

11. Galloway 2004.

12. Surprisingly, Mihaly Csikszentmihalyi, who proposed a theory of psychological flow, isn't prominent, though his name does show up in the corpus.

13. The title of Tyler's 2008 article "A Procrustean Probe" alludes to one of the bandits that Theseus had to dispose of in his Herculean labors. Procrustes was a smith who would fit people to an iron bed by hammering them out or cutting them down.

14. Kücklich 2003.

15. Eskelinen 2001.

16. Rockwell's conference report is available at http://www.philosophi.ca/pmwiki. php/Main/InteractingWithImmersiveWorlds2009. Aarseth has a video version of a similar talk about the "Narrative Theory of Games" available at http://vimeo. com/7097715.

17. Janet Murray says something similar in her 2005 paper "The Last Word on Ludology v Narratology in Game Studies."

18. Murray 2005.

19. Taylor 2003.

20. Yee 2009.

Chapter 9

1. This is a translation of Wang Zhiben's commentary on the last panel of the scroll provided by *Perry in Japan: A Visual History* project at http://library.brown.edu/cds/perry/scroll_bul.html.

2. For more on this history see Ericson 1996.

3. Fish 2011.

4. Fish 2012b.

5. This is the theory put forward by Stephen Ramsay in *Reading Machines* (2011b).

6. Baird 2004, p. xv.

7. Baird 2002, p. 13.

8. Busa 1980, p. 83.

9. Ibid.

10. The question of who was the first to use text analysis is interesting, as it asks us to look back over text techniques before the computer. We should also question whether Busa, despite his heroic status, is the first computing humanist. A case could be made for Andrew Booth, who was building and using computers at Birkbeck College in the late 1940s and the 1950s and who is often considered a pioneer of linguistic computing. (See http://theoreti.ca/?p=1608.)

11. Tasman 1957, p. 249.

12. Ibid.

13. Tasman 1957, p. 256.

14. Ibid.

15. The cards included a "mark sensing area for use of scholar in selecting, collating, printing, or revising information" (Tasman 1957, p. 251). This zone on the right of each card had bubbles for pencil marks like those in standardized tests that the scholar could use to annotate the cards. For more on the punch card, see Lubar 1992.

16. Mendenhall 1887, p. 238.

17. After this, and after a stint at the University of Tokyo, Mendenhall conducted a study in which Shakespeare's works were compared against those of Bacon and Marlowe. That time-consuming study was supported by a wealthy patron who paid for the manual labor of two secretaries who counted words. A short history of Mendenhall's method as applied to Shakespeare can be found at http://marlowe-shakespeare.blogspot.ca/2009/02/on-mendenhall-and-compelling-evidence.html.

18. On Agatha Christie's rich vocabulary, and more generally on stylistics and cognition, see Lancashire 2010. Lancashire deploys cognitive studies to rescue stylistics from postmodern critique. On Juola's forensic stylistic study of *The Cuckoo's Calling* for the *Sunday Times*, see Juola 2013. After the *Sunday Times* received a hint that Rowling was the real author of *The Cuckoo's Calling*, it commissioned Juola to assess whether the text could have been written by Rowling. In Juola 2013 he nicely summarizes the theory and methods he applied to show that Rowling was a likely to have been the author.

19. Smith 1985.

20. Smith 1978, p. 327.

21. Ibid.

22. Ibid., p. 339.

23. Smith (1978, p. 343) makes the point that "diachronic distributions, Fourier Analysis, Principal Component Analysis, state diagrams, and CGAMS are all models that may be used to explore thematic structures and relations." It should be noted that Smith's article was published three years before Parunak's "Prolegomena to Pictorial Concordances" (1981), the first sustained discussion of what today we would call textual visualization. Parunak was aware of Smith's groundbreaking work and referenced Smith's experiments.

24. Barthes 1972, pp. 214–215

25. Ibid., p. 216.

26. Ibid., p. 215.

27. In "The Visual Concordance" Rockwell (2001) called the new representation a monster is the old sense of something stitched together, like Frankenstein's monster, from dissected parts. The concordance of passages is just such a monster—a new text stitched from other texts. A visualization can be thought of as an even more abstract monster: you don't even have the original parts to stitch, but graphical features are automatically composed into a new interpretive work.

28. The same issue of *Literary and Linguistic Computing* contained a fine paper by John Bradley on what humanists do (Bradley 2003). That paper led to the Pliny software, which combines note-taking and analytics. Pliny is available at http://pliny.cch.kcl.ac.uk/.

29. Rockwell 2003a, p. 213. In an afterword to that issue of *Literary and Linguistic Computing*, Thomas Corns (2003) nicely summarized the call for playful text analysis: "We need tools that can confront us more starkly with what the text is by showing us what it could have been. … In a controlled way, we could generate phantom texts around the target text that would disclose the characteristics of its working parts. None of this leads to 'proof,' but it may lead to insight."

30. During the session, Paul Fortier, who chaired the ACH/ALLC 2002 panel at which we first came out of the serious closet, commented on the direction in which our papers were going.

31. Fish 2012b.

32. Ibid.

33. Ibid.

34. See Fish 1980.

35. See Ramsay and Rockwell 2012 for an earlier discussion of how tools can be thought of as a theoretical lens or model.

36. As Heidegger would put it, tools such as spectacles and hammers are ready to hand, and can be picked up and used without theorizing.

37. Masterman 1962, pp. 38–39.

38. Ibid., p. 38.

39. Ibid., p. 44.

40. This is my translation from the Italian on page vi of Perilli and Fiormonte 2011. It first appeared in a blog entry (http://theoreti.ca/?p=4333).

41. Tito Orlandi and other Italian digital humanists are not as well known to the English-speaking DH community as they should be. They did pioneering work (as did Father Busa), and they theorized what they were doing. For a list of Orlandi's publications, see http://rmcisadu.let.uniroma1.it/~orlandi/pubinf.html. "Is Humanities Computing a Discipline?" is one work by Orlandi that is available in English (http://computerphilologie.uni-muenchen.de/jg02/orlandi.html).

42. An interesting and initially testy exchange about this between McCarty and Orlandi led to a friendly discussion about what are some of the questions of the Digital Humanities. See Orlandi's summary at http://rmcisadu.let.uniroma1. it/~orlandi/mccarty1.html (1999).

43. Who doesn't miss fiddling with clay or balsa? Modeling as a paradigm nicely counteracts the accusation that what we are doing is "cold" and "abstract," making the Digital Humanities more a craft than a calculation.

Chapter 10

1. For a good description of the history of the text, see the second chapter of Carabelli 1972.

2. For more on scepticism, see http://plato.stanford.edu/entries/skepticism and Annas and Barnes 1985.

3. This tradition goes back to the Greeks—see Annas and Barnes 1985 or http:// plato.stanford.edu/entries/skepticism-ancient. In Hume's dialogue they talk about Pyrrhonian scepticism which developed a practice of investigation designed to undermine any argument so as to lead to peace of mind. We will argue that Philo demonstrates an updated version of this in the dialogue.

4. This chapter is an artifice as it isn't an actual transcript of what we did so much as a fiction describing how one can proceeded in theory if uninterrupted. In point of fact, this research was started in the 1990s by Geoffrey Rockwell and John Bradley when they were experimenting with visualization (1996). For more authentic examples of how people have used Voyant, see http://docs.voyant-tools.org/about/ examples-gallery.

5. The Gutenberg edition is available at http://www.gutenberg.org/ebooks/4583. We used the "Plain Text UTF-8" version at http://www.gutenberg.org/cache/epub/ 4583/pg4583.txt. We checked all quotes against the Tweyman print edition, and we have used page numbers from that edition. It should be noted that the Gutenberg version doesn't identify the edition on which it is based, and that it differs in minor ways from the Tweyman edition (which is based on the handwritten manuscript in the National Library in Edinburgh).

6. For the purpose of this study, we will use the term "chapters" to identify the segments of the *Dialogues*.

7. Our colored version of the *Dialogues* is available at http://hermeneuti.ca/sites/ hermeneuti.ca/files/DialoguesConcerningNaturalReligionbyDavidHume.html. The version divided into parts in Voyant is available at http://voyant-tools.org/? corpus=hume.dialogues.by.book&stopList=stop.en.taporware.txt. A version divided by speakers in Voyant is available at http://voyant-tools.org/?corpus=hume. dialogues.by.speaker&stopList=stop.en. taporware.txt.

8. We have found that we almost always want to go beyond what a tool such as Voyant can do when pursuing questions. That is an argument for learning different tools or some basic programming skills.

9. The *Dialogues* consist of an introductory letter by Pamphilus and twelve parts. In some editions the parts are called books. Here we stick with Tweyman's labels, though in some of our visualizations you will see thirteen sections (the introduction plus 12 parts.) In other visualizations you will see ten divisions that represent 10 percent chunks of the text.

10. Here we define a visualization as a visual representation of information generated by a computer (as opposed to an illustration drawn by hand). There is a rich literature on visualizations (including pre-computer visualizations). Edward Tufte's books (1983, 1990) contain many beautiful examples.

11. We borrow the term "pictorial concordance" from the first article written about textual visualization in *Computers and the Humanities*: "Prolegomena To Pictorial Concordances" (Parunak 1981.) In that article Parunak recognizes the pioneering work of John B. Smith, notably the 1978 article "Computer Criticism."

12. On the Visible Man and the Visible Woman, see http://americanhistory.si.edu/collections/search/object/nmah_214319.

13. Howard Rheingold documents this tradition of thinking of computing as a way to extend our capacities in *Tools for Thought* (1985). One of the most important proponents of augmenting our intellect was Douglas Engelbart, who not only wrote a report titled Augmenting Human Intellect (1962) but also developed an innovative system, called NLS, that demonstrated his ideas. An edited video of a 1968 demonstration of NLS is available at http://sloan.stanford.edu/mousesite/1968Demo.html.

14. Tweyman edition (Hume 1991), p. 172.

15. Pamphilus concludes this narrative framing of the dialogue as follows: "I confess, that, upon a serious review of the whole, I cannot but think, that PHILO's principles are more probable than DEMEA's; but that those of CLEANTHES approach still nearer to the truth." (p. 185) This judgment is from the end of the text, the descriptions of Philo and Cleanthes at the beginning (p. 96).

16. Linguistic and stylistic analytics are typically not designed to assist in the interpretation of the text so much as for the purpose of using the text to interpret some other phenomenon, such as language use in a community or the style of an author.

17. See, for example, Mossner 1977 or Foley 2006.

18. This search uses regular expressions to find both "sceptic" and "skeptic" and to find different endings. For more on regular expressions, see http://etext.lib.virginia.edu/services/helpsheets/unix/regex.html.

19. Hume 1991, p. 97.

20. Ibid., p. 99.

21. Ibid., p. 99.

22. We produced this graph by using the Collocate Clusters tool in a different "skin" of Voyant. See http://voyant-tools.org/?corpus=hume.dialogues.by.speaker&stopList=stop.en.taporware.txt&skin=collocates. This skin is a different arrangement of Voyant tools that is optimized for exploring words that collocate with (i.e., appear near) a key word.

23. Hume 1991, p. 120.

24. Ibid.

25. Ibid.

26. Foley (2006) is an exception. He explains Philo's reversal in chapter 13 as Hume showing us how a character like Philo, no matter how sceptical, will revert to some level of belief in divine design if indoctrinated from an early age. In effect, Philo exemplifies how someone educated in the fashion described at the beginning of the *Dialogues* will be comfortable arguing skeptically, but will revert to the piety he was taught when young and impressionable.

27. If we were to take this line of inquiry further, we would look to Hume's writings on and his history of intellectual manners. What did Hume have to say about intellectual society and wit? How is he supposed to have behaved in society? Did that matter to him?

28. Hume 1991, p 185.

29. Ibid., p. 185.

30. Ibid., p. 96.

31. Ibid.

32. Ibid.

Chapter 11

1. From the 1957 movie *Desk Set* (our transcription).

2. Oakeshott 1959, p. 11.

3. Plato, *Phaedrus*, sections 274e–275a.

4. Ibid., sections 275d and 275e.

5. "I started working through a few titles. First, two broad-spectrum and established periodicals, *Yearbook of English Studies* and *Review of English Studies:* not a single article appeared in the 1980s using computer-aided or computer-based approaches." (Corns 1991, p. 127)

6. Milic 1966, p. 4.

7. The MONK (Metadata Offer New Knowledge) Project developed text-analysis tools that were coupled with a large collection so one easily try mining techniques within an environment that included prepared texts. For more on the MONK Project, see http://monk.library.illinois.edu/.

8. This quote is from "Computing and reading," a summary of the series of five lectures. The summary is available at http://www.mccarty.org.uk/essays/McCarty,%20 Lecture%20series%2020100328.pdf; slides and podcasts of the lectures are available at http://www.mccarty.org.uk/.

9. Corns 2003.

10. The Datablog is introduced at http://www.guardian.co.uk/news/datablog/2009/mar/10/blogpost1. The *Guardian* has also issued an e-book about data journalism, *Facts Are Sacred: The Power of Data* (Rogers 2011).

11. Heidegger 2002, p. 64.

Bibliography

Aarseth, E. 2001. Computer game studies, year one. *Game Studies* 1 (1).

Aarseth, E. 2002. The dungeon and the ivory tower: Vive la difference ou liaison dangereuse? *Game Studies* 2 (1).

Anderson, C. 2008. The end of theory: The data deluge makes the scientific method obsolete. *Wired* 16 (7).

Anderssen, E. 2014. Big Data is watching you: Has online spying gone too far? *Globe and Mail*, October 2 (http://www.theglobeandmail.com/life/relationships/big-data -is-watching-you-has-online-spying-gone-too-far/article20894498).

Annas, J., and J. Barnes. 1985. *The Modes of Scepticism: Ancient Texts and Modern Interpretations*. Cambridge University Press.

Auer, K., and R. Miller. 2002. *Extreme Programming Applied: Playing to Win*. Boston: Addison-Wesley,.

Baird, D. 2002. Thing knowledge—function and truth. *Techné* 6 (2).

Baird, D. 2004. *Thing Knowledge: A Philosophy of Scientific Instruments*. Berkeley: University of California Press,.

Bamford, J. 2009. *The Shadow Factory: The Ultra-secret NSA from 9/11 to the Eavesdropping on America*. New York: Anchor Books.

Barbaro, M., and T. J. Zeller. 2006. A face is exposed for AOL searcher No. 4417749. *New York Times*, August 9 (http://www.nytimes.com/2006/08/09/technology/09aol .html).

Barthes, R. 1972. *The Structuralist Activity: Critical Essays*. Evanston: Northwestern University Press.

Beck, K. 2000. *Extreme Programming Explained: Embrace Change*. Boston: Addison-Wesley,

Blair, A. M. 2010. *Too Much to Know: Managing Scholarly Information before the Modern Age.* New Haven: Yale University Press.

Bogost, I. 2012. *Alien Phenomenology, or What It's Like to Be a Thing.* Minneapolis: University of Minnesota Press.

boyd, d., and K. Crawford. 2012. Critical questions for Big Data. *Information, Communication & Society* 15 (5): 662–679.

Bradley, J. 2003. Finding a middle ground between 'determinism' and 'aesthetic indeterminacy': A model for text analysis tools. *Literary and Linguistic Computing* 18 (2): 185–207.

Brockman, W., L. Neumann, C. Palmer, and T. Tidline. *Scholarly Work in the Humanities and the Evolving Information Environment.* Digital Library Federation, 2001.

Brunet, É. 1989. L'exploitation des grands corpus: Le bestiare de la littérature française. *Literary and Linguistic Computing* 4 (2): 121–134.

Burgess, T. 2009. *Pontypool Changes Everything.* Toronto: ECW.

Burton, D. M. 1981 a. Automated concordances and word indexes: The fifties. *Computers and the Humanities* 15 (1): 1–14.

Burton, D. M. 1981 b. Automated concordances and word indexes: The early sixties and the early centers. *Computers and the Humanities* 15 (2): 83–100.

Burton, D. M. 1981 c. Automated concordances and word indexes: The process, the programs, and the products. *Computers and the Humanities* 15 (3): 139–154.

Burton, D. M. 1982. Automated concordances and word-indexes: Machine decisions and editorial revisions. *Computers and the Humanities* 16 (4): 195–218.

Burton, D. 1984. Review essay: *Index Thomisticus. Computers and the Humanities* 18 (2): 109–120.

Busa, R. 1980. The annals of humanities computing: The Index Thomisticus. *Computers and the Humanities* 14 (2): 83–90.

Bush, V. 1945. "As we may think." *Atlantic Monthly*, July: 101–108. http://www.theatlantic.com/magazine/archive/1945/07/as-we-may-think/303881.

Caillois, R. 1961. *Man, Play, and Games.* New York: Free Press.

Canadian Academies. 2006. The State of Science and Technology in Canada (http://www.scienceadvice.ca/en/assessments/completed/science-technology.aspx).

Carabelli, G. 1972. *Hume e la retorica dell'ideologia.* Firenze: La Nuova Italia Editrice.

Churchhouse, R. F. 1972. Computer Applications in the Arts and Sciences. Lecture, University College, Cardiff (http://www.chilton-computing.org.uk/acl/literature/reports/p016.htm).

Clement, T. M. 2008. "A thing not beginning and not ending": Using digital tools to distant-read Gertrude Stein's *The Making of Americans*. *Literary and Linguistic Computing* 23 (3): 361–381.

Cline, E. 2011. *Ready Player One*. New York: Random House.

Corns, T. N. 1991. Computers in the humanities: Methods and applications in the study of English literature. *Literary and Linguistic Computing* 6 (2): 127–130.

Corns, T. N. 2003. Afterword. *Literary and Linguistic Computing* 18 (2): 221–223.

Crane, G. 2006. What do you do with a million books? *D-Lib Magazine* 12 (3).

Crawford, C. 1984. *The Art of Computer Game Design*. Berkeley: Osborne/McGraw-Hill.

Deegan, M., and W. McCarty, eds. 2012. *Collaborative Research in the Digital Humanities*. Farnham: Ashgate.

Descartes, R. 2006. *A Discourse on the Method of Correctly Conducting One's Reason and Seeking Truth in the Sciences*, tr. I. Maclean. Oxford University Press.

Dewey, C. 2014a. 9 answers about Facebook's creepy emotional-manipulation experiment. *Washington Post*, July 1 (http://www.washingtonpost.com/news/the-intersect/wp/2014/07/01/9-answers-about-facebooks-creepy-emotional-manipulation-experiment).

Dewey, C. 2014b. After eight years with Facebook's News Feed, there's no such thing as "TMI." *Washington Post*, September 23 (http://www.washingtonpost.com/news/the-intersect/wp/2014/09/23/after-eight-years-with-facebooks-news-feed-theres-no-such-thing-as-tmi).

Dreyfus, H. L. 1979. *What Computers Can't Do: The Limits of Artificial Intelligence*. New York: Harper Colophon.

Duhigg, C. 2012. How companies learn your secrets. *New York Times*, February 16 (http://www.nytimes.com/2012/02/19/magazine/shopping-habits.html).

Eaton, C., D. Deroos, T. Deutsch, G. Lapis, and P. Zikopoulos. 2012. *Understanding Big Data*. New York: McGraw-Hill.

Ebitz, D. 1988. Connoisseurship as practice. *Artibus et Historiae* 9 (18): 207–212.

Eco, U. 1992. *Interpretation and Overinterpretation*. Cambridge University Press.

Elliot, J., and T. Meyer. 2013. Claim on "attacks thwarted" by NSA spreads despite lack of evidence. ProPublica, October 23 (http://www.propublica.org/article/claim-on-attacks-thwarted-by-nsa-spreads-despite-lack-of-evidence).

Engelbart, D. 1962. Augmenting Human Intellect: A Conceptual Framework. SRI Summary Report AFOSR-3223 (http://www.dougengelbart.org/pubs/augment-3906 .html).

Ericson, S. J. 1996. *The Sound of the Whistle: Railroads and the State in Meiji Japan*. Cambridge: Harvard University Press.

Eskelinen, M. 2001. The gaming situation. *Game Studies* 1 (1).

Executive Office of the President. 2014. Big Data: Seizing Opportunities, Preserving Values (http://www.whitehouse.gov/sites/default/files/docs/big_data_privacy_report _may_1_2014.pdf).

Feinstein, D. 2013. Continue NSA call-records program. *USA Today*, October 20 (http://www.usatoday.com/story/opinion/2013/10/20/nsa-call-records-program-sen -dianne-feinstein-editorials-debates/3112715).

Ferruci, D., A. Levas, S. Bagchi, D. Gondek, and E. Mueller. 2011. Watson: Beyond Jeopardy! IBM Research Division Report (http://bmi205.stanford.edu/_media/ ebrown-2.pdf).

Fischer, M. 1971. The KWIC Index concept: A retrospective view. In *Key Papers in Information Science*, ed. A. W. Elias. American Society for Information Science.

Fish, S. 1980. What is stylistics and why are they saying such terrible things about it? In Fish, *Is There a Text in This Class? The Authority of Interpretive Communities*. Cambridge: Harvard University Press.

Fish, S. 2011. The old order changeth. Opinionator blog, December 26 (http://opin-ionator.blogs.nytimes.com/2011/12/26/the-old-order-changeth).

Fish, S. 2012 a. The digital humanities and the transcending of mortality. Opinionator blog, January 9 (http://opinionator.blogs.nytimes.com/2012/01/09/the-digital -humanities-and-the-transcending-of-mortality0.

Fish, S. 2012 b. Mind your P's and B's: The digital humanities and interpretation. Opinionator blog, January 23 (http://opinionator.blogs.nytimes.com/2012/01/23/ mind-your-ps-and-bs-the-digital-humanities-and-interpretation).

Floridi, L. 1999. *Philosophy and Computing: An Introduction*. London: Routledge.

Foley, R. 2006. Unnatural religion: Indoctrination and Philo's reversal in Hume's *Dialogues Concerning Natural Religion*. *Human Studies* 32 (1): 83–112.

Frasca, G. Simulation versus narrative: Introduction to ludology. In *The Video Game Theory Reader*, ed. M. Wolf and B. Perron. London: Routledge, 2003.

Friedman, T. 1995. Making sense of software: Computer games and interactive textuality, http://www.duke.edu/~tlove/simcity.htm. This is an edited version of an essay that appeared in *CyberSociety*, ed. S. G. Jones (SAGE, 1995).

Friedman, V. 2007. Tag clouds gallery: Examples and good practices, *Smashing Magazine*, November 7.

Gadamer, H. G. 1985. *Truth and Method*, tr. J. Weinsheimer and D. G. Marshall. New York: Crossroad.

Galloway, A. R. 2004. Social realism in gaming. *Game Studies* 4 (1).

Gellman, B. "Is the FBI up to the job 10 years after 9/11?" *Time*, May 9 2011. http://content.time.com/time/printout/0,8816,2068082,00.html.

Gellman, B., and T. Lindeman. 2013. Inner workings of a top-secret spy program. *Washington Post*, June 29 (http://apps.washingtonpost.com/g/page/national/inner-workings-of-a-top-secret-spy-program/282).

Gellman, B., and L. Poitras. 2013. U.S., British intelligence mining data from nine U.S. Internet companies in broad secret program. *Washington Post*, June 6 (http://www.washingtonpost.com/investigations/us-intelligence-mining-data-from-nine-us-internet-companies-in-broad-secret-program/2013/06/06/3a0c0da8-cebf-11e2-8845-d970ccb04497_story.html).

Glickman, R., and G. Staalman. 1966. *Manual for the Printing of Literary Texts and Concordances by Computer*. University of Toronto Press.

Greenacre, M. J. 1984. *Theory and Applications of Correspondence Analysis*. London: Academic Press.

Greenblatt, S. 2011. *The Swerve: How the World Became Modern*. New York: Norton.

Greenwald, G. 2013. NSA collecting phone records of millions of Verizon customers daily. *Guardian*, June 6 (http://www.theguardian.com/world/2013/jun/06/nsa-phone-records-verizon-court-order).

Greenwald, G. *No Place to Hide: Edward Snowden, the NSA, and the U.S. Surveillance State*. Toronto: Signal, 2014.

Harpham, G. 2006. "Science and the theft of humanity." *American Scientist* 94 (4): 296–298.

Harris, J. 2011. Word clouds considered harmful. Nieman Lab, October 11 (http://www.niemanlab.org/2011/10/word-clouds-considered-harmful).

Hayles, N. K. 1990. *Chaos Bound: Orderly Disorder in Contemporary Literature and Science*. Ithaca: Cornell University Press.

Heidegger, M. 1953. *Being and Time*, tr. J. Stambaugh. Albany: State University of New York Press.

Heidegger, M. 1971. The thing. In Heidegger, *Poetry, Language, Thought*, tr. A. Hofstadter. New York: Harper & Row.

Heidegger, M. 2002.The age of the world picture. In Heidegger, *Off the Beaten Track*, tr. J. Young and K. Haynes. Cambridge University Press,.

Hockey, S. 2000. *Electronic Texts in the Humanities*. Oxford University Press.

Horton, R., M. Olsen, and G. Roe. 2010. Something borrowed: Sequence alignment and the identification of similar passages in large text collections. *Digital Studies / Le champ numérique* 2 (1).

Howard-Hill, T. H. 1979. *Literary Concordances: A Guide to the Preparation of Manual and Computer Concordances*. Oxford: Pergamon.

Huizinga, J. 1938. *Homo Ludens: A Study of the Play-Element in Culture*. Boston: Beacon, 1950

Human Rights Watch. 2014. With Liberty to Monitor All: How Large-Scale US Surveillance Is Harming Journalism, Law and American Democracy (http://www .hrw.org/reports/2014/07/28/liberty-monitor-all-0).

Hume, D. 1991. *Dialogues Concerning Natural Religion*, ed. S. Tweyman. London: Routledge.

IDC. 2012. The Digital Universe in 2020: Big Data, Bigger Digital Shadows, and Biggest Growth in the Far East (http://www.emc.com/collateral/analyst-reports/idc-the-digital-universe-in-2020.pdf).

Jockers, M. L. 2013. *Macroanalysis: Digital Methods and Literary History*. Urbana: University of Illinois Press.

Jonas, J., and J. Harper. 2006. Effective Counterterrorism and the Limited Role of Predictive Data Mining. Policy Analysis No. 584, Cato Institute (http://www.cato .org/publications/policy-analysis/effective-counterterrorism-limited-role-predictive -data-mining).

Joyce, J. 1968. *A Portrait of the Artist as a Young Man: Text, Criticism, and Notes*, ed. G. Chester Anderson. New York: Viking.

Juola, P. 2013. Rowling and "Galbraith": An authorial analysis. http://languagelog. ldc.upenn.edu/nll/?p=5315.

Jurafsky, D., and J. H. Martin. 2000. *Speech and Language Processing: An Introduction to Natural Language Processing, Computational Linguistics, and Speech Recognition*. Upper Saddle River: Prentice-Hall.

Juul, J. 2011. Games telling stories. *Game Studies* 1 (1).

Kenny, A. 1982. *The Computation of Style*. Oxford: Pergamon.

Kenny, A. 1992. *Computers and the Humanities*. London: British Library.

Kirk, J. A. 2009. Word frequency use or misuse? In *What's in a Word-List? Investigating Word Frequency and Keyword Extraction*, ed. D. Archer. Farnham: Ashgate.

Kirschenbaum, M. G. 2008. *Mechanisms: New Media and the Forensic Imagination.* Cambridge: MIT Press.

Kirschenbaum, M. G. 2010. What is Digital Humanities and what's it doing in English Departments? *ADE Bulletin* 150: 55–61.

Kücklich, J. 2003.Perspectives of computer game philology. *Game Studies* 3 (1).

Lancashire, I. 1986. Concordance programs for literary analysis. *ACM SIGCUE Outlook* 19 (112) 54–61.

Lancashire, I. 2010. *Forgetful Muses: Reading the Author in the Text.* University of Toronto Press.

Laney, D. 2001. 3-D Data Management: Controlling Data Volume, Velocity and Variety (http://gtnr.it/15NbqwH).

Latour, B. 2000. When things strike back: A possible contribution of "science studies" to the social sciences. *British Journal of Sociology* 51 (1): 107–123.

Liu, A. 2012. Where is cultural criticism in the digital humanities? In *Debates in the Digital Humanities*, ed. M. Gold. Minneapolis: University of Minnesota Press.

Lodge, David. *Small World: An Academic Romance.* London: Secker & Warburg, 1984.

Lubar, S. 1992. "Do not fold, spindle or mutilate": A cultural history of the punch card. *Journal of American Culture* 15 (4): 43–55.

Lucretius. 1969. *The Way Things Are: The De Rerum Natura of Titus Lucretius Carus*, tr. R. Humphries. Bloomington: Indiana University Press.

Lyman, P., and H. R. Varian. 2003. How Much Information? (http://www2.sims.berkeley.edu/research/projects/how-much-info-2003).

MacAskill, E. 2013. Edward Snowden, NSA files source: If they want to get you, in time they will. *Guardian*, June 10 (http://www.theguardian.com/world/2013/jun/09/nsa-whistleblower-edward-snowden-why).

Manovich, L. *The Language of New Media.* Cambridge: MIT Press, 2001.

Manyika, J., M. Chui, B. Brown, J. Bughin, R. Dobbs, C. Roxburgh, and A. H. Byers. 2011. Big Data: The Next Frontier for Innovation, Competition, and Productivity (http://www.mckinsey.com/insights/business_technology/big_data_the_next_frontier_for_innovation).

Masterman, M. 1962. The intellect's new eye. In *Freeing the Mind: Articles and Letters from the Times Literary Supplement during March–June, 1962.* London: Times.

Matthews, D. 2013. America's secret intelligence budget, in 11 (nay 13) charts. *Washington Post*, August 29 (http://www.washingtonpost.com/blogs/wonkblog/wp/2013/08/29/your-cheat-sheet-to-americas-secret-intelligence-budget).

Mayer-Schönberger, V., and K. Cukier. 2013. *Big Data: A Revolution That Will Transform How We Live, Work, and Think*. New York: Houghton Mifflin Harcourt

McCarty, W. 1993. Handmade, computer-assisted, and electronic concordances of Chaucer. *CCH Working Papers* 3: 49–65.

McCarty, W. 2005. *Humanities Computing*. New York: Palgrave Macmillan.

McCarty, W. 2007. Beyond the Word: Modeling Literary Context (http://www.mccarty.org.uk/essays/McCarty,%20Beyond%20the%20word.pdf).

McKinnon, A. 1989. Mapping the dimensions of a literary corpus. *Literary and Linguistic Computing* 4 (2): 73–84.

Mendenhall, T. C. 1887. The characteristic curves of composition. *Science* 9 (214): 237–249.

Michel, J.-B., et al. 2010. Quantitative analysis of culture using millions of digitized books. *Science* 331 (6014): 176–182.

Miles, M. Descartes's method. 2008. In *A Companion to Descartes*, ed. J. Broughton and J. Carriero. Oxford: Blackwell.

Milic, L. 1966. The next step. *Computers and the Humanities* 1 (1): 3–6.

Moretti, F. 2007. *Graphs, Maps, Trees: Abstract Models for Literary History*. London: Verso.

Moretti, F. 2013a. The end of the beginning: A reply to Christopher Prendergast. In Moretti, *Distant Reading*. London: Verso,

Moretti, F. 2013b. Network theory, plot analysis. In Moretti, *Distant Reading*. London: Verso.

Mossner, E. C. 1977. Hume and the legacy of the *Dialogues*. In *David Hume: Bicentenary Papers*, ed. G. P. Morice. Edinburgh University Press.

Murray, J. H. 2005. The Last Word on Ludology v Narratology in Game Studies (http://inventingthemedium.com/2013/06/28/the-last-word-on-ludology-v-narratology-2005).

Murray, J. H. *Hamlet on the Holodeck: The Future of Narrative in Cyberspace*. Cambridge: MIT Press, 2008.

Oakeshott, M. 1959. *The Voice of Poetry in the Conversation of Mankind*. London: Bowes & Bowes.

Obama, B. 2008. A More Perfect Union. Transcript of speech from *Huffington Post*, March 18 (http://www.huffingtonpost.com/2008/03/18/obama-race-speech-read -th_n_92077.html).

Oppy, G., and D. Dowe. 2011. The Turing test. In *The Stanford Encyclopedia of Philosophy*, ed. E. N. Zalta (http://plato.stanford.edu/archives/spr2011/entries/turing-test).

Orlandi, T. Informatica, formalizzazione e discipline umanistiche. 1997. In *Discipline umanistiche e informatica: Il problema della formalizzazione*, ed. T. Orlandi. Rome: Accademia Nazionale dei Lincei.

Orlandi, T. 1999. The Scholarly Environment of Humanities Computing: A Reaction to Willard McCarty's Talk on "The computational transformation of the humanities" (http://rmcisadu.let.uniroma1.it/~orlandi/mccarty1.html).

Orlandi, T. 2002. Is humanities computing a discipline? *Jahrbuch für Computerphilologie* 4: 51–58.

Pannapacker, W. 2009. The MLA and the digital humanities. Brainstorm blog (http://chronicle.com/blogPost/The-MLAthe-Digital/19468).

Pantelia, Maria. 2000. Nous into chaos: The creation of the thesaurus of the Greek language. *International Journal of Lexicography* 13 (1): 1–11.

Parrish, S. M., ed. 1959. *A Concordance to the Poems of Matthew Arnold*. Ithaca: Cornell University Press.

Parunak, H. V. D. 1981. Prolegomena to pictorial concordances. *Computers and the Humanities* 15 (1): 15–36.

Pearce, C. 2002. Sims, BattleBots, Cellular Automata God and Go. *Game Studies* 2 (1).

Perilli, L., and D. Fiormonte, eds. 2011. *La macchina nel tempo: Studi di informatica umanistica in onore di Tito Orlandi*. Firenze: Le Lettere.

Plato. *Phaedrus*, tr. H. N. Fowler. 1925. http://data.perseus.org/citations/urn:cts :greekLit:tlg0059.tlg012.perseus-eng1:227a.

Plato. 1961. *The Collected Dialogues of Plato Including the Letters*, ed. E. Hamilton and H. Cairns. Princeton University Press.

Poitras, L., M. Rosenbach, and H. Stark. 2014. 'A' for Angela: GCHQ and NSA Targeted Private German Companies and Merkel. Spiegel Online (http://www.spiegel .de/international/germany/gchq-and-nsa-targeted-private-german-companies-a -961444-druck.html).

Potter, R. 1991. Statistical analysis of literature: A retrospective on computers and the humanities, 1966–1990. *Computers and the Humanities* 25 (6): 401–429.

Power, D. J. 2002. What is the true story about data mining, beer and diapers? http:// dssresources.com/newsletters/66.php.

Powers, R. 1996. *Galatea 2.2*. New York: Harper Perennial.

Pratchett, T. 1998. Doom. alt.fan.pratchett Usenet Group (https://groups.google
.com/forum/#!msg/alt.fan.pratchett/FvOcPGokWW4/jPzghK77yTEJ).

Priest, D., and W. Arkin. 2011. *Top Secret America: The Rise of the New American Security State*. New York: Back Bay Books.

Ramsay, S. 2003. Toward an algorithmic criticism. *Literary and Linguistic Computing* 18 (2): 167–174.

Ramsay, S. 2008. *Algorithmic Criticism. A Companion to Digital Literary Studies*, ed. S. Schreibman and R. Siemens. Oxford: Blackwell.

Ramsay, S. 2011 a. On Building (http://stephenramsay.us/text/2011/01/11/on
-building).

Ramsay, S. 2011 b. *Reading Machines: Towards Algorithmic Criticism*. Urbana: University of Illinois Press.

Ramsay, S. The hermeneutics of screwing around; or what you do with a million books. In *Pastplay: Teaching and Learning History with Technology*, ed. K. Kee. Ann Arbor: University of Michigan Press, 2014.

Ramsay, S., and G. Rockwell. 2012. Developing things: notes toward an epistemology of building in the digital humanities. In *Debates in the Digital Humanities*, ed. M. K. Gold. Minneapolis: University of Minnesota Press.

Rheingold, H. 1985. *Tools for Thought: The People and Ideas behind the Next Computer Revolution*. New York: Simon & Schuster.

Risen, J., and L. Poitras. 2013. N.S.A. gathers data on social connections of U.S. citizens. *New York Times*, September 28 (http://www.nytimes.com/2013/09/29/us/nsa
-examines-social-networks-of-us-citizens.html?hp&_r=0&pagewanted=all).

Rockwell, G. 2001. The visual concordance: The design of Eye-ConTact. *Text Technology* 10 (1): 73–86.

Rockwell, G. 2003a. What is text analysis, really? *Literary and Linguistic Computing* 18 (2): 209–219.

Rockwell, G. 2003b. *Defining Dialogue: From Socrates to the Internet*. Amherst: Prometheus Books.

Rockwell, G., and J. Bradley. 1996. Watching scepticism: Computer assisted visualization and Hume's *Dialogues*. In *Research in Humanities Computing 5*, ed. G. Perissinotto. Oxford: Clarendon.

Rockwell, G., and J. Bradley. 1998. Eye-Contact: Towards a New Design for Text-Analysis Tools. Computing in the Humanities Working Paper (http://journals.sfu
.ca/chwp/index.php/chwp/article/view/A.4/61).

Rockwell, G. and K. Kee. 2011. The leisure of serious games: A dialogue. *Game Studies* 11 (2).

Rockwell, G., G. Passmore, and J. Bradley. 1997. TACTweb: The intersection of text-analysis and hypertext. *Educational Computing Research* 17 (3): 217–230.

Rockwell, G., S. Sinclair, S. Ruecker, and P. Organisciak. 2010. Ubiquitous text analysis. *Poetess Archive Journal* 2 (1).

Rodriguez, H. 2006. The Playful and the Serious: An Approximation to Huizinga's *Homo Ludens*. *Game Studies* 6 (1).

Rogers, S. *Facts Are Sacred: The Power of Data*. London: Guardian Faber, 2013.

Rosen, J. 2005. *The Naked Crowd: Reclaiming Security and Freedom in an Anxious Age*. New York: Random House.

Rouse, R. H., and M. A. Rouse. 1982. *Statim invenire*: Schools, preachers, and new attitudes to the page. In *Renaissance and Renewal in the Twelfth Century*, ed. R. L. Benson and G. Constable. Cambridge: Harvard University Press.

Ryan, M.-L. 2001. Beyond myth and metaphor: The case of narrative in digital media. *Game Studies* 1 (1).

Schreibman, S., R. Siemens, and J. Unsworth, eds. 2004. *A Companion to Digital Humanities*. Oxford: Blackwell.

Schwartz, G. 1988. Connoisseurship: The penalty of ahistoricism. *Artibus et Historiae* 9 (18): 201–206.

Searle, J. 1980. Minds, brains, and programs. *Behavioral and Brain Sciences* 3: 417–457.

Shaftesbury, Earl of. 1963. *Characteristics of Men, Manners, Opinions, Times, etc.* Gloucester: Peter Smith.

Shore, J., and S. Warden. 2007. *The Art of Agile Development*. Sebastopol: O'Reilly.

Simons, J. 2007. Narrative, games, and theory. *Game Studies* 7 (1).

Sinclair, S. 2003. Computer-assisted reading: Reconceiving text analysis. *Literary and Linguistic Computing* 18 (2): 175–184.

Smith, J. B. Image and imagery in Joyce's Portrait: A computer-assisted analysis. In *Directions in Literary Criticism: Contemporary Approaches to Literature*, ed. S. Weintraub and P. Young. University Park: Pennsylvania State University Press, 1973.

Smith, J. B. 1978. Computer criticism. *Style* 12 (4): 326–356.

Smith, J. B. 1984. A new environment for literary analysis. *Perspectives in Computing* 4 (2/3): 20–31.

Smith, J. B. 1985. Arras User's Manual. TextLab Report TR85-036, Department of Computer Science, University of North Carolina, Chapel Hill.

Suits, B. 1978. *The Grasshopper: Games, Life and Utopia*. University of Toronto Press.

Svensson, P. 2010. The landscape of digital humanities. *Digital Humanities Quarterly* 4 (1).

Tasman, P. 1957 Literary data processing. *IBM Journal of Research and Development* 1 (3): 249–256.

Taylor, L. 2003. When seams fall apart: Video game space and the player. *Game Studies* 3 (2).

Thesaurus Linguae Graecae. 2009. Project history (http://www.tlg.uci.edu/about/history.php).

Tompa, F. W. 1996. An Overview of Waterloo's Database Software for the OED. Computing in the Humanities Working Papers B, no. 13 (http://projects.chass .utoronto.ca/chwp/tompa/index.html).

Tufekci, Z. 2014. Engineering the public: Big data, surveillance and computational politics. *First Monday* 19: 7 (http://firstmonday.org/ojs/index.php/fm/article/view/4901/4097).

Tufte, E. 1983. *The Visual Display of Quantitative Information*. Cheshire: Graphics Press.

Tufte, E. 1990. *Envisioning Information*. Cheshire: Graphics Press.

Turner, V., D. Reinsel, J. Gantz, and S. Minton. 2014. The Digital Universe of Opportunities: Rich Data and the increasing value of the Internet of Things (http://idcdoc-serv.com/1678).

Tyler, T. 2008. A Procrustean probe. *Game Studies* 8 (2).

Unsworth, J. 1997. Documenting the reinvention of text: The importance of failure. *Journal of Electronic Publishing* 3 (2).

Unsworth, J. 2003. Tool-Time, or "Haven't We Been Here Already?": Ten Years in Humanities Computing. http://people.brandeis.edu/~unsworth/carnegie-ninch.03 .html.

Unsworth, J. 2005. New Methods for Humanities Research. http://people.brandeis .edu/~unsworth/lyman.htm.

Unsworth, J. 2010. The State of Digital Humanities. Address to Digital Humanities Summer Institute, University of Victoria (http://www3.isrl.illinois.edu/~unsworth/state.of.dh.DHSI.pdf).

Wang, X., and M. Inaba. 2009. Analyzing structures and evolution of digital humanities based on correspondence analysis and co-word analysis. *Artery Research* 9: 123–134.

Wilkens, M. 2012. Canons, close reading, and the evolution of method. In *Debates in the Digital Humanities*, ed. M. K. Gold. Minneapolis: University of Minnesota Press.

Wolf, G. 2003. The Great Library of Amazonia. *Wired*, November.

Wright, J. A., Jr. 2008a. Transcript of speech to NAACP from CNN, April 27 (http://www.cnn.com/2008/POLITICS/04/28/wright.transcript).

Wright, J. A., Jr. 2008b. Transcript: Rev. Jeremiah Wright speech to National Press Club from SunSentinel.com, April (http://www.sun-sentinel.com/news/local/south-florida/chi-wrighttranscript-04282008,0,2350259.story).

Xenophon. 1920. *Xenophon in Seven Volumes, 4*, ed. E. C. Marchant. Cambridge: Harvard University Press.

Yates, F. A. 1966. *The Art of Memory*. University of Chicago Press.

Index

Printed in the United States
by Baker & Taylor Publisher Services